Acknowledgments

With the creation of a book, but more specifically, in the discerning of a call, a vocation, a "conversation" with a community becomes very important and necessary. I felt acutely the need to test what I was experiencing within a community of faith. In many ways, those who have been involved with this book have provided this dialogue in community.

Before any words formed on paper, there was the living out of God's call to preach. I spent hours with trusted friends and guides in classroom and chapel at the Lutheran seminary, over coffee or lunch in a restaurant, over a glass of wine in someone's living room, in the back pew of a church, on long walks. All these encounters of trust and challenge helped to crystallize the story that unfolded first in my life and then on these pages. At the risk of excluding some, I name in particular some of my friends from seminary days: Bruce Ehlert, Anita Jantz, Kristian Graupe, Anne Zimmerman, Donna Smalley, Henri and Erna Funk, Peter Van Katwijk, and Anne Keffer. The faculty at the Lutheran Seminary had unwavering faith in my gifts, callings and abilities, in particular professors Bill Nelson, Gertrude Buck and Jann Boyd. Many times they saw God's calling and activity long before I acknowledged it. Their challenges confused and surprised me at times, but these kindled a process of discovery that led me to places never visited before, both within myself and in the Church at large.

The support and guidance of trained spiritual directors has been vital along the way. I thank in particular Sisters Margaret Dick, Louisa Brost, Pauline Greenizan, and Janet Malone; Antoinette Voete Roeder; and Fathers Leo Mann OMI, George Morris SJ, and Doug Jeffreys OMI. Their prayerful feedback and keen sense of observation helped me to trust and to grow the courage necessary to let God's plan unfold.

Long before this manuscript made its way to Novalis, I nervously sent a first draft to a wide variety of people. This consultation process produced unanticipated fruits for me, which affirmed the importance of discernment by the faith community. Ordained and non-ordained, women and men, Catholic and Protestant contributed observations, affirmations, questions and challenges: Jim Schmeiser, Ron Rolheiser, Mary Marrocco, Gilbert Chevrier, Joyce Salie, Mary-Anne Lewis Jamin, Dean Sarnecki, Bruce Ehlert, Betty Marsh, Doug Jeffreys, Betty Boechler, George Morris, Ron Baerg, David Tumback, Denis Rolheiser, Sarah Donnelly, Zita Maier, and a couple more who prefer to remain unnamed. They splattered their comments and questions on every page. These marked-up review copies serve to keep alive the grace-filled memory of a collaborative effort. Each one offered a unique perspective that I took to heart in order to further refine and flesh out the words in the story. Without their loving commitment and their faith in me, this book might not have reached the store shelves, nor would I be the person I am today.

The Battlefords Ministerial Association deserves a very special thanks. After I graduated from the Lutheran Seminary, this group of 25 clergy in my home community welcomed me in their midst. Their friendships and their invitations to help prepare ecumenical gatherings gave me a privileged inside view into their life as pastors. They also believed in and affirmed my call to preach. A number of them opened the pulpit in their churches to me, something I never dreamt could or would happen. Particular thanks goes to pastors Ean Kasper, Roger Haugen, Bill Hall, Hazel Arbon, Ron Baerg, and Betty Marsh. I know the value placed in Protestant circles on the Word proclaimed and preached, and I know that the open pulpit is a great sign of trust. I will never take such invitations for granted.

My work as editor of *Our Family* magazine laid some very important groundwork for the writing of this book. I owe a special thanks to the Missionary Oblates of St. Mary's Province, who hired me as editor of the magazine, a position which came as a total surprise to me. I never thought of myself as a good writer, in particular since English is not my first language. It was only through the trust and challenge of the Oblates, and the feedback from readers of the magazine, that my confidence and skill grew. My editors at Novalis, Kevin Burns and Anne Louise Mahoney, then helped me build on my editorial experience; they became invaluable coaches. I have learned much, and continue to learn much, about the art of writing because of them.

Finding the Treasure Within

Finding the Treasure Within

A Woman's Journey
into Preaching

Marie-Louise Ternier-Gommers

NOVALIS

Cover design: Christiane Lemire
Cover painting: "Mediator" by Regina Coupar (http://reginacoupar.com)
Layout: Suzanne Latourelle and Caroline Gagnon

Business Office:
Novalis
49 Front Street East, 2nd Floor
Toronto, Ontario, Canada
M5E 1B3

Phone: 1-800-387-7164 or (416) 363-3303
Fax: 1-800-204-4140 or (416) 363-9409
E-mail: cservice@novalis.ca

National Library of Canada Cataloguing in Publication

Ternier-Gommers, Marie-Louise
    Finding the treasure within : a woman's journey into preaching /
Marie-Louise Ternier-Gommers.

Includes bibliographical references.
ISBN 2-89507-306-6

    1. Ternier-Gommers, Marie-Louise 2. Lay preaching. 3. Catholics–Canada–
Biography. 4. Sermons, Canadian (English) I. Title.

BV4211.3.T47 2002   251'.092   C2002-902967-8

Printed in Canada.

We acknowledge the financial support of the Government of Canada through the
Book Publishing Industry Development Program (BPIDP) for our publishing activities.

5 4 3 2 1   06 05 04 03 02

Contents

The cross is a condition of every holy work.
God himself is at work in what is a cross for us.
Only through it do we reach a certain
authenticity and profundity of existence…
Only he (she) who has suffered for his (her) convictions
attains in them a certain force,
a certain quality of the irrevocable,
and also the right to be heard and respected.
Yves Congar

The identity of the Christian as witness
is marked by the unavoidable and
distinctive presence of the cross.
There can be no authentic witness without it.
Pope John Paul II

Dedication

To Jann
— teacher, priest, mentor —
through whose witness
God led me home
to my own calling

A special thank-you goes to my local bishop, Most Reverend Blaise Morand. We spent much time talking, asking questions, exchanging ideas and experiences, and praying for guidance. New and unsettling as it must have been to listen to me, Bishop Morand always received me with the greatest respect and interest. It is not easy for a bishop to be in a leadership position in today's Church, nor is it easy for an ordinary person to be an instrument of God's Spirit in this time of change and transition. I thank you, Bishop, for the trust you continue to put in me. I pray that, with God's help, I will continue to be worthy of this trust.

Another special thank-you goes to Fr. Ron Rolheiser, well-known writer and speaker, a priest with the Missionary Oblates of St. Mary's Province, for whom I worked as editor of their beloved magazine, *Our Family*. Involved in the first round of reviews before the manuscript was accepted for publication, Fr. Ron believed in the message of this personal story and in the importance of sharing it. He eased my fears about being misunderstood and criticized, saying that he learned from experience that it is impossible to write something that will be liked and understood by everyone. The best efforts will fall short, he said, so all we can do is write from a steadfastness in faith and a trust in our experience of God's activity, with help from others if necessary. The rest is up to God's Spirit.

Last but not least, a final thanks goes to my family: my husband, Jim, and our three children, Rachelle, Daniel and David. They have watched this journey from up close. Not always understanding at first, yet always supportive, my family has marvelled at God's activity in my life despite all my fears and misgivings, which they heard me express often. It is their trust, encouragement and faith, and especially that of Jim, that gave me the inner freedom to explore new territory both in the Church and with God.

As I look at this long list of acknowledgments, it becomes clear that we are all the product of the faith that others have in us. Let us therefore not underestimate the power we have to build each other up for God's reign with the love, the care, the respect, the encouragement and the comfort we can offer each other every day.

Foreword

Contemporary psychology describes a certain kind of person as "generative." Such a person, it tells us, constantly generates life and energy rather than draining them away. Ultimately, that is what makes people archetypal adults: they feed the life around them rather than feeding off that life. This is also true in spiritual and ecclesial terms. What makes someone mature in the areas of faith and church is precisely that kind of generativity. A mature believer creates spiritual energy rather than diminishes it.

Creating spiritual energy is not always easy to do, of course, especially in difficult or painful situations. Leibnitz once said that we do not live in the best of all possible universes. That is true for all families, communities and churches. We are forever caught up in situations that are less than ideal, full of tension, and fraught with potential for self-pity and bitterness.

When such situations arise, we may be tempted to run away and distance ourselves from the tension ("This isn't worth it!") or to stay but grow bitter, resentful, angry and tense. Neither of these responses is generative.

So what can we do when we find ourselves living in a family, a church or a community that is less than ideal? We are invited to help carry that situation and transform it.

How do we do this? By standing in it as Mary stood under the cross of Jesus – neither fleeing, nor bitter, nor weak. What was she doing there? Overtly, it would seem, very little. She was not trying to stop the crucifixion or even protest her son's innocence. She did not, it appears, say anything at all. She stood. That was significant. Standing, for the Hebrews, was a position of strength. Mary was not prostrate in front of the cross in weakness; she did not seem to be bitter.

So what was she doing? She was helping to hold, carry and transform the tension, bitterness, anger and darkness of that moment. Unlike the crowd, which was caught up in spontaneous emotion, she did not give back in kind – anger for anger, hatred for hatred, bitterness for bitterness, an eye for an eye. Rather, like a water filter removes impurities and gives back only the pure water, Mary held the anger and hatred and gave back only graciousness and love. Real transformation inside of any relationship – friendship, marriage, family, church, community – takes place only when someone standing under the situation holds within herself or himself the injustice and bitterness and gives back graciousness, blessing and love. This is what generates life. In the Bible, it is called "pondering."

Marie-Louise Ternier-Gommers, in her autobiographical reflection *Finding the Treasure Within: A Woman's Journey into Preaching,* does precisely this sort of biblical pondering. Her journey into preaching, which parallels the journey of many women today, was not an easy one; at times she was tempted towards flight or bitterness. She opted for neither.

Experiencing simultaneously the call to minister in the Church and some major historical and institutional blockages to that call, she chose a generative response, a biblical response, the slow road, the road less taken, the road that avoids both bitter self-pity and passive resignation. She follows her conscience and her call, is true to herself and true to her God, even as she works within the structures of her church.

What is her secret? Ah, but that would be telling! The book is her formula. It is a good story, a true story, a hope-filled story. It is a story that needs to be told because it models how any of us, faced with a situation that does not seem fair, can find the way that leads through the narrow gate, the generative gate that opens the doorway to new life.

Ronald Rolheiser omi

June 2002

Introduction

The beginning of the third millennium is a trying time for the Christian family. In Roman Catholic circles, an article written some 35 years ago might as well have been written today. Back in 1967, Avery Dulles, SJ, who is now a Cardinal, compared the historical character of the Catholic Church in the past few centuries to key stages in faith development. Leaving behind a relatively uncritical and protected "childhood" mentality (before Vatican II), the North American Catholic Church in the past 40 years has passed swiftly from this rather benign and obedient phase into a turbulent adolescence, opening the third millennium with the challenge to grow into full maturity.[1] Others speak of a major shift in world views, spurred on by a rapidly changing contemporary culture, increased contact with other world religions, and a healing of denominational rifts in the Christian family. Whether we live in the academic world of theology or in the world of rural parishes and remote missions, underground shifts are shaking the Church, just like plates rub deep in the earth's belly and cause an earthquake.

This book reveals just such a fundamental shift. In some places the story features sharp contours and clear lines, yet in other places the ground shakes deep beneath the surface, making everything feel incomplete, unstable and blurred. Language proves highly inadequate when attempting to name and contain the new thing God's Spirit is effecting. I ask the reader for a spirit of patience, openness and courage, and a willingness to seek the faithfulness behind the struggle. I share as a child who inadvertently took an unknown turn in the road and finds herself in a new part of town. I share as an adolescent, whose critical faculties work overtime, whose enthusiasm for the new and untried makes her adrenaline flow, and whose self-centred tendencies get her caught in pain and disappointment at times. I share as an emerging adult in faith, who yearns for wisdom, clarity and the capacity to live the pain with integrity in a hurting yet redeemed world.

Despite the fear of inadequate naming, I believe my experience of liturgical preaching is a witness to the "Word-made-Flesh" and to the power of resurrection faith in Jesus Christ our Lord. Standing in the company of the first disciples who were startled by the reality of the risen Lord, I too am slow to understand what is happening. Hiding in the upper room, I too fear the authorities. Feeling the power of the Spirit, I nevertheless feel courage, love and wisdom infuse my words, my gestures, my heart. In the revealing light of this faith, I continue to love and respect that which I scrutinize and question. Committed to discerning God's spirit, I pray for ongoing surrender and humility, placing the good of the community before my need to be right. I offer my childlike wonderment about the greatness of God, wrapped in an adolescent zeal for the renewal of the Church and the whole earth, gently held by maturing wisdom and sacrificial love.

To experience zeal for the spreading of the Gospel and for the proper functioning of the Church is not new for a woman like me. I stand in the company of countless women who gave their lives, their hearts, and sometimes their material wealth to build up the Church throughout history.

Even today, very few parishes would function properly if women withdrew their active participation: the cleaning, the coffee, the office work, the pastoral visiting, the altar serving, the sacristy work, and the music (to name but a few essential tasks) would simply not get done. For many years I too have been a part of the army of female volunteers that kept a parish humming. However, this radical giving of self seldom, if ever, earns women roles in leadership, liturgical or otherwise, in the Church. Historically, women's contributions, however extensive, are viewed as voluntary sacrifices of love that do not lead to any institutional recognition in terms of formal authority, liturgical leadership or decision-making influence on matters of doctrine and theology. My claim of being called to liturgical preaching is therefore constitutively different from all the usual female contributions. This claim places me not only in the liturgical leadership of the faith community, whether ordained or non-ordained, but also employs my insights in Scripture, theology and life from a distinctly female point of view in ways that give value, authority and respect to women's perspectives everywhere.

As a Roman Catholic woman, my claiming a call to preach, therefore, leaves me caught in a contradiction, a paradox, a conundrum. Roman Catholic teaching upholds the prohibition on the ordination of women to Holy Orders, and the same teaching does not allow claiming such a call in any formal way apart from ordained ministry. A quick conclusion could lead one either to deny the action of God in this matter or to deny the validity of the Church's teaching on women's ordination. Yet, in many ways, either denial risks short-circuiting God's plan for both the Church and for me. In this book, I attempt to share hope and inspiration, witnessing to God's unlimited creativity in working within church structures and rising above these structures.

The shifts presently felt in both the Church and the world are reflected here. Old terms and understandings are being re-evaluated and redefined. The barriers between denominational linguistic worlds are breaking down. My ecumenical formation in theology and ministry has resulted in my adopting language that does not always fit into exclusively Catholic categories. For example, I studied at a theological institution called a "seminary."[2] Unlike a Catholic seminary, which is place of formation for ordained priesthood, the Lutheran seminary I attended welcomed a wide range of students preparing for ministry in the Church: women and men, married and single, people beginning their first, second or third career, ordained and lay people, Lutherans and Roman Catholics, and many other traditions. I speak of Eucharist when referring to the Catholic Mass, to the Lord's Supper, Holy Communion or Holy Eucharist. I speak of preaching in the pulpit during worship when referring to breaking open the Word from the ambo or lectern in the liturgy. I speak of sermons, homilies and reflections. I have grown comfortable with a theology of preaching that includes both lay and ordained, that is both eucharistic and non-eucharistic, and that is learning to move back and forth between different denominational worlds. Being formed in a theological setting that speaks openly about the possibility of a woman's call to ordination, I learned to shed fear and ignorance on an issue that remains unresolved for many Catholics.

It ought not to surprise readers, especially Catholic readers, therefore, that they may at times share in the confusion of living between worlds, and may at times share in the pain, wondering whether they are dealing with adolescent impatience, real injustice, or a Spirit-filled birthing. I do not pretend to offer answers and fixed conclusions, but rather search for the questions by revealing pieces of an ongoing journey. Catch the spirit of childlike wonderment, adolescent risk-taking, and adult wisdom peeking around the corner once in a while. Our God is a God of ongoing creation and regeneration. If nothing else, we are all called, each in the particular features of our lives, to bear witness to this universal gift of a loving Creator.

In a spirit of prayer, faithfulness to both God and the Church, and openness to the Spirit, our only task is to share what we come to know as true and good. As we grow to know God intimately we learn to recognize the features of God's activity, features that always point to a liberating spirituality – liberating for both God and ourselves. Kenan B. Osborne, OFM, writes:

> A spirituality which takes into critical account the view of God presented in traditional Catholic Christian spiritualities has not yet been fully explicated, but there is a pressing need to "liberate" God from the human made constraints which disallow God from being sovereignly free. Humans do not tell God how God can be God. Human beings, Christians included, listen, both in the sounds of creation and in the sounds of revelation, for God's own voice telling us what the sovereignty and freedom of God is all about. God is not a Roman Catholic. God is not even a Christian. God is not Jewish. God is not Islamic. Rather, God is a God of all. God is a God in whom women as well as men can believe. God is a God in whom the marginated and the poor, as well as the comfortable citizens, can believe. Indeed, only that understanding of God which sees God as preferentially the God of the poor, the God of the marginated, the God of the second-rate, will stir up any embers of human faith.
>
> This approach to a loving God who loves the entire world and who loves each and every part of creation, and human creation above all, is revealed throughout the wide canvas of creation. When a given religious leadership attempts to speak *in persona Dei*, such statements will be tested against a creation that also speaks *in persona Dei*. Such state-

ments will be tested against the voice of the Spirit, which enters into the very heart and conscience of each and every human person, a voice that also speaks *in persona Dei*. Women as well as men can speak *in persona Dei*, and sometimes women can speak more clearly. The marginalized and the poor speak *in persona Dei*, and most of the time in a very loud and powerful way. Only a spirituality that honours the Spirit of God in all will be a spirituality of the third millennium.[3]

The story in this book bears witness to the way God can speak in a liberating fashion through one woman in the ministry of preaching. The sermons offered here claim to speak *in persona Dei*. And yet, they are merely the written part of an entire event, each of which represents a personal landmark in my journey with God. Preaching is mostly an oral endeavour; a written text of something that was originally spoken aloud does not have the same impact. There is nothing like "being there" and "doing it." A big aspect of preaching lies in the delivery of the words: the body language, the pace and tone of voice, the silences, the eye contact.

Each chapter features one sermon or homiletic reflection preached in the past eight years. (I use the term "sermon" when the preaching took place in a non-Catholic church. "Homiletic reflection" is used for those texts preached in a Roman Catholic non-eucharistic liturgical context. I avoid using "homily" in order to comply with the Vatican instruction on the involvement of the laity in priestly ministries. However, the term "preaching" refers to the same activity in both contexts.) I have assumed that there is no difference in how the preaching is experienced, whether it is called a homily, a sermon, or a homiletic reflection. Whenever I thought it necessary, I used a fictitious name for certain individuals who have played a significant role in this journey in order to protect their privacy.

I have made extensive use of my own journal entries in this book. Journal writing helps me in many ways: it provides a safe outlet for strong feelings and intimate experiences, writing out intense moments helps to articulate the journey of becoming a person of faith, and writing itself can be an intimate form of prayer. Having a log that documents my inner journey with God also helps to clarify and to claim where God is moving in my life, especially when I reread entries after some time has passed. Putting into words something that is often so beyond words fosters trust and confidence that God is active and close, even in the painful times.

Just as earthquakes reveal the strata and substrata of the earth's geological makeup, each sermon or homiletic reflection contains several layers of story and meaning. There is the direct story and meaning conveyed in the preaching of the words. Those who preach on a regular basis, whether ordained or lay, may find insights to incorporate into their own preparation and preaching. The narrative section in each chapter intends to break open the stories and meanings behind each sermon or homiletic reflection, revealing my own spirituality, my struggles with the Scripture texts, my relationship to the church through the act of preaching, and my attempts to formulate a response to God. This layer in particular reveals that God does not abandon anyone. Once God raises up gifts in ordinary women and men, ways do open to use these gifts in the Church, even if those ways are not always according to the set rules. In the end, the Church is all the richer for God's activity of opening unexpected doors.

The feminist reader will find that this story of giving birth to, of liberating, my female Catholic voice in the task of preaching is glaringly lacking in feminist analysis and terminology. There are several reasons for this absence. First, I simply had little occasion, apart from reading books, to grow and learn in an explicit feminist social, academic and spiritual context. Because of this, I am still "in process," connecting my experience with a feminist perspective. The incompleteness of this process is evident whenever I show difficulty stepping out of traditional and limiting mindsets. Sometimes I really do feel like a fish trying to study the properties of the water she swims in. Second, I found the elements necessary for liberation and birthing in the person of Jesus and in the Scriptures that witness to his mission of bringing about God's reign here and now. Thus my journey is first and foremost of a deeply spiritual nature, with its own demands of accountability and integrity. This spiritual grounding provides me with a prism through which I evaluate and test everything else, including feminism. Even in the absence of feminist terms and concepts, I hope that the reader steeped in a feminist world view and spirituality will still recognize the movements of inner liberation. In places I do draw on insights from Christian feminist authors. Third, the few brushes I had with feminism moved me into a position of caution. While my Christian spirituality leads me to embrace values and goals similar to those of feminism, and offers me critical tools for analysis and reflection in the same way that feminism does, I experienced the latter too much in an unbridled form. Uncontrolled forms of any ideology run the risk of being driven by our own personal hurts and anger, ego trips, insecurities and fears, or political agendas of power, even in Christian circles. Several times I have experienced feminism as divorced from a solid spirituality that could provide some measure of depth and accountability outside of itself, and could caution it about its own traps. This may well be one reason for the suspicion of things feminist that I observe in many who sit in our church pews on Sunday mornings. Fourth, the little feminist analysis I have been exposed to, including Christian feminism, seems quick to name the sins of patriarchy, but rarely admits to sins of its own. We are all sinful creatures, women and men. To promote feminism as the absolute good feels dishonest and arrogant. Fifth, the door between my Christian spirituality and feminism remains open, inviting an ongoing process of interactive reflection, evaluation and appropriation of the two. Most importantly in this process, however, is that my relationship with Jesus informs and sheds discerning light on my feminism, not the other way around.

St. Thérèse of Lisieux deserves special mention here, as she became a steady companion on this journey of uncovering the treasures of God. Even though the external features of her life story are vastly different from mine, it is the "substrata" in her life that bear a striking resemblance to my experience, in particular her deep conviction of the authenticity of her call despite those around her who dismissed, ridiculed and ignored her. The external pressures to deny her calling did not detract Thérèse or make her bitter or angry. Instead, she drew from the wellspring of her calling even before she was allowed to enter Carmel, letting God's love take hold of her whole being and of the way she related to those who were trying to dismiss her. It is thus that Thérèse became so remarkable in her virtues, capable of fostering patience, perseverance, courage, gentleness and wisdom. I share the story on these pages with the strong conviction that God can use the experiences of one individual, provided her driving force is love. Therefore, with Thérèse of Lisieux, I offer this book to the Church in love: "I have found my place in the bosom of the Church and it is you, Lord, who has given it to me. In the heart of the Church [...] I will be love."[4]

PART I

In the Beginning...

Awakening the Voice

Tired from the dusty walk
dizzy from the day's heat
she rests, sitting by
the well…
drawing voiceless water
day after day
lifeless drudgery
quenching thirst for
a mere few moments…
only a sleeping voice can
contend with lifeless water
halting her weeping soul
from speech
silent, whispering, yearning
hurting, aching voice…
"Give me some water…"
Startled out of
daydreaming humdrum
He asks her the
unthinkable, impossible
He really wants her
voiceless water…?
Querying Him unlocks
her voiceless soul
her own aching bestowed
dignified speech
in the lavish stream
of Love's Living Water
handing right perspective in
unconditional love and
integrity
opening her anew to
Being in being…

She runs to tell
proclaiming what and Who
she has seen and heard
Living water restoring
power of voice
authority of speech
rooted in the One
who touched her
in the One who
sent her...
daydreaming humdrum
rolling into
voice filled life

(inspired by John 4:1-30)

CHAPTER 1

Quickening

You did not choose me
but I chose you.
And I appointed you to go and bear fruit,
fruit that will last,
so that the Father will give you
whatever you ask in his name.

(John 15:16)

Just as I did not come to Canada planning to marry and live here, so I did not go to the Lutheran Seminary to be prepared for ministry and to learn how to preach. I intended to take only those courses that would prepare me to work in the field of pastoral counselling. For a while I managed to do this, despite the fact that I literally devoured all theology, liturgy and church history classes.

My hunger to learn about the things of God had lain dormant for many decades. Growing up after Vatican II in the Netherlands, I was active in youth ministry as a teenager and wrote homiletic reflections for youth masses. As a young adult I set out on a quest to search for meaning that took me abroad, first to Taizé and L'Arche in France, then to Canada, fostering a faith that was eagerly seeking understanding. Walking into the classes on theology, liturgy and spirituality fanned the flames. It felt new and exciting, yet familiar. Then came my first course on preaching. At first I was a reluctant and impatient student, even feeling slightly annoyed that such a class was required for my degree. Just as Sarah did when overhearing the strangers say that she would have a son in her old age (Genesis 18:9-12), I laughed in secret at the absurdity of my situation. Here I was, a Roman Catholic woman, learning from the Lutherans how to preach

God's Word in the pulpit! I knew this combination was ludicrous and that I would probably not learn very much, let alone ever apply such learning. What was even more absurd was that the professor was an ordained Lutheran woman, the first ordained woman I had ever faced in such a close encounter.

Despite my outright annoyance at the lack of course clarity and organization, I decided rather quickly to view the class as a good challenge to my own spiritual journey and to my relationship with my own church tradition. Life in my mid-thirties was pulling me more inward, pressing for more reflection and introspection. I had learned to become a good sport, seeing the potential for growth in every situation. Even if I was not going to be a preacher, I told myself, I could always find enough to reflect on and pray with, thus allowing the material to help me grow. Furthermore, I never doubted my belonging in the Roman Catholic Church; I experienced my church as my home away from home. Knowing myself to be deeply nourished by the Church's sacraments, spirituality and social teachings, I fully expected this class to strengthen my denominational identity. With that resolve added to my study goals of pastoral counselling, what could possibly go wrong?

Soon the preaching course moved beyond my comfort zone. It did not take long before I needed to risk the security of knowing who I was and who I was called to be. The paradox of learning more, and learning more deeply, became apparent. Gaining greater insight into the task of good preaching did not make my listening to Sunday homilies any easier. Developing a critical ear started to spell despair. More often than I care to admit, I heard big gaps in Sunday homilies: those featuring the preacher more than God's Word, those that kept things too "nice" so as not to offend the listeners, those that divided people easily into camps of "them" and "us," those that perpetuated gender stereotypes, those that excluded by sheer omission and silence, those used for spreading personal agendas, those that even left God's Word untouched altogether. Many times I left Mass still hungry, even though I had received communion. Now I wondered about the reasons for that hunger: there were, in fact, very few homilies that fed me spiritually. Receiving communion without nourishing words to sustain me left me wanting more. I gained some understanding of and sympathy for people who say they "don't get anything out of church," even by those who come with sincere intent and a hungry heart. I felt deep sadness and frustration. I started to hark back to the days of ignorance in the best sense of that word – it felt more comfortable not to know so much. Yet in very clear and somewhat unexpected ways, I had taken another new turn in the road and found myself in new territory. God led me into a process from which there was no turning back.

I had had such moments before. Every time I embarked on a new adventure – in my teens, that meant crossing the border of my country – the butterflies in my stomach went wild. I was irresistibly drawn to what lay beyond, yet the unknown terrified me. I kept reaching for wider horizons until, at age 22, I stepped on an airplane for the first time and flew across the ocean to Canada, leaving behind the security and my sense of belonging in the Netherlands. Even though I could not predict how, I knew intuitively that travelling to a new world would change me forever. I met Jim, a Saskatchewan farmer, while travelling with a mutual friend. Why did we decide to marry? Maybe foolishness, maybe a common dream, maybe a deep desire to live out our love in a sacramental way. Whatever the reason, walking down the aisle to marry him initiated me into two unknown worlds: marriage and rural farm life (I had been raised in the city, where we lived above a store!). The alluring promises of love and happiness helped to keep the butterflies in my stomach under wraps. But now, as I stepped into the world of theological studies, and into the preaching class in particular, the butterflies were back with a vengeance.

I never questioned my belonging in the Roman Catholic Church. Growing up in the southern part of the Netherlands made my entire religious culture Catholic. I didn't meet a Protestant until I came to Canada. Travelling through this vast country at age 22, I remember writing home that in Canada, there seemed to be a different church on every street corner. I had never seen anything like that before. As far as I was concerned, the world was Catholic. Without ever knowing anything else, I loved being part of this Catholic Church. Being a Catholic teenager in the Netherlands after Vatican II was fresh and exciting. The changes could not happen fast enough for the younger generation. Once I was living in Canada, this love for my Catholic tradition was deeply affirmed, even when I was studying with the Lutherans. I cherished the Church's liturgies, sacraments, ways of keeping and passing on the Good News of the Gospel, and teachings on justice and morality. Throughout my life, these nourished a personal faith in God and in Jesus that grew deep roots within me. They challenged me and guided me in developing my creative potential, in making major decisions, and in adopting a set of life-giving beliefs and values. Even if there were many different traditions in Canada, I had no desire or need to leave the Roman Catholic Church.

I came to my studies out of deep love and commitment to both my faith and my own church tradition. Choosing to study at a Lutheran seminary instead of a Catholic college was merely motivated by practical reasons of distance and family responsibilities at the time. As a woman, I always found a meaningful place within my Catholic tradition. I considered my contributions in the parish, from cleaning to liturgical ministries and the choir, worthwhile and satisfying. I had little understanding and sympathy for those who were calling the Church to task for its practice of exclusion and discrimination against women. Unconsciously, I had every intention of sticking to my own study agenda without considering the possibility that God might have different callings and challenges in mind.

Crazy as it felt, a question began to surface: Did I have a call to preach? I was raised in a church tradition where there was no expectation, let alone possibility, that preaching could ever be part of my ministry. Until I enrolled in this class on preaching, the religious Catholic climate kept such a question at bay. I started to discover that church structures greatly affect our experience of God's call and our ability to respond to that call. If church structures do not permit the experience of being called by God to preaching or to ordained ministry or both, and do not permit the discernment and the response to such a call, then such questions may not necessarily surface in a person's consciousness. If they do, naming that experience can create deep turmoil if the name of the call is one that is not permitted by the powers that be. For the first time ever, I started wondering if this is what happens when a Roman Catholic woman dares to claim being called by God to preach or to ordained ministry.

The crucible of God's call now took shape in a theological learning setting, among my Lutheran sisters and brothers. As such I became part of a church structure where God's call to me, a woman, was an accepted possibility that was invited to be discerned in a serious manner. Having an ordained woman as teacher and role model became the greatest blessing and the most disturbing challenge: there in front of me, there in my hearing, was the possibility. Her witness unsettled me deeply, for a variety of reasons that only surfaced over time. This female pastor modelled a theology of worship and preaching profoundly rooted in God through Christ in a way that few Roman Catholic priests I knew could rival. Ironically, she was more sacramental and liturgical than most Lutherans. "I'm a closet Catholic," she used to quip. How could this be, for my church teaches that God does not call women to the ordained ministry of Word and Sacrament? If God did not call this woman, then how could she witness to Christ risen in such a profound way through her teaching, her eucharistic presiding and her preaching ministry? These questions resembled those debated by the Pharisees and Scribes about the power with which Jesus himself cast out demons and healed the sick:

> Some of them said, "He casts out demons by Beelzebul, the ruler of demons." Others […] kept demanding from him a sign from heaven…. But he knew what they were thinking and said to them, "Every kingdom divided against itself becomes a desert…. But if it is by the finger of God that I cast out demons, then the kingdom of God has come to you." (Luke 11:15-16, 20)

I felt like the Pharisees, questioning my professor's call and the validity of her ministry. Her witness broke me open by surprise into a new view of life, of faith, of the Church. Considering myself a faithful daughter of the Roman Church, I had difficulty holding together the Roman Catholic teaching on women's ordination and this woman's powerful and clearly authentic witness as an ordained minister. Until this class, I had managed to keep the question of women's ordination at a comfortable distance. Now it stared me in the face in the most incarnational form possible, and I felt deeply affected and challenged. This was no longer merely an intellectual and theoretical issue. This was now a person, and I was involved with this person. No academic treatise or any discussion on the topic had ever had this kind of effect on me. Where was God taking me?

I had spent a big part of my life living my faith "on the outside." I was active in the Church at various levels; I got involved in social justice causes; I was committed to a simple life off the land. As far as I was concerned, I had given Jesus everything I had. Not expecting any "new" demands from God, and being fairly new at growing in faith from a place within myself apart from my outside commitments, I was most uncomfortable with the shaking of my foundations. Even the faithful presence of a skilled spiritual director did not ease my fears. Something of great significance was occurring, and I did not know what it was.

I feared allowing the discernment. What if I did find God's call? A deep, intuitive knowing suggested that this was a faint but sure possibility. For did I not devour the knowledge of the holy things of God, fuelling a fire in my heart to serve God's people in God's Church?

> I wrote to my bishop today, telling him of my educational endeavours, telling him of my desire to serve our Church with the fruits of my formation. I don't know if he cares to know, but I need for him to know…. The tears splashed between the lines reveal an aching desire for blessing, for prayerful support. Why? Why is this so important? I am just going to school, like any other university student. I started out wishing to become merely a pastoral counsellor. I am doing this for fun, out of personal interest, for myself, right?… Wrong. Like the first disciples, shocked at the news of Jesus' resurrection, I am getting more than I bargained for, and I panic. I had no idea that God's alluring Word could take me to such a painful place, could literally make me go crazy inside, because responding to God's call feels terrifyingly bold. And thus the cross of Christ is the unchosen burden, the one I least expect to find. (Journal entry)

A Catch-22 situation started to emerge. Opening myself up to learning to proclaim God's Word in preaching, and to the possibility of God's call, deeply jeopardized my comfortable sense of denominational belonging. As a woman – and a married one at that – I had no place or privilege to preach the Word of God in my own Church. Who would I be in my church? I remembered Mary Magdalene with unsettling yet warm and deep affection. Her announcement of Jesus' resurrection was received by the disciples as "the idle gossip of women" (Luke 24:11). How could I speak and claim my voice? Would my words be heard as "idle gossip" as well, or could I be heard as a voice called to address God's people?

I never meant for this faith business to creep into my life so intimately. But already on an emotional level, my illusion of wholeness started to crumble. Painful achings for belonging, approval, peace and union turned out not to be fulfilled by the mere doing of the right thing. I had three healthy and happy children, a dedicated and hardworking husband, a home on the shores of a beautiful little lake, and an active social life, and still I argued with God about the emptiness. The last thing I wanted was to add more painful longings, especially regarding my place as a woman in the Church. Yet there I was in the palm of God's hand, where God's gentle love gripped my heart in irresistible ways. I had no choice but to keep going.

The first sermon I preached in class showed that I still had a long way to go. I had not quite shed my initial distrust of the course and my expectation that I would not learn a lot. My sermon on the story of the forgiving father and prodigal son from Luke 15:1-32 resembled a comprehensive class essay rather than a sermon. I still pity the professor and my classmates who sat through my 25-minute treatise. The professor tried hard to be positive: "Well, at least we know that you have thought about the text extensively!" I had yet to learn the difference between writing a text meant for reading, and writing a text meant for oral delivery. Being a complex thinker, I had yet to learn how to trim my thoughts ruthlessly. I still needed to learn that I could not possibly say it all in one sermon; every Scripture text overflows with meaning, abundantly more than we can ever express in human words. And I had yet to become aware of the importance of body language and places of silence in the sermon, of the pace and tone of my voice, and of the deliberate and careful weaving together of thoughts and words in a way that the listener could follow. So much for thinking that there was not much to learn.

Nevertheless, my voice was changing, my heart heard new songs, and I was desperately looking for new ways to sing, even though I remained unsure about how, where and when to sing. One of our textbooks, *A Little Exercise for Young Theologians*, by Helmut Thielicke, proved immeasurably helpful: "During the period when the voice is changing we do not sing, and during this formative period in the life of the theological student he/she does not preach."[5] These words gave me permission to let the process take its course without the pressure of needing to share answers I did not yet have. For now, remaining faithfully rooted in God and prayerfully alert to the inner movements was sufficient. I prayed and learned, learned and prayed, continuously offering to God the deep stirrings of my heart. The accompaniment of my spiritual director was an integral part of the journey; without her insightful and objective feedback, I could not have mustered the courage to let God's activity unfold. Without her prayerful stance towards what I brought to our conversations, I would not have learned how to discern the hand of God in the tumultuous stirrings of my soul.

I felt the quickening of new life, yet I feared claiming it. Nothing would ever be the same again. I mourned deeply the loss of denominational comfort that I had known for so long. Not that there was anything leading me to believe God was taking me out of the Roman Catholic Church and into the Lutheran one. On the contrary, the deeper I moved into the theological, spiritual, historical and liturgical heritage of our Christian tradition, the greater the realization of my strong Catholic identity. I did not just belong to the Catholic Church, I was Catholic in my bones. My love for the sacraments grew, my appreciation of liturgy deepened, my awareness of the richness of Catholic spirituality increased. I was rediscovering "home" and entering it as if for the first time, with a reverence and love too deep for words.

Therefore, if my denominational belonging was so strongly affirmed, what started to threaten that same belonging? For the first time ever I came face to face in a most personal way with what feminism has termed "the silence of women in the Church." I never was a strong or vocal supporter of feminism per se, although I am aware that the freedoms I enjoy as a woman are probably the fruits of women's fights for equality and recognition. The snippets of feminism to which I was exposed were not appealing: too radical, too anti-Church, too simplistic, or too man-hating. The feminism I observed at a distance seemed to be without a spiritual base and, as Joan Chittister notes, "without a spiritual base that obligates it beyond itself [...] it can become just one more intellectual ghetto that the world doesn't notice and doesn't need."[6] I did not belong in a feminist camp and always felt that the Church was still the best place to be, even if the voice and role of women in this Church left much to be desired. Besides, talking with women candidates for ordination from other traditions made me aware that even though their churches claimed equal roles in ministry for women and men, all was not well in the practical living out of that equality.

This was my position for a long time. Women's ordination was not really my issue, and that was not about to change because I studied at a seminary. Yet great restlessness and inexplicable pain, sadness and anger started to invade my peaceful sense of Roman Catholic belonging. For the first time ever, tears welled up in my eyes each time a woman presided at worship. When others spoke about the role of women in the Church, a big lump formed in my throat. Feelings of exclusion crept into my ecclesial comfort zone as my desire to serve in ministry grew. I greatly distrusted these feelings, arguing that I had indeed been among the Lutherans for too long.

But these were not the only feelings wreaking havoc with my peace of mind. There were other feelings, deep and bursting with new life in ways I had not known before. Learning to preach claimed my whole being in a new way. I discovered parts of myself that I did not know existed. The pulpit felt strangely familiar and comfortable; there was something undeniably right about my presence in that sacred space. The process of preparing to preach and delivering the sermon challenged me more than anything else had previously, pushing me into prayer and solitude with God in a way that nothing else did. The personal and spiritual growth, the sense of ministry and the deep love for the preaching task became new sources of life. In giving all I had to the task of preaching, I found life in abundance. I started to feel in my bones the meaning of Jesus' words: "For those who want to save their life will lose it, and those who lose their life for my sake will save it" (Luke 9:24). With this sense of awakening to new life, I preached the last sermon for my preaching course to the entire seminary community in a healing worship service with anointing.

Sermon for Worship Service at Lutheran Theological Seminary

John 12:1-8

My friend Dan was 32, a loving husband to Gayle and a good father to his four young children. He was dying of skin cancer. We all knew it was a matter of weeks. Dan asked for the sacrament of anointing in his local Roman Catholic parish. In the presence of his wife, children, relatives and many friends, the priest traced the sign of the cross on Dan's forehead with oil. We remembered and claimed God's promise of life that Dan had first heard at his baptism. We were there to show Dan our love and support – the communal blessing to carry Dan through. His anointing became a celebration of his life, and of our life together.

We chose to be with him in the face of his death, in the face of the reality that we too will die. It was not easy to be there with Dan. Throughout the anointing service I got caught up in my own grief over losing Dan. I was still trying to bargain with God to keep him with us. The hot, silent tears on my cheeks spewed anger. My heart yelled, "Why is this happening?" Observing the many who cried, I realized that for once my tears were not out of place.

Is this how you feel, Mary, as you anoint Jesus' feet? Do you know what you are doing? Is your behaviour out of place, unbecoming of a woman in your time? Are you crying hot tears too? Why pour out such precious, costly perfume at a seemingly inappropriate time? Do you know that soon your beloved friend and companion will be no more? Your action goes against all norms of custom and propriety. You "waste" costly perfume. You proceed to wipe Jesus' feet with your hair! You are vulnerable, pouring out your heart's treasure.

Your vulnerability, like tears, embarrasses onlookers. Mary, your act is unexpected and shocking. The rich fragrance lingers long after. The disciples grumble about the price of perfume, thinking of the money which could have been made. They do not see the blessing between you and Jesus. They do not see healing in your radical giving of self. They do not see God's anointing of God's people through your action. Caught up in our own worries we can miss the meaning, just as I risked missing the blessing of Dan's life because the pain over losing him started to overwhelm me.

But Jesus does not miss anything. Jesus reveals the meaning of this simple yet profound offering. Jesus receives Mary's extravagant act in the face of his impending death. Human as he is, Jesus needs and gratefully accepts this support, this sign of thanksgiving.

As Jesus lets Mary anoint and comfort him, he is anointing her with the oil of God's steadfast love, poured out for her in his own life. For our lives are so intertwined, and so are our deaths. Jesus' death is forever intertwined with every human death. Mary's action is an extravagant celebration of life in the face of death.

Jesus anticipates our grief-stricken spirits. Seeing our grief, Dan was the one comforting us, realizing that we were the ones feeling the loss. After all, focused on Christ's promise of life, he had heaven to look forward to. Dan accepted our grief, and returned it to us as blessing. Anointing us with his peace, he sent us forth into our lives to be fruitful bearers of God's Word. The fragrance of that anointing moment lingers in my heart.

And in the same way, the fragrance of Mary's perfume on Jesus' feet lingers here in Saskatoon, here at this seminary. What is this perfume? Where do we smell it? How does it get smeared on us? How does its fragrance penetrate our lives?

The oil of baptism intertwines our lives and our death with Christ's life and with Christ's death. God's chrism of baptism binds our resurrected lives to Christ. Blessing, anointing, is still offered to us, as gift to give and to receive. God's immeasurable outpouring of love, like Mary's costly perfume, heals loss and grief, and binds us together in life and in death. This communion in Christ is the fragrance that permeates our lives.

As with Mary's extravagant anointing, at times we must intentionally bless the communion we share in Jesus Christ. Christ's own resurrection is the fragrance of hope lingering on in our lives. This is cause to stand still, to look death and all our little deaths in the face. In the face of death we remember, we claim and we celebrate God's promises. This is cause to stand with Christ in the face of all suffering and loss.

People who believe that anointing is reserved only for our deathbed are mistaken. Anointing is an event that brings our whole selves before God now, to be poured out in Christ – like Mary's costly perfume. Anointing one another in this community reminds us to recognize our radical healing and radical commissioning to live and serve in Jesus Christ, our Lord. Anointing with oil is a blessing that celebrates life; life of the Anointed One, here and right through death.

Dan died two months after that anointing liturgy. I do miss him. But my life remains intertwined with his. My grief over losing him bore fruit in the process of my becoming a Canadian citizen. Dan's death here in Saskatoon solidified the sense that Canada has indeed become my home – the place where death and life meet in truth.

Extravagant blessing, extravagant love. This is our God, who creates our kinship with one another through Christ. Jesus' death and resurrection reveal that the God of life-giving Love is indeed our home – the place where death and life meet in truth.

God blesses our woundedness into wholeness. Anointed into healing, God calls us to go forth in God's abundant Spirit. Our presence here at the seminary, our offering of ourselves through anointing, claims God's love for us and for all of creation.

In this love may we live, bound to one another. In God's extravagant anointing, may we mend our brokenness. May we thus be poured out for God's world in God's Spirit. Amen.

After the service I sat in my professor's office and cried. Never before had I felt such an intense mix of passion, love and terror all at the same time. Never before had I felt so alive or found such an unexpected treasure, a treasure revealing who I was in God. I cried because the treasure, beautiful as its features were, terrified me. The professor's comment that I was one of a few in a class of twenty students who seriously wrestled with the call to preach only made the pain worse. She asked how it felt standing in the pulpit, breaking open God's Word. Through my tears I answered: "I felt like I was tasting forbidden fruit, because, according to my tradition, God does not call women in this way. Yet it felt so right. I have come alive in a new way, with an even more burning desire to serve my church. But how?" The annoyed and reluctant student from the start of the course had changed into a woman who experienced God's call to preach and felt acutely that this call could not be claimed publicly. I was that woman, and I cried. Seeing my pain, my professor responded: "Don't worry. I do not believe God raises up gifts and then drops you like a hot potato. And besides, sit tight – your Church needs you sooner than it would like to think."

Those words proved to be prophetic, but at the time I did not know it. All I knew was that both the call to preach and the gift of preaching were not mine to keep, to hide, or to boast about. Rather, God's own gifts are always given for the sake of, and for service to, the faith community. It baffled me how God's call and gift to break open the Word in preaching could ever bear fruit in my tradition. I felt like Mary, when the angel visited her, announcing she was to give birth to God's own beloved son. Mary's question became the one big burning question in my heart: "How can this be?" (Luke 1:34) I concluded the preaching course with the acute awareness that the courage to name the call and claim the gift of preaching would forever alter my relationship to my beloved Roman Catholic Church. I feared deeply that somehow I was about to lose everything on which I had staked my very being. "When what is amazingly and bewilderingly new intrudes the living rooms of our souls, it is time to realize that something wonderful has happened, yes, but that life as we knew it will also never again be the same,"[7] says Chittister, and I knew in my bones what those words meant. Yet, with Mary, the mother of God, I fell into the arms of this God who makes the impossible possible.

CHAPTER 2

Gestation

For it was you who formed my inward parts;
you knit me together in my mother's womb.
My frame was not hidden from you,
when I was being made in secret,
Intricately woven in the depths of the earth.

(Psalm 139:13, 15)

Learning about preaching opened up many issues well beyond the classroom. The power of words, and the way words are used, became visible in its many dimensions, not least of which was the role of words in shaping our reality and our belief systems. Moreover, words used in the public sphere – and preaching is a public activity – always have a political aspect that far exceeds their local and personal setting. The faith community's role in the preaching process became one of the first revelations for me. My preaching was possible only because the seminary's faith community called me forth to do so. The course requirements and the student body itself invited me into the pulpit. There was no other reason that I should be preaching.

This was unlike my understanding of most other choices in my life. Nothing ever depended so much on outside circumstances to legitimate what I chose to do. Quite the contrary, I thought myself reasonably free from others to do the things I did, free to refuse what I did not like, and so on. To realize the need to be "free for" the faith community in order to minister through preaching was a brand new idea. This felt like too much dependency at first. Yet the movement was clear: without the "fiat" of the community, I had no right to preach.

I pondered repeatedly these words of Jesus: "Your faith has saved you; go in peace" (Luke 7:50) and "When he saw their faith, he said, 'Friend, your sins are forgiven you'" (Luke 5:20). I always wondered why Jesus, the Son of God, "needed" our faith before he could perform miracles. Jesus is God; therefore Jesus could act independently from us. Yet he seemed to seek faith in those coming to him, and the success of his healing ministry seemed to hinge on the measure of that faith. I started to understand more fully that Jesus' healing is an incarnational healing; it needs to be invited into our lives of our own free will, and it needs to be received at a deep level. Jesus' ministry of healing and teaching becomes manifest in the flesh and bones of its recipients. This is the God of incarnation, the God of Jesus of Nazareth.

Somehow these words of Jesus shed some light on my new experience. I learned that preaching arises from the community's call. My preaching apprenticeship took place within a community of faith, the student body, who affirmed and validated both call and gifts. Without the affirmation and invitation to preach, given in freedom, there was no call to discern and no response required. Just as Jesus needs active faith in the person asking for healing, I needed a community of faith to mandate and to actively receive the preached Word of God. The preacher can never grab the authority to preach, whether ordained or not: this authority is always handed over by the community. This is the antithesis of standing on one's own soapbox – something the pulpit should never be!

God is present in the assembly gathered for worship. The preacher arises out of that assembly, and is sent to the Scripture text on behalf of the faith community. I hold a position of peculiarity that comes with being the one called. It is a fragile place, a place of intense listening, a place of vulnerability where the Word of God seizes me before addressing the assembly. As the Word speaks to my heart, the community is being addressed. Like Moses coming down from the mountain, I return to the community and speak that which I have seen and heard. In the end, I trust and pray that the words spoken serve God's Good News and reach the hearts of people. But there is never a guarantee, and no two people respond in the same way.

Once the words have left, they take on a life of their own, carried by the Spirit of God. Born out of a deeply personal engagement with God's Word, the words, once spoken, nevertheless cease to be mine. It is a strange and often frightening experience. Barbara Brown Taylor captures well the delicate work of the preacher in her book *The Preaching Life*:

> Watching a preacher climb into the pulpit is a lot like watching a tightrope walker climb onto the platform as the drum roll begins. The first clears her throat and spreads out her notes; the second loosens his shoulders and stretches out one rosin-soled foot to test the taut rope. Then both step out into the air, trusting everything they have done to prepare for this moment as they surrender themselves to it, counting now on something beyond themselves to help them do what they love and fear and most want to do. If they reach the other side without falling, it is skill but it is also grace – a benevolent God's decision to let these daredevils tread the high places where ordinary mortals have the good sense not to go.[8]

Preparing to preach on Scripture texts not of my choosing – the Lectionary determines the choice – requires great discipline in listening anew, setting aside all the things I would like to say or think I should say. The attentive listening is especially important for texts that are most familiar, for I risk assuming that I know what the text communicates even before spending time with it. The listening happens three ways: one, to the text itself in its historical setting, its theological, pastoral and spiritual meaning; two, to the community about to be addressed here and now – its composition, its joys and sorrows, its crises and questions; and three, to my own inner responses, both to the text and to the community, my own preoccupations and discomforts with either, my questions and hurts, my connecting points and my dissimilarities with both.

The Word of God confronts our existence each time we engage with it. Preparing to preach involves a process that closely resembles an examination of conscience. I learned the meaning of David Buttrick's phrase "confessional exploration":

> If we intend to voice attitudes in a sermon, we must be cautious. We should never attempt to represent an attitude which we cannot find within ourselves or which we flatly

reject. If we try to express an attitude that we do not have, our language will usually ring false. And if we speak an attitude that we despise, our hostility will almost always creep into our language as sarcasm or slight ridicule. As preachers…we are children of a social world, a world which we internalize (along with our listeners)….Thus, when we articulate an attitude, we are not engaging in theatrics (as if) playing a role. Instead, we are voicing an attitude which is *in us*, an attitude which we share with our congregation on the basis of our common humanness in a common worldmind. Though we may not be *of* the world, we are all emphatically *in* the world.[9]

Far from "theatrics," the preparation process required an honesty that left me feeling stark naked before God and, in some way, before the faith community. Every step in prayer and study brought a personal challenge. If the Biblical text addressed certain sinful behaviours, I searched my own life for similar sins. If the texts spoke about the unbelief of the people, I wondered about the strength of my own faith. If the story featured someone in need of Jesus' healing, I sought out my own wounds in need of healing. When certain parts of a given text evoked strong feelings, I learned to pay special attention, trying to understand the reasons for their presence. This was especially hard with negative, uncomfortable and angry feelings.

I used to "let it all hang out" when such feelings overtook me in daily life. This way of handling emotions created havoc with my significant relationships more than once, and proved to be most unhelpful when praying with a Scripture text for the purpose of preaching. Now a new inner discipline was required to explore the origin of the strong feelings, to affirm them when necessary and to put them at the service of the task ahead. Many a time I felt my own inadequacy; I was a klutz in handling feelings, people, myself and situations even though I appeared to have it all together. To speak God's Word in the full knowledge of my own sinfulness made me feel incredibly small and humble.

Coming to the Scripture texts for the purpose of preaching, therefore, seemed more demanding than coming to the same texts for personal devotion. Ideally, even when praying with the Scriptures for private spiritual growth and nourishment, we take the text seriously. However, praying with the texts in order to preach created an urgency and an added responsibility to be real with God in order that I could be real with the congregation I was addressing. As David Buttrick said, a ring of falseness is inevitably communicated if we have not struggled, and been honest with, the text ourselves. I cannot invite my listeners into a conversion of heart if I am not open to conversion myself.

These insights, realizations and experiences developed over my remaining years of studies. Sometimes the learning process was painstakingly slow and difficult, yet at the same time it was undeniably challenging and life-giving. It was the discovery of the life-giving potential in the arduous task of preaching that kept me spellbound, and that kept fuelling the fire within, the fire to serve my church in the ministry of preaching, however unusual that seemed for a Catholic woman. I still had no idea how I would be able to live out this ministry.

God's call to preach does not necessarily imply a call to ordained ministry. However, with the exception of some Catholic women, such as Hildegard of Bingen, Catherine of Siena and Teresa of Avila, who were outstanding preachers in their own right, historically most "lay preaching" developed in Protestant circles, if at all. The history of the Evangelical churches, for example, includes many women, especially in the nineteenth century, who claimed a call to preach without tying this to ordination. Outside the definition of liturgical preaching, there are many Catholic women even today who "preach" by sharing stories of call from God and response in service: these include Marguerite Bourgeoys, Mother Teresa, Catherine Doherty, Dorothy Day and Joan Chittister. Most of these well-known women were single or religious, including Catherine Doherty, who chose to live a celibate marriage. It is somewhat peculiar that married women are missing from the list. Even given the abundance of Catholic women witnessing powerfully to the Gospel with their lives, according to Roman Catholic teaching, God does not call women to ordained ministry and the Church does not consider itself as having the authority to ordain women. I adhered to that doctrine as best I could while attempting to interpret, and make sense of, my preaching experience and my perceived call from God to do so. For Catholics the preaching ministry in the liturgy of the Eucharist is intimately tied to ordination – whether priest, bishop or deacon. Theologically and liturgically, Jesus Christ is fully present, and his life is broken and poured out for us in both the proclaimed and preached Word of God, and in the eucharistic sacrifice of bread and wine:

> [...] preaching is not "telling my story," not "my moment," not "choosing my text." It is a communal ritual undertaking, the texts read in the meeting and the whole (eucharistic) action [...] brought to contemporary rhetorical focus as a pattern for life. (Preaching) is at once a symbol of the faith of the community and a symbol of that word of life always coming from outside of us, surprising us. Preaching fulfills the promise of these symbols only by speaking of Jesus Christ, crucified and risen, as the meaning of the scriptures and of the (eucharistic) table, as the only grounds for our community, and as God's word of life....[10]

Tension emerged in me from living in several understandings: a Protestant acceptance of the possibility of women being called to sacramental ministry, and therefore to the preaching of the Word; a Catholic prohibition that my experience could not possibly be interpreted as a call to ordination; an Evangelical understanding of the validity of lay preaching without ordination; and, at least in theory, a renewed Catholic reappraisal of the call to all the baptized to serve in both the Church and the world. When it comes to preaching in the liturgy, Roman Catholics regard the call to exercise this ministry as synonymous with the call to Holy Orders:

> By means of the homily the mysteries of the faith and the guiding principles of the Christian life are expounded from the sacred text. The homily [...] is to be highly esteemed as part of the [eucharistic] liturgy itself.[11]

> The pastors of the Church, by their willing fidelity to the norms and directives of the Church, and in a spirit of faith

which abandons all personal and individual preferences, are in an especial way the ministers of the common liturgy. By their example, by their deep understanding, by their daunt-less preaching, they can bring about that flowering growth which the renewal of the liturgy requires. They will listen to the needs of the present day in a way which is far from secularism and an arbitrary attitude which would seriously threaten the liturgical reform.[12]

Our Lutheran and Anglican sisters and brothers also ordain their ministers to the ministry of "Word and Sacrament." Both aspects need one another in order to represent Christ fully to the faith com-munity and in order to bind us together as Christ's body on earth. Except for deacons, Roman Catholic understanding regards preaching and celebrating the sacraments as one single call to ordained priest-hood. Though not impossible, it is extremely difficult to consider a call to preach God's Word in isolation from a call to celebrate the sacred mysteries of the faith. Moreover, the learning and discerning context at the Lutheran seminary had no intention to separate preach-ing and ordination into two different calls. However strange it felt, I entered critical reflection and personal discernment on the one pos-sibility that my tradition did not formally recognize.

I thought I knew where I was going with my studies: my ulti-mate goal was to become a deeply Spirit-filled, prayerful, competent and effective counselling professional. My academic goal was a Mas-ter's degree in pastoral counselling. However, as I moved through the process of academic learning and challenge, I discovered the paradox of cross and resurrection in a new and frightening way. What started out as a clear response in a certain direction, and a delightful revelling in my ability to learn and grow, turned into some-thing much bigger than my own life, becoming a catalyst for unset-tling and unexpected questions. The treasures I was starting to dis-cover extended far beyond being the faithful parish volunteer. Claim-ing my identity, integrity and calling as woman in the Church started to challenge loyalties to the beloved religious home of my youth and adulthood, and not because I had become indoctrinated with Lutheranism.

Trying to hold together my Roman Catholic doctrinal and theological understanding on the question of women's ordination with my new, deep, personal experience of call and of preaching, was therefore an excruciating task. Either I worked hard to deny the validity of what God was doing in order to safeguard my Roman Catholic belonging, or I balanced on the edge of the denominational abyss, mustering the courage to claim God's call to the preaching ministry and therefore, it seemed, to ordained ministry. The formation process did not just affect what I did, what I thought, what I desired – God's call and the preaching experience was forming me ontologically, that is, affecting who I was becoming in my very being. It was not something I could put on like a set of clothes for a given occasion, and take off when I chose. In the deepest sense of the word, God led me home to myself, to what God was calling me to be. The authenticity, the renewed creativity and vision, the depth and fullness of life, the seemingly boundless energy unleashed, and the growing intimacy with God through Jesus Christ were all fruits of God's Spirit. Nevertheless, the learning and discerning were often seriously obstructed by my own resistance and fear. Allowing questions of call to the ministry of liturgical preaching to emerge truly felt like risking a betrayal of my tradition, precisely because of my church's teaching on ordination. God could take everything else, but I was bound to remain a faithful daughter of the Church. I now wished I could be content serving coffee after Mass.

I preached a few more times in the seminary chapel for morning worship. Praying with the biblical texts in preparation for preaching set me ablaze. I got bouts of nervousness every time, and the preparation process consumed me. It was hard to understand how something that was so demanding and created so many unsettling questions nevertheless drew me so totally that I gave everything I could to the task before me. Somehow, in and among the intensity of the process, I discovered a wellspring of life so full and overflowing that I could not stay away. Preaching held the promise of life to the full. Once I experienced it, this promise drew me back into the discipline of preparing, drew me into the questions and nervousness, because the rewards were like nothing I had ever known before.

When preparing the following sermon, I became aware of seminary life in new ways. The movements in the sermon were evoked by walking through Mark 10:17-22 over and over again, and having the text interact with the reality of seminary life. As a member of the student body I spent enough time with other students to know that many shared my experiences. We organized a food drive for one of the students and his family when they ran out of money for groceries. We mourned the sudden death of a fellow student. We had endless discussions about the questions arising from our theology classes. We explored together the reasons for leaving behind jobs, hometowns and security, all to follow a beckoning from God into ministry. I could say the following things precisely because I was a member of the community addressed and featured in the sermon.

Sermon for Lutheran Theological Seminary Worship

2 Corinthians 3:1-6, Mark 10:17-22

"Teacher! Teacher!" I yelled as I ran across the classroom, almost stumbling over my own feet. Today was report card day. I was excited. Had I done all the right things to get good marks? Mom and Dad had promised me a new bike if I passed my grade. Wow, what a reward! I worked hard for this all year. Now it was time for the glory…

Ah, those early school days… We learned a lot back then, and not only in reading and arithmetic. We learned good work habits. We learned to work for what we got. Early life lessons weave distinct threads through our adult years. At our workplace we ask: What must I do to meet job expectations? In university we ask: Professor, what must I do to pass the course? In family life we ask: What must I do to live with others in reasonable harmony? These are good things. Building blocks of personal growth, of competence, of community. So it is no surprise that when we come to Jesus, the first question on our mind is: What must I do to inherit eternal life?

Teacher, teacher… Does this work all the time? With zeal and self-confidence we set out to face the big questions in life. Convinced of our own competence we set out to make the world a better place – whatever our situation and whatever we understand that phrase to mean. We are all basically good people. We align ourselves with the "right" political issues, both in the Church and outside of it. We are immersed in social justice, we speak in tongues, we pray for the sick and the hungry, and we study the Holy things of God. Those of us in seminary fit this profile a bit too well. With a church structure that supports our notion of being called, it is so easy to feel that we are doing the "right" thing. We can even be heard to echo the words of the young man in the Gospel: "Well, Lord, I have kept all the commandments since my youth." After all, I was endorsed by my synod, sent by my parish, encouraged by my family, so what more is there to do, Lord?

Few of us expect, or look forward to, the torment in our souls when Jesus looks at us and loves us. Like the young man who asked Jesus what to do, few of us are prepared for Jesus' shocking invitation to go and sell all… Us? The ones in seminary? Have we not given everything already by coming here? What more do you want, Lord?

"Teacher, teacher" starts to sound bittersweet and hollow when life delivers the inevitable blows of living. In that sense, seminary is not a good hiding place. We sit with one another in times of illness and poverty, overcome with helplessness and despair – How will I pay the bills while going to school? We hear one another's anguish – Am I in the right place, doing the right thing? Is God still with me? We even face, and mourn, death itself among our very own in this place of learning. We lean on one another's shoulders, crying tears of grief and pain, sharing doubt and confusion. And we debate – oh, we can debate – and critique the very learning structure that is challenging us. No, seminary is not a good hiding place, not from the world, or from Jesus.

Well, maybe we can handle the thought of selling all in order to follow Jesus. Many of us can feel that we have done exactly that. We may have given up a good job, sold our house, moved across the country – all to come to seminary. And so we honestly believe that we let Jesus look at us and love us…until our faith itself gets a good shaking. Convinced that we have done all the right things – kept all the commandments, teacher – we can resist and even object to the painful questions in systematics, ethics or biblical studies. We came here to have our faith affirmed. We did not ask to have holes poked in our carefully thought-out belief system. How dare "they" undermine *my* faith?

And the emptying, the selling all, continues, layer after layer after layer... For we, of all people, need to clothe ourselves fully with Paul's words: our competence does not come from ourselves. If we believe that our competence is so important, then our faith has become works righteousness and self-glorification. That is why Jesus' loving gaze continues to strip us bare, layer after layer after layer.

As we are called to be ministers of a new covenant, the Spirit of the living God gets written – not with ink or on stone tablets, but applied with a branding iron onto our human hearts. Scarred with that loving look of God, we learn to see, hear, taste, smell and touch life anew.

With humility and slowly emerging clarity, we recognize what Paul means when he says that the letter of the law alone not only injures, but can kill...including in no small measure our own strong views – whether they be religious, social or political, whether liberal or conservative, whether left, right or centre. When that loving look of Christ really sets eyes on our soul, we can expect, first, inner turmoil – for we too have so many possessions. If we have the courage to stick it out in this loving gaze of God, our hearts will be branded with the Spirit of Life. In that Spirit of the living God we are set on fire with passion and compassion for and in the world.

Teacher, teacher, what must we do to inherit eternal life? After the initial shock and grief over losing our possessions – and not just material ones – we surrender and follow Jesus. Stripped, emptied, exposed and disempowered, we become a "letter of Christ." As ministers of the new covenant, we become the ones through whom Jesus looks upon the world and loves that world right into the heart of God. Such is the confidence that we have through Christ towards God. Amen.

I became an astute observer of the "movement" of call and response: the faith community saying in one form or another, "Preach to us"; God's blessing of that call by the tangible presence of God's guidance and grace in the prayerful preparations; and my response to the call through the energy and commitment to the task, unleashed in the prayerful preparation and the preaching discipline:

> I am getting so nervous that I fear I will pass out in the pulpit. Not because I'll be speaking to a group of people, but more because of what it means to preach God's Word to the faith community... The need for prayer, for blessing, for being sent, aches in my soul. Preaching is not meant to be my personal thing – I sense this all over. Preaching needs the blessing of the community, the prayer and support of a mentor, and the mandate from the One who is being proclaimed. The seminary community endorses my preaching by its invitation and its presence around me. My professor endorses my preaching by her example and by her encouraging feedback on my draft sermons. God calls and endorses my preaching by the fire kindled in my whole being when bringing myself to the biblical texts for the purpose of preaching. (Journal entry)

Slowly, paying attention to the learning, the feedback from others and my personal inner movements, I grew stronger in my ability to discern a definite call from God and from the faith community. Jesus went to Nazareth and could not do any healing there because of lack of faith (Luke 4:16-30). While my experience of God's call grew and developed, I wondered what it would be like to preach in my own Church tradition. Would God's Word be heard, or would people be too preoccupied with the sight of a woman in that sacred space?

CHAPTER 3

Labour and Delivery

"Peace be with you.
As the Father has sent me,
so I send you."
When he had said this,
he breathed on them and said to them,
"Receive the Holy Spirit."
(John 20:21-22)

Our experiences – and the way we interpret them – are culturally and religiously determined. As long as our interpretations, and the values attributed to them, fall within accepted cultural and religious norms we hardly notice being hemmed in or limited. Until something or someone clearly does not "fit." I think back to the start of our married life.

Jim and I found a strong common bond in countercultural choices of lifestyle. We made our living off the land operating a small organic market garden. We heated the house and cooked meals with wood heat, preserved most of our food for the winter (canning and freezing), and managed our bodily needs without modern plumbing (rainwater becomes very precious for more reasons than one!). Our making those choices as active Catholics had many people puzzled and even slightly uncomfortable. Our choices clearly fell outside the accepted cultural and religious norms. According to fellow Catholics we lived like lopsided hippies, back-to-the-landers who were just a bit "odd" coming to church on Sundays. It seemed incomprehensible to live in opposition of mainstream culture and call that opposition "inspired by the Gospel." According to the "real" back-to-the-landers, who lived on marginal bush land north and east of our region, we didn't really buck the system since we remained part of a church that spans 20 centuries. It did not occur to them that our Christianity inspired the same countercultural choices as they made; turning away from organized religion was part of their protest. Jim and I felt out of place in both circles. We felt regret that some of our friends decided it was necessary to throw the baby out with the Christian bathwater. We shook our heads at fellow Catholics who seemed to feel totally unchallenged by the Gospel in their affluent, middle-class lifestyles. Where was the social conscience that revolted against injustice, that cried out over the exploitation of the earth, and that worked diligently to assure equal distribution of the earth's resources? It was an uncomfortable place to be, yet life off the land was rich in real-ness and potent with spiritual meaning for us both. However, culturally, and even religiously, we felt "displaced."

Such a sense of displacement can occur in one's prayer life. Praying to God, whether privately or communally, we ask the Holy Spirit for insight, guidance and wisdom. Prayer moulds our disposition to God, developing in us an open heart and mind. However, our ability to recognize the Holy Spirit's work is heavily influenced by what the Church tells us. In other words, we readily recognize and appreciate the Holy Spirit in our lives as long as the insights gained are within the parameters of "revealed truth." For the most part, the Holy Spirit's activity occurs in unobtrusive ways, until one day, the insight, guidance and wisdom received find no place within what is culturally and religiously acceptable, through ways that are "not always in the book."[13] For a Roman Catholic woman like me, discovering a call and gifts that lie beyond the church's understanding of "revealed truth" was therefore unsettling, because at first glance it did not "fit" and I risked feeling displaced as a result. Even though we have been trying to recover, ever since Vatican II, a renewed understanding of our baptismal call as laity, much work remains to be done to get the attitudes and mentality of those in the pews to fully embrace such a theology of gifts and ministry connected to baptism. A recent article quoted laity as not only called to minister *ex-ecclesia* (i.e., in their secular place in the world), but increasingly to minister within the Church.[14] Even at that, generally speaking, liturgical preaching is still not considered one of these ministries. Despite all conventions and Church teachings, the call to liturgical preaching continued to make itself known to me, and I felt thrown off balance. The ways of knowing God, myself, others and the Church changed dramatically, leaving me unsteady on my feet at age 40 – a toddler all over again:

> Needing to hide among my own people, and shrouding in a mist of silence the fullness of who I am becoming – two descriptions of how I felt in a couple of church settings this past weekend. New dance steps, and my Partner takes me along the dance floor – I feel unsteady, oh I feel unsteady. Strange experiences, yet disturbingly revealing the next phase of this journey with God. I take note of the dramatic inner changes, but I feel like I am watching a movie – this is happening to someone else. And a big part of me still wants to run, and pretend this is make-believe. (Journal entry)

The last year of studies, now almost seven years ago, proved to be one of revelation and of mourning in preparation for graduation, which launched me into a dark and unknown future, or so it felt. The illusion of pretending was ripped away and I was forced to face that God had been revealing something much fuller, much more creative and engaging than my initial goal of pastoral counselling. What God was revealing affected in profound ways my self-identity and mission. These seven years of study and formation were not about becoming a pastoral counsellor. Rather, this place that prepares women and men for ministry in the Church was leaving its mark on my very soul. God was calling me to a form of leadership in my church. And I still panicked, asking how this could be. All I could feel was displacement.

Not that serving the Church was a new concept for me – far from it. All through my studies, I remained active in my own Roman Catholic parish, along with my husband, Jim. I was on the local and diocesan liturgy committee. I represented my parish on the diocesan pastoral council, and helped facilitate workshops on liturgy-related matters and on pastoral care. I sang in our church choir and went on pilgrimage to a local Marian shrine. As a member of our parish women's group, I brought many a dish of food to church lunches and suppers. Along with many others behind the scene, I was one of the trusted volunteers who kept the church going. Our bishop knew Jim and me and our three children by name. Along with the habits of brushing your teeth at night and doing chores around the house, our children absorbed through example and lifestyle an active church involvement, family-centred prayer, and social justice commitments both big and small.

Nor did the new callings and challenges come out of the blue. The learning built on natural interests and abilities, deepening my desire to serve the Church. What until now were theoretical questions about the place of women in my church tradition started to take on features of my own experience. One day a fellow student remarked how wonderful it was that my Church endorsed my studies at a non-Catholic seminary. I replied that he forgot to ask a preliminary question: Did my church care whether I studied theology and ministry? The answer to that question was no, which made his comment nonsense. I was not sent by my church to study ministry. I was not formally supported to do so, and I had no hope of being sent or supported, financially or otherwise. This little, seemingly innocent remark set off a disturbing train of thought, producing new feelings of exclusion. Priestly ministry, which was understood as the calling of celibate men, now started to emerge out of the historical, psychological and theological/spiritual landscape of my own life – something outside of acceptable "revealed truth," or so it seemed. How was this possible? How could I make sense of these experiences within the parameters of Roman Catholic Church teaching? Was this about a call to ordained ministry or was it something else: an intensification of my baptismal call to serve in ministry as a lay person, as addressed in Pope Paul VI's *Evangelii Nuntiandi* (1975) and in the U.S. Bishops' *Lay Ecclesial Ministry* (1999)? If it was the latter, then how was the experience of priestly call for celibate men different from what I was experiencing?

> Lay ministers speak often and reverently of their call or vocation to ministry, a call that finds its origin in the call of God and its confirmation in the appointment of a specific ministry within the Church. These ministers often experience such a call within, and sometimes transcending, a vocation to married, single, or religious life.[15]

The U.S. Bishops go on to admit that the Church has not yet sufficiently spoken, defined or ordered such an experience of call by lay people. My personal story seemed to confirm the ambivalence and newness felt throughout the Church. Being intentional about my theological, pastoral and spiritual formation effected a change in my understanding of call to service in the Church. The need for "vocational discernment" became compelling:

> During the course of our earthly sojourn our vocation comprises three aspects: a self-identity, or who the Lord calls us to be; a lifestyle, or how the Lord calls us to become ourselves in God; a mission, or what the Lord calls us to do for God and others.... The faith process whereby we listen to God, sift out our various interior leanings and try to name the Lord's particular invitation to us we term "vocational discernment." We cannot do the Father's will until we first listen to him, and we cannot know what the Father desires of us until he furnishes us some insight into his design. In vocational discernment...we seek enlightenment from God with regard to our self-identity, lifestyle and mission.[16]

As for my vocational lifestyle, I had embraced the sacrament of matrimony. I was married at 23 and started a family two years later. Living this sacrament moulded my self-identity and to a large extent, my mission in the world. Now a shift seemed to occur in my sense of mission in the Church, part of the third element of vocation as identified by Coomb and Nemeck. The shift in both experience and understanding of my call or mission in turn affected my self-identity, and my relationship to the Church, in profound ways.

The changes in my own life took place at a time when our diocese faced an increasing shortage of priests to serve the 87 parishes spread across a large geographical area across the province. Our bishop used every opportunity to address the people on this topic, to bring home the severity of the situation, and to spur everyone on to pray for vocations to the ordained priesthood. In light of his urgent call for help, and in light of my studies and formation, remaining a faithful parish volunteer did not feel adequate anymore. I was filled with anticipation, eagerness to serve, and frustration, all at the same time:

I can no longer ignore that I am submitting myself to a formation process preparing me for leadership in the Church. Being thus seized by the call of the Gospel to choose life in Christ upsets my applecart, spilling the apples all over my carefully tidied alleys and pathways, forcefully throwing out the well thought-out goals. The Gospel of Life still has the power to roll the stone away from the tombs we bury ourselves in, even if those tombs are church traditions that compromise the proclamation and practice of the Gospel. With shock and pain I realize that my theological, psychological and political position in the Church is one of silence and invisibility. My practical stance in the Church is one of being willing to offer my gifts in times of absolute emergencies, a poor substitute for "the real thing." I am slowly taking my place with the many women who feel in their bones the blatant discrepancy between this injustice and the person of Jesus who offered women and men God's promise of life in abundance. Again I kick and scream silently as I open my eyes to the blinding call of the Gospel to me, a woman in the Roman Catholic Church. I had no idea that it could hurt so much when one has more to offer God's church than bringing the pumpkin pies to the church supper, when all that is wanted and asked for are the pumpkin pies. I'm not even good at baking pies. (Journal entry)

Since our diocese seemed in such dire need of pastoral leadership, and I was about to complete my formation, I informed the bishop of my availability. I sincerely hoped and prayed that the training I had received and the gifts that had been awakened could now be put at the service of our beloved church. If I was a celibate male with these experiences of call, ordained priesthood would likely be a serious option to consider. Yet even without this option, new forms of parish pastoral ministry were emerging in other dioceses in order to compensate for the shortage of ordained ministers. I had a real sense that God was working to effect these new forms, through my training and in the creative responses in specific pastoral situations emerging in other dioceses. Working for and in the Church would no longer be a volunteer task alongside my other work. I was called to make ministry in the Church my primary focus, even though its final form remained unclear.

Very early on in this study venture, something inside told me that it was important to write to the bishop on a regular basis, keeping him apprised of the formative happenings in my life. I wrote to him out of a clear sense that I was being prepared for the Church, and that this formation was not for myself. I felt both accountable to, and dependent on, the local bishop, as pastoral ministry is exercised through his mandate. I wrote my letters expecting a reply. None came. It was only years later that I learned that unless my letter requested a reply on a concrete issue, the bishop would likely not respond. Yet we met at diocesan meetings and events, socializing and chatting. I found it most unusual, and hurtful, that nothing was said by him about my written communication.

> The bishop attended the afternoon meetings. I expected him to acknowledge receipt of my resume and letter, especially since he speaks so often about the severity of the pastoral leadership crisis. But there was nothing. Not that he was unfriendly or negative – no, we chatted quite casually and cheerfully. And in his public talk he praised women's volunteer contributions to the Church. He was, however, silent about the pastoral call I put out there to be received and considered. It is this omission that hurt so deeply. The pastoral part of my being was rendered invisible by the bishop's friendly, yet dismissing silence. Pain pierced my soul like a dagger. At Mass the bishop spoke about service to the Church, about the lack of priests, and the need to pray for vocations … Tears burnt behind my eyes the whole time, but how could I explain such tears to those around me… I swallowed the pain, big gulps at a time, choking me. (Journal entry)

I wondered whether this is what Joan Chittister called "being seduced by a reverence that applauds [women] but limits them" and "[Women] are eulogized for staying in their proper places, for being sufficiently docile and properly deferent, but they are also degraded by the false protectionism, veneration, paternalism, and denigration that [a patriarchal] system offers."[17]

This was the atmosphere in which I prepared for graduation. I mourned deeply ending the years with my Lutheran sisters and brothers – so much deep and unexpected spiritual, intellectual and psychological growth had occurred during my time among them. Now came the time to leave the nest and try out my new wings. Terror filled my heart at the thought of being thrown back into my church with a professional formation for pastoral leadership. At the same time I was excited over accomplishing an enormous task. Years of driving back and forth to classes (a four-hour round trip twice a week) had taken its toll. My husband had been supportive of and interested in my studies all along, but balancing the roles of mother, wife, homemaker and student had left me exhausted. The end was near, and it was time.

> I am slowly catching the graduation fever; it is indeed an exciting occasion that has been seven years in the making. And I am coming to terms with closure of this phase in my life. I have started to apply for jobs. Mentally I am preparing for the next step, and it is time. I am growing into a readiness to both welcome and enter into this next step – whatever this will be. The pain about leaving Lutheran Theological Seminary is turning from a mourning pain into a labour pain: something new is being born. Do you not see it yet? (Journal entry)

As if the formation for pastoral leadership was not sufficient, the seminary community insisted on reaffirming God's call one more time, in case it had not yet sunk in. As the ten graduates prepared the closing graduation liturgy, they asked me to preach at the eucharistic celebration. Shivers went down my spine. I joked, asking out loud if they really wanted a Roman Catholic woman to preach at a Lutheran graduation (there was also a Mennonite and a Pentecostal among the graduates, and not all the Lutherans were planning to be ordained). With fear and trembling, I accepted. This time the pain of wrestling and praying with the Scripture texts seemed more intense than ever. I found myself face to face with God's call in a most poignant, compelling way – a call that contrasted sharply with my place as a woman in the Church.

The chosen Scripture texts spoke of being called and sent forth – no surprise for a seminary graduation. However, one question haunted me: How could I preach in a way that included myself, someone who is part of a church that has no structural place either for the discernment of this call or for being sent forth out of this call? What was God doing, putting me in this burning place of ministry? The seminary community had affirmed and mandated this call one more time, but who or what would call forth the gift once I left this place of formation?

By this time, I was conducting workshops on preaching with a Catholic priest, Father Leonard. Spending hours together driving to workshop locations gave us the opportunity to collaborate and to get to know each other. I was also looking for a spiritual director. Even though I was not keen on having a Catholic priest fulfill this role, Father Leonard's respect, openness and appreciation prompted me to seek him out for spiritual direction. It was the first time I had entrusted my soul's journey with God to a man – not to mention an ordained minister in my own tradition. I entered this aspect of our relationship with apprehension, fear and misgivings. It became clear, however, that God was asking me in no uncertain terms to frame my story squarely within my tradition. What better way than with a Roman Catholic priest, in the sacramental encounter of confession?

There were several reasons for sacramental confession. Coming to terms with God's call to preach made me more aware of my own sinfulness. I tasted vividly the temptation to make this my own ego trip, pushing the Scripture texts around according to my own preferences, and revelling in the "glory" of being called. I knew I could not let such temptations take hold, because it would destroy both the call and God's activity. Rather than satisfy these ego trips, I needed to foster a spirit of humility and receptivity, much like Mary when she submitted to God's plan: "Do with me according to your will."

I also had a strong sense that my personal experience with God somehow belonged within the larger story of the Church. I remained aware that I had not gone looking for this call, nor had my ego dreamed it up. Instead, God came looking for me and pried open my clenched fist, which nervously tried to hang on to its own agenda. Surrendering to God now made the most total claim. Enormous tension arose between total and full engagement with God and the need to let go at unprecedented depth of soul. I knew I could not possibly negotiate this phase of the journey alone. Even though I was deeply alone with God in this experience, I needed help, guidance, strength, forgiveness. I turned to the sacrament of reconciliation with renewed desire.

Because the nature of God's activity in this matter seemed so difficult to place in my tradition, I felt strangely at odds with my Church, and this at a time when I felt I was being led deep into the heart of that same church. I was worried that in claiming God's call to preach I placed myself outside traditional church teaching, since what I was doing came close to violating church teaching on the ordination of women. Never in my life had I willingly violated church teachings, not even on family planning. On the contrary, up to now I had experienced the rules of the Church as facilitating a maturing and liberating faith. I felt extremely uncomfortable with the possibility of contradicting the powers that be. Some form of reconciliation was essential, if I was to increase my trust and courage in letting God's plan unfold. The sacrament of forgiveness and healing beckoned me.

The *sensus fidelium*, the consensus of the faithful, expressed in its teachings, its liturgy, its spirituality, is what guides the Church throughout the centuries. Historically, the Church has used these expressions to discern the activity of God in the experiences of individual Christians. The witness of any person, including saints, becomes part of the Church, authenticated by the Church, often after the person's death. I placed great faith in the Church's wisdom and scrutiny to preserve the depth and richness of our Christian faith. I believed it remained the Church's sacred task to discern the authenticity of anyone's call and anyone's spiritual life, and I was no exception. It was completely in keeping with this understanding of the Church's role that I needed to place my experience with God in the Church. The first option to do this presented itself through the sacramental encounter of confession and forgiveness.

Father Leonard received me with incredible respect. Filled with God's grace, he received the questions in my mind, the joys in my heart, the pain in my body, and the tears in my soul. He helped me look at my journey in terms of the paschal mystery of Christ's own death and resurrection. The hallmark of God's presence is the crucified and risen Jesus, who emptied himself in order to be filled with God's resurrection living. The yearning to serve God in our church burned in my heart; at the same time, this yearning felt like the emptying of my own ambitions, goals and agency. The pain of the cross emptied and emptied me, while God filled the emptiness with new life in the risen Christ.

In many ways, I am mourning – deeply mourning. And I mourned most of this year, whether I was consciously aware of this or not. I am mourning the loss of the illusion of control over my life journey. I am mourning my forever inadequate understanding of God, self and others. I am mourning the loss of a place of learning that not only supported me but actively called me forth in ways I had never dreamed possible, challenging me to claim the gifts and passion that have now seen the light and that will no longer retreat into darkness. I mourn the thick mist on the journey with God, which makes it impossible to see more than one step ahead of me. I mourn the loss of clear and cherished self-concepts, the loss of the comfort and reassurance these once gave me. I mourn the loss of my ego's freedom. (Journal entry)

Preparing the graduation sermon and the spiritual direction work with Father Leonard were intense, painful and yet filled with the pushing of the Spirit, much like labour pains a woman feels when her time has come. I was haunted by painful questions, by a growing and more acute awareness of my place in the Church, and by a deep fear of my future in that Church.

How could I possibly preach on being called and sent forth in a way that included me, since I was *not* being called and sent forth by my Church? Many times in the sessions with Father Leonard I sat and cried as I sifted my way through the Scriptures, the yearnings in my heart, and the seminary community to be addressed on this joyous occasion. Out of the turmoil, through prayer, solitary reflection and the talks with Father Leonard, eventually emerged a deep understanding of baptism: our threefold baptismal anointing into Christ's own ministry as priest, prophet and king. I grew in my understanding that I could claim my call to preach as arising out of this baptismal anointing, and that this call was valid and legitimate. I climbed into the pulpit that festive day, reassured that I stood on solid ground with God and with the Church.

Sermon for Graduation, Lutheran Theological Seminary
Isaiah 6:1-8, Colossians 3:12-17, John 20:19-21

It has been a long road to this place, this time, this graduation — for some of us as long as nine years… right, Henri? We think of the trials of discernment, the obstacles and the challenges — all to pursue a call to ministry and come to seminary. Would we do it again? Probably yes. For amid the struggles, we have found a pearl of great price. The pearl of God's call to give our lives in loving service is mysterious, unsettling, and irresistible.

Even after all the years in seminary, God's calling voice remains an alluring mystery. Most of us are not sure if we have ever clearly heard it. Initial wonderment over a call to ministry often comes in a cryptic message. You know, God's voice is like a message that jars, and causes us to reflect. Like the person who says to us, out of the blue: "Have you ever considered full-time ministry?" Who, me? Or like a recurring dream about celebrating Eucharist, or about serving God in a special way. And what about discovering notes of an unsung melody asleep in our soul, awakened by the new reading of a familiar Scripture passage. Who, me? Pursuing what we believe God calls us to is not simple. Often it is just easier to continue with life, to go on as we have always done. Don't disturb our family life. Don't give up that business career. Don't change the lifestyle. Yet God knocks. God's hand keeps sketching ideas in our hearts. We become restless. We pray. We wonder what God asks. We try to name the experience. All we have are weeks of daily living: raising our children, paying the bills, going to school and work, going to church, struggling to find times of quiet. What do our hopes and dreams mean? Where is God taking us? Ideas form in our minds, desires move into our hearts, luring and drawing us…

Discerning a call to ministry is one struggle; following a call is another struggle. Obstacles abound: doubt, confusion, finances, social sacrifices, geographical and emotional displacement.

Yet the yearning to serve God's people haunts us, driving us into these struggles.

The burning dream in our heart drives us to forge a way. God, having claimed us in baptism, claims us for life. Just so, God confronts and invites us daily. When we realize this, we find ourselves poked and prodded, called to watch and wait and work with God.

God claims us. God wants us to serve. At first, we protest or run the other way. We are not worthy, we are "unclean." We are too old or too young. We are not gifted. We are wounded from living. We are stuck in a limited understanding of God's calling activity in the world. We want to be safe – untouched. Then, the living fire of baptism burns away our excuses. The hot coal of baptism leaps up and overtakes our limited understandings. The Living One renders us clean, burning away all that is unworthy. This living fire moulds and transforms us, from the inside out. In baptism God claims us. And some of us God claims for ministry in the Church, for the world. God courts us with such diligence that the only way we find peace is to say: "Here I am, send me."

Those who study for this ministry, those who have said to their synods, church boards and bishops, "Here I am; send me," end up in this place, at seminary. Here, there is more fire, the refiner's fire of seminary formation. We learn, we wrestle, we weep a bit. We are torn down and built up. As we are about to leave now, the future stretches out before us. Some are going north, some west. Some to wheat fields and lonely country roads. Some are going to cities and flood plains. Sometimes we are afraid, and doubtful. At times it looks safer to stay within the walls of the seminary – to go back to the books, to avoid the risk of making a mistake, to avoid the anxiety of being the new pastor in town. Here is the known; our future is unknown.

Wanting to lock the doors of this place, we could cling, in fear. But the Christ who comes and stands among us today says to each of us: "Peace be with you." This is the God who stands with us in our human vulnerability. In and with family, friends, mentors and teachers, in the assembly of the baptized, Christ offers us peace.

Around this table of bread and wine Christ's love surrounds us – and we who venture into new callings receive the Holy Spirit with all who share in Christ's feast.

Therefore, new graduates and freshly minted servants of Christ's church, be spurred on. Fred, Donna, Mel, Lohn, William, Phil, Marie-Louise, Henri, Benti and Joan: receive Christ's peace. Be sent. For Christ is the one who, being sent, now sends us. Be sent forth, in all the wonder and diversity of the Church catholic. Live out your calling as ordained priest. Live out your calling as pastoral and compassionate presence in places of need and suffering. Live out your calling in places pushing you into prophetic speech, in and outside the Church. Live out your calling in intimate connection to your sisters and brothers in Christ in the world. Christ calls and uses us all: as priest, prophet and king; as administrator, musician, healer and teacher.

As ministers of the Gospel we are set among the people of God. We are called by God from among the baptized. We reflect and seek Christ in the world we serve. And we need to receive the ministry of others. As servants of the Gospel we invite others into the fullness of their own baptism. This freedom in Christ gives peace. Nothing more, nothing less. What started out as a cryptic message, a baptismal promise and a baptismal struggle has now become a necessity of life. To live in the peace and fullness of Christ, we take up our baptism and bear God's Word into the world, each according to our gifts.

Life in service to the Church, life in the Church, brings pain and joy. There is praise and blame; there are challenges and aches for healing and mercy. We find food and experience hunger as we face our own ups and downs. Nonetheless, in Christ, we may embrace the ministries given, and face the challenges and hurdles. We may remain steadfast in our faith, knowing that Jesus Christ has gone before us in all things, and is with us always.

Christ's promise of peace transfigures our moving into places of ministry with zeal and trembling awareness. We hear Paul's ancient words of encouragement as fresh words, as God's words to us. Joan, Benti, Henri, Marie-Louise, William, Lohn, Phil, Mel, Donna and Fred – be steadfast; be filled with compassion; be filled with gentleness, both towards others as well as towards yourselves. Work to embody the God-given unity of the Spirit in the bond of Christ's peace. Thus, one faith is revealed in the one Body. Know that in the Lord no labour is in vain.

After all is said and done, God's calling activity remains an alluring mystery. Yet this pearl of great price is tangible in this place, at this celebration, with these graduates. We respond by offering our lives in service of the Gospel, and discover life given to us in turn, in full measure, overflowing… Mysterious, unsettling, and indeed, irresistible… Here I am, Lord… send me. Amen.

I left the pulpit with the distinct impression that I had just given birth in full view of the assembly.

Incredible relief, joy and peace washed over me, the kind I knew so well from the times I successfully delivered each of my children. The service continued while I held the treasure of my call with great delight and gratitude. For this moment at least, I rejoiced in what God had accomplished beyond my wildest dreams. Still wrapped in the joy of graduating, I shared the sermon with my own bishop a month later. It felt like showing him the "newborn." In the privacy of our encounter he listened, he saw, and he heard. His face showed surprise and wonder as he looked at me and said, thoughtfully and respectfully: "You are not just talking of a job – you are talking of a vocation." Then and there he prayed a blessing, and together we asked God to guide us.

CHAPTER 4

Feeding the Newborn

Jesus came to his hometown
and began to teach people in their synagogue,
so that they were astounded and said:
"Where did this man get this wisdom and these deeds of power?"
And they took offence at him.

(Matthew 13:54, 57)

During my seven years of studies, I remained quite active in my local church. However, until the call to preach became the clear voice of God, I had never imagined myself preaching in my Catholic tradition. Somehow that remained the unquestioned domain of the priest, and of my own husband whenever we celebrated Sunday liturgy without Eucharist. It simply never occurred to me that I could preach. Instead, I made my preaching debut in the nearby United Church community, as a result of a friendship with the pastor there. This struck me as ironic – as a Catholic I could not officially occupy the role of liturgical preacher in my own church, but as a non-member of the United Church I could preach in their pulpit. To be honest, I became afraid to "go back to Nazareth," remembering what happened to Jesus. It was safer to go to another church, preach to another community. But God would not have it this way.

Our parish priest was overburdened with the pastoral and sacramental care of six parishes. *Sunday Celebrations of the Word with Communion* (using reserved sacrament)[18] in the absence of a priest became a regular feature in our Catholic community's worship pattern. As opportunities to preach opened up out of sheer need, the words of my homiletics professor echoed in my mind: "Sit tight – your church needs you sooner than it likes to think." In my last year at seminary I had had the opportunity to preach in a non-eucharistic Catholic worship service. This was not easy. If I had trembled preaching at seminary, I surely trembled now, and for many reasons.

Many Catholics simply have never seen a woman in the role of liturgical preacher. Before I even opened my mouth, I was acutely aware of the "something new" offered to the listeners because I was a woman. It was definitely easier to simply bring my less-than-perfect pies to the church suppers. I did not particularly want to break open people's intimate experience of faith and church, but I felt pushed into this place. I had no desire to make a political statement by my presence in the pulpit, nor did I wish to flaunt my skills in inappropriate ways. With trembling I realized, however, that the features of God's activity were undeniably present. Mary Catherine Hilkert and a few other women seasoned in the preaching ministry helped me to see these features. In her book *Naming Grace: Preaching and the Sacramental Imagination*, Hilkert links the experience of a woman in the role of liturgical preacher to the startling newness that the proclamation of Christ Jesus crucified and raised from the dead continues to bring to the faith community:

> All Christian preaching centers around the proclamation that the one who was crucified has been raised and lives among us now in and through the power of the Spirit. But there is a unique way in which women's preaching of the gospel shares in the very mystery of the resurrection. The resurrection is the ultimate surprise and overthrow of former categories and limitations. The proclamation of the good news is an event in which the mystery of the gospel happens again here and now. For many in the Christian churches today, witnessing the word of God enfleshed by women is just such a parabolic experience. Their categories and expectations are shattered as God once again proves to be "doing a new thing" (Isaiah 43:19).[19]

Carol M. Noren makes similar observations with a different emphasis in her book *The Woman in the Pulpit*.[20] She opens her Introduction with the following words: "The Sunday morning service is different when a woman preaches. Church members know this instinctively. Women clergy know it, though past encounters with prejudice may make them reluctant to acknowledge and work with the differences." I knew what both Hilkert and Noren spoke about, since I felt in my bones these differences and the potentially subversive nature of taking on the preacher's role. I was as reluctant as the prophet Jeremiah, desperately wanting to drag my feet, asking why and complaining that God was not leaving me alone:

O Lord, you have enticed me, and I was enticed.
You have overpowered me, and you have prevailed.
I have become a laughingstock all day long;
everyone mocks me.
[…] If I say, "I will not mention him,
or speak anymore in his name,"
Then within me there is something like a fire burning
shut up in my bones.
I am weary with holding it in,
and I cannot.
(Jeremiah 20:7, 9)

With Jeremiah, my constant companion in those early days, I lamented about being seduced and overshadowed by God. All I had originally wanted was to be trained in pastoral counselling! Yet God startled me into a new endeavour with so much more. I started to understand the beauty of ignorance in the best sense of that word: it would have been better never to know what I know and feel now, and simply to stick with the usual volunteer work. When I took on the role of liturgical preacher, God shattered all human-made categories, possibly breaking open the listeners' experience in unexpected ways. Once the door of personal experience opened, there was no turning back. We cannot miss what we have never had; that explains in part why the ordination of women is a non-issue for some, or even an unacceptable concept for others. My preaching opened the door ever so slightly, even if I was not politically motivated to do so, and even for those who had not given much thought to the matter. And that is what made me tremble, raising the adrenaline to peak heights, urging me to run away. Pick on someone else, God. I do not want to be the one that stirs the pot:

> My life has been irrevocably changed – how this will manifest itself remains unclear. How do I now live – aware and yielding to the call – my relationships, my belonging in the Church, my new ministry? This call, and God's loving voice inviting my response, is not mine to control. Living in the heart of God and the Church is bigger than my own life – and this shows on the outside. God's own passion oozes out of me, and others take note and are struck. This has already started to happen in people's reactions to my preaching. Sometimes their remarks embarrass me, as if I am caught naked since they see deeply into my soul when God's presence is communicated in my passionate words. (Journal entry)

I read the words of Jesus in Matthew's Gospel:

> You are the light of the world. No one after lighting a lamp puts it under the bushel basket, but on the lamp-stand, and it gives light to all in the house. In the same way, let your light shine before others, so that they may see your good works and give glory to your Father in heaven. (Matthew 5:14-16)

I felt as if I was encountering the words for the first time, and they took on monumental meaning. I had no choice but to share with the faith community what I understood was given by God for the sake of that same faith community. Plagued by fears and worries of all sorts, I nevertheless responded and let my light shine.

Reactions to preaching in my own parish were, and remain, strong. The responses, at first surprisingly positive, related both to the fact that I was a layperson and a woman, and to the quality of my homiletic reflections. I felt uncomfortable with the comments. How could I start explaining what happened for me in the act of preaching? I started to realize how "easy" it was to offer something better than and different from most of the homilies people hear on a given Sunday with Eucharist. I realized that I probably could not do such a good job if I preached every Sunday, trying to squeeze preparation time into an overloaded pastoral schedule. My understanding of and compassion for the tasks of parish priests grew. Even though my life was equally overburdened with family and study/work commitments, somehow preparing to preach remained a fresh and inviting task for which I was always able and eager to make time. However, if I had to preach 52 times a year, I too might feel depleted at times.

It took continued grounding in prayer and surrender to God to absorb both the preaching experience in my own church and people's reactions. It felt as if I had learned to walk all over again in a house that was both familiar and strange. My self-identity changed, my sense of call and mission changed; as a result, my relationship to everything around me changed. Nothing felt comfortable, nothing felt easy or familiar anymore. The only place left to call home was the inner sanctuary where God whispers in the heart, that space deep inside where no other human being can go. Being a relational extrovert, I both feared and felt uncomfortable in that inner space. I was used to finding a friend or a mentor to reach out to, but now these options seemed inadequate and unfulfilling. For if I attempted to share with another, even my spiritual director, of my venture with God, no one could really enter my experience. Despite my attempts to put words on this intense process, they remained inadequate. No one really had a sense of the depth and the extent of this venture into preaching. How could I explain that in the preaching process I not only journeyed into Scripture, but also found myself in a rather unprotected and "forbidden" place. Unprotected not only from the demands of God's Word, but also from criticism and misunderstanding. Forbidden because the institutional protection of ordination, which traditionally clothes and recognizes this kind of call, was simply not available to me. I was exploring uncharted territory, and how I wished for a path to follow. But there was none – I had to make my own path. As Carol Noren puts it:

> Because the word of God is what a preacher wrestles with in the pulpit, and because it is a living word, every sermon is God's creation as well as the creation of the preacher and the congregation. All three participate, with the preacher as the designated voice. It is a delicate job for the one in the

pulpit.... If the preacher leans too far one way, he will side with the text against the congregation and deliver a finger-pointing sermon from on high. If the preacher leans too far the other way, she will side with the congregation against the text and deliver a sermon that stops short of encountering God.[21]

I felt this balancing act acutely. Every homiletic reflection carried in it, and was carried by, my entire experience of God's call and my response, as well as my awareness of the congregation's daily life. Without making explicit reference to it, I felt God's breath as I spoke to the faith community. At first, the authority that seized me in the preaching act startled me. Is this what my homiletics professor referred to when she said: "Don't talk about the Scriptures, *do* the Good News." Or was this how many nineteenth-century evangelical women legitimized their preaching ministry? Carol M. Noren quotes one such woman, Phoebe Palmer, in her famous exhortation:

> And now, my dear sister, do not be startled, when I tell you that you have been ordained for a great work. Not by the imposition of mortal hands, or a call from man, no Christ, the great head of the church, hath chosen you, and "ordained you, that ye should go and bring forth fruit."[22]

For nineteenth-century women like Palmer, a call to preach did not automatically constitute a call to ordination, as is consistent with the evangelical, non-sacramental traditions. However, what did it mean that I, a Roman Catholic woman, experienced a similar type of authority? Was this not priestly authority in its deepest sense? My friend Ron, an Anglican priest, commented: "You sound quite Protestant in claiming a call to preach as divorced from a call to sacramental ministry. This does not strike me as a Roman Catholic understanding." He was right. I risked sounding Protestant, and maybe even seemed in sync with these nineteenth-century evangelical women who regarded their call to preach as independent from any church sanction or ordination of sorts. But ordained priestly authority was something I was not free to claim. What was I to do? God shattered my self-imposed limitations and pushed me into a daring new venture. I grew more attuned to how I carried call, gift and response in my body (see Chapter 8). Only God and I knew the arduous preparation process that preceded every reflection before it was delivered. Only God and I knew of the tears between the lines every time the Scriptures confronted me more deeply than I was willing to allow.

I read St. Paul with renewed insight. His words became my "letter of introduction" and my defence:

> When I came to you, brothers and sisters, I did not come proclaiming the mystery of God to you in lofty words of wisdom. For I decided to know nothing among you except Jesus Christ, and him crucified. And I came to you in weakness and in fear and in much trembling. My speech and my proclamation were not with plausible words of wisdom, but with a demonstration of the Spirit and of power, so that your faith might rest not on human wisdom but on the power of God. (1 Corinthians 2:1-5)

My most ardent prayer before each preaching experience was patterned on the words of John the Baptist in the Gospel of John: "That I may decrease, so that Christ in me may increase, and therefore that the people will hear, taste and see God" (John 3:30). If God was not in my ministry, then everything I said or thought or felt was in vain and was not even worth writing down, let alone listening to. I am aware that such claims can be made with misguided motivation and intent. It becomes a matter of faith and trust while taking seriously the need and importance of appropriate checks and balances. I learned to find the places on the preaching tightrope where the balancing was particularly delicate. The relationship between the Word of God, my personal life, and the life of the faith community created paradoxical tension. While the Word of God needed to be listened to on its own merit, I could only do the listening from within my own world view, and within the framework of my life experience. Yet the communal experiences of the faith community covered a gamut of world views and experiences that far exceeded my private life. In order to open the Scriptures as wide as possible, I needed to open myself wide to the vast array of views, joys and sorrows of the entire faith community. The balancing was especially delicate when I was moved to use examples from my own life as part of the homiletic reflection. David Buttrick has this to say on the topic:

The problem with (most personal illustrations)...is that they overlook an illustration's *main purpose*, namely, to illustrate. While we hold no brief for depersonalized illustrations, we are suspicious of the current trend....A personal illustration [...] will (almost) always split the congregational consciousness. To be blunt, there are virtually no good reasons to talk about ourselves from the pulpit.[23]

Personal examples can be used, but there is a danger that the personal example may draw attention to the preacher and away from the Gospel. Besides, one can be personal but never private. Sad to say, this distinction is not always carefully observed. The intention may be quite good, but it is easy to overdo the personal sharing in a homily. When that happens, people walk away having heard more about the preacher than about the Good News. Most of the time I do not risk this balancing, but in the following reflection I used an example from my personal life. Jesus' words about dividing families for the sake of the Gospel hit too close to home. I just hoped and prayed that my example might serve the Good News, and not the other way around.

Homiletic Reflection in My Home Parish

Jeremiah 38:4-6, 8-10; Hebrews 12:1-4; Luke 12:49-56

With the smoke of forest fires clouding our days this past week, we might get really jarred by Jesus' words today: bringing fire to the earth — yeah, right. With people being evacuated from their homes, and millions of acres covered with blazing flames, we may feel like saying to Jesus: Hold those flames a minute, please. We've got enough fire destroying our land and our crops and threatening our people. What do you mean, you came to bring fire to the earth, and how you wish it were already kindled? These words sound pretty sour right now in Western Canada, in poor taste. Try something else, Jesus, but not fire — please.

The present forest fire situation can make us forget about the life-giving qualities of fire. With choking smoke tickling our nostrils we may forget that God's love itself is the fire of life. A long-standing symbol in the Church for new life in Christ, fire *is* the life-giving activity of the Holy Spirit. Just as the destructive power of fire shows no mercy, neither does the life-giving power of God's fire. And both Jesus and Jeremiah knew what it is like to have God's passion burn like a fire in your chest, setting your whole being ablaze.

If anyone was a reluctant prophet, it was Jeremiah. Forever dragging his feet, even complaining to God that he had been seduced by God. Jeremiah tried to get rid of the fire of God's Spirit within him. Not that he feared that this kind of fire would destroy him, just like a forest fire would. No, Jeremiah dragged his feet because he knew how unpopular God's prophetic words would make him. So despised was God's news coming through Jeremiah that he was threatened with death more than once. If God's fire in his heart did not destroy him, the people he was called to address would certainly destroy him. It is not that God wishes to sow division, strife and conflict. Rather, God's fire is literally an all-or-nothing deal, and most of us cannot handle that kind of radical living. That was true in Jeremiah's time and in Jesus' time, and it is true in our time. Despite all the whining and complaining to God, Jeremiah let God's fire shine through him in such a way that the people around him would rather destroy him than listen to God. Jesus infuriated the establishment of his time because of his radical, all-inclusive love and compassion. Like the people in Jeremiah's time and in Jesus' time, we too have great difficulty with that much commitment to love, even though we were claimed for this Love in our baptism. When we claim our life to be on fire with God, even our own family and our church family can turn against us.

I had a brush with the kind of fire Jesus talks about when I was a teenager. At that time, I did not connect my experience to the Gospel. As a teenager, I was both critical of and attracted to religion: I wanted something out of it but was not sure how to plug into it. Then I got involved in a campaign to raise awareness about leprosy victims in Africa. I was on fire to help, and to offer a financial contribution of my own. Since my personal resources were limited, I thought I had found the ideal "sacrifice": I would forgo my sixteenth birthday party and donate the money allocated to the party to the leprosy fund instead. When I made the suggestion to my parents, I was unprepared for their response: I was told that the money was not mine to dispose of. If I did not want a party that was my decision, but my parents kept the power to decide where the money went. What did I think we were, a philanthropic institution?

My parents' response confused me. They had raised us as faithful Catholics. Now I wanted to do something inspired by my compassion for others, and I was accused of being too idealistic.

My parents were good people, and they still are. They loved us children, and they worked very hard to care for us. What I did not understand at that time was that they had been raised in a passive and duty-bound church. They had never learned to take their faith with them when they left church on Sunday morning. They had never been shown how to let the power of Jesus set them on fire in daily acts of love for those who needed it most.

The incident around my birthday party was the first of many faith-driven decisions in my life that deeply divided me from my parents. It took a long time to accept the hurt this caused, and to understand the reasons for the divisions from a faith perspective. I now recognize this division as the kind Jesus talks about today. It happens all the time to those who make radical commitments to love. I think about Pauline Vanier, Jean Vanier's mother: she used to recall how she thought her son had gone out of his mind when he left a successful career in the Navy to move in with two handicapped fellows in a tiny village in France. Today we know Jean Vanier's work across the world as the L'Arche communities. I think of a friend of mine: she is so keen to awaken her fellow parishioners to a deeper faith that she tried to introduce them to a Bible study – only to have her enthusiasm viewed with distrust. It is very hard to get knocked down by the very people to whom we feel closest – especially because of the fire of God burning in our heart.

It is not that God desires to cause us grief and conflict with those close to us. After all, Jesus is and always will be the Prince of Peace. But the peace Jesus gives is not an absence of conflict.

Quite the contrary, as we hear today. The peace of God is like a sword that divides families, and even churches. The division is caused by our refusal to embrace that costly commitment to discipleship.

The strife comes because of our refusal, not because of God's vindictive wishes. Jesus knew what that human refusal did to the prophets who came before him, such as Jeremiah. Jesus knew that such human refusal of fullness of life would deal him a similar lot. And sometimes it seems that in 2000 years of Christianity, our human refusal still condemns Jesus to death, without having to point fingers at those outside the Church.

"I came to bring fire to the earth, and how I wish it were already kindled!" Even though Jesus is wary of the baptism he is yet to undergo, which is his death, and even though he knows full well our capacity to refuse God's fire of love, he nevertheless continues to beckon us into this fire.

For the passion of God is a fire that does not destroy. The passion of God is a fire that brings life in overflowing measure. To let God's fire run through every vein of our being, we are to be committed totally. God's fire purifies, cleanses, and sets us ablaze. Jesus shows us what that blazing fire of love looks like. That is why we are encouraged by the words in Hebrews to always consider Jesus "so that you may not grow weary or lose heart." Jesus "disregarded the shame of the cross" – we are called to disregard the shame of our sin while our eyes of faith are fixed on the One who persevered and showed us the way into God's own heart.

Dietrich Bonhoeffer was one of those contemporary Christians who persevered to the point of shedding his own blood. A Lutheran pastor in Germany during the Second World War, he publicly denounced Hitler and harshly criticized Hitler's treatment of the Jews. Because of his outspoken faith, Bonhoeffer was imprisoned in a concentration camp. He was killed just days before the camp was liberated by the Allied Forces. Before he was imprisoned, Bonhoeffer wrote sermons, reflections, books. While in the concentration camp, he kept writing.

His writings were smuggled out of the camp and circulated in the churches. His autobiography is aptly called *The Cost of Discipleship*. Speaking on the fire of Christ as burning in the Church, he said: "The church cannot tolerate setting limits to love and service. For wherever there is human need and suffering, there is Christ. It is thus that the church truly invades the life of the world."[24]

Christ cannot tolerate lukewarm faith. The world cannot benefit from lukewarm faith. We pray that we may receive that fire of Christ in our hearts, and allow it to set us ablaze with limitless and passionate love. It is through the fire of love in our hearts that Christ truly invades the life of the world. Amen.

PART II

Growing in Fear and Wisdom

Forbidden Healing

I am the woman
bent over and
not knowing it for
a long time
inadvertently wandering into
the synagogue, the
men's circle
forbidden fruit
for a woman…
Yet Jesus
Jesus sees and calls
and heals
me, a woman
calls and heals without
request or permission
fire in my soul enflames
all, and Jesus
sees, calls and frees the
fire
sets me free to
stand tall and praise God
in the midst of the
assembly of men
upsetting everyone's
carefully constructed
applecart…
(Inspired by Luke 13:10–17)

CHAPTER 5

What Are Saints?

I am the vine, you are the branches.
Those who abide in me and I in them
bear much fruit,
because apart from me
you can do nothing.

(John 15:5)

To look on the life of those who have faithfully followed Christ is to be inspired with a new reason for seeking the city which is to come…, while at the same time we are taught to know a most safe path by which, despite the vicissitudes of the world, and in keeping with the state of life and condition proper to each of us, we will be able to arrive at perfect union with Christ, that is, holiness. God shows…in a vivid way his presence and his face in the lives of those companions of ours in the human condition who are more perfectly transformed into the image of Christ. He speaks to us in them and offers us a sign of this kingdom, to which we are powerfully attracted, so great a cloud of witnesses is there given and such a witness to the truth of the Gospel.[25]

When it comes to admiring others for their virtues and ideals, I have never ventured far from the Christian world. Yet it took quite a while before I could truly drink from the store of memories and stories of our revered communion of saints. With all the changes in the Dutch church in the 1960s and 1970s, the popular forms of piety of older Catholics, such as the rosary and benediction, did not appeal to me. I had little sense of the loss that the abandonment of these devotional practices represented to the older generation. For lack of direction, I briefly turned to non-Christian writers of wisdom. With a teenage soul hungry and searching for meaning, there was something compelling about Hermann Hesse's *Siddhartha*. Some old and basic truths span religious traditions, and when we encounter them, our soul recognizes them as true and essential. I recognized something in *Siddhartha* that I could not explain at the time. Now I see that Siddhartha, a young and handsome man, spent his entire life looking for the formula for ultimate fulfillment in life. He tried everything, including being a warrior and the love of woman. But each time his heart remained restless and still seeking. In the end, he befriended an old man who operated a ferry across the river. Siddhartha told the old man of his quest. The old man replied that he had learned everything about life and the sacred from the water in the river. Intrigued with the wisdom and peace the old man radiated, Siddharta decided to stay and live with him. Slowly, his understanding grew: fulfillment in life, and union with the sacred, is not an exterior object to pursue; rather, it becomes an inner space of holiness from whence all outside reality is radically transformed. Once the old man died, Siddhartha took over operating the ferry. Like the old man, he too grew in wisdom and peace.

Like Siddhartha, who spent many years pushing ahead on this quest for a home, I too hoped that some day I would arrive. My parents thought I was too idealistic. If that is true it is because others showed me time and again that my spiritual hunger and my ideals were not unrealistic in the eyes of God. If it had not been for these women and men, these role models in the faith, I doubt if I would have come as far as I have on my journey with God.

When preparing to preach on All Saints' Day in my parish on the Saskatchewan prairies, my mind and heart wandered back to the people who have lit up the path in the 47 years of my life. Many remain unnamed, but we live on in one another's hearts and lives because our encounters have made a distinct mark.

At first there was my Aunt Jeanne in the town of Zundert, at the Belgian border. She prided herself on living in the birthplace of the famous Dutch painter Vincent van Gogh. Van Gogh became my favourite artist; perhaps I felt a personal tie. Aunt Jeanne always showed me a world bigger than the one I knew from home and school. She took me to cultural events like concerts, plays and Holiday on Ice –

things my parents did not make time for. She taught me how to appreciate beauty, art and style. She took me abroad, to France, for the first time when I was twelve. She married a foreigner and loved travelling. All things became possible; encouraged by her example I pushed boundaries and crossed borders. The sky was the limit.

There was Rud, the diocesan youth pastor in the nearby city of Breda, who spurred me on in social justice projects and teen retreats. The three-day Pax Christi treks on foot became annual highlights in my adolescent years. Rud welcomed the questions and doubts of teenage faith; he listened to my criticisms and fears, showing me places and possibilities where I might find answers. The international monastic community of Taizé, which attracts tens of thousands of young people every year, was one such place that Rud revealed to me. I fondly recall the many hours we spent talking in the car while travelling to and from this special place in Burgundy, France. My numerous stays on that hill of prayer and encounter – with God, the brothers and the youth from other countries – became pivotal experiences in my spiritual formation.

There was our dear parish youth choir in my hometown of Rijen in the province of Noord-Brabant. Some of us sang better than others, but that didn't matter. We were a community of friends who shared song, laughter, birthdays, camp-outs and critical Scripture reflections. The liturgical renewals encouraged a strong social justice focus, and we used this focus in our monthly youth masses as much as we could. I remember how one time we chose the Vietnam War as our focus; for the occasion we placed a machine gun in the sanctuary. Another time, with creation as the theme, we introduced the parish to liturgical dance. It was in the midst of this group of people that I was encouraged to write my first "sermons." Even though we did not call our sharing at Mass "preaching," the dynamics I experienced then are the same I experience now in the pulpit.

There was my dear friend Nanny in The Hague, with whom I wandered the North Sea beach for hours, sharing dreams for a better world. We laughed and cried on those beaches, sometimes bathing ourselves in the silent beauty of the sunset (and one time a sunrise) over the water. We met at a time when both of us were dissatisfied with our young lives in middle-class jobs; our hearts longed for more and our wings waited impatiently to try new flying patterns.

There was Brother Roger Schutz, founder of Taizé, and the ecumenical community of brothers there, who fuelled the idealism in my heart with compelling messages from the Gospel. Every Friday evening Brother Roger spoke in the church after evening prayer, with simultaneous translation outfits set up in different parts of the church. It was in Taizé that I tasted first-hand the universality of Christ's church. The most lively corner of the campground was always where the Italians were: their boundless joy and musical enthusiasm were magnets, creating community across languages and cultures. It was in Taizé that my heart was moved to the core by the Gospel invitation to place my life, my trust, my future totally and unequivocally in God's hands. Thousands of young people a week in the summer, and anywhere between 20,000 and 25,000 at Easter, from all over the world shared food, music, prayer, Eucharist, tears and laughter. Because I was fluent in four languages, I often functioned as the translator in the discussion groups during the day. According to our conversations, the Church of tomorrow would look very different than what we had known.

Having made a strong commitment to give my life to God while in Taizé at age 19, I looked for a way to give concrete expression to this surrender. I found this expression in Jean Vanier's L'Arche community north of Paris, France, where I spent one year. Living with the mentally challenged taught me, slowly and at times painfully, the importance of *being* over *doing*. One of the women in my house was Edith. She lived in a world of silence, with only her eyes to communicate. Her quiet demands and piercing looks invited me into another form of relationship, one that makes love shine through in a purer and less altered form than in the so-called normal world. Because of my awkwardness in this radical form of loving, Edith led me home to parts of myself that were as bruised and broken as parts of her were. Risking to love her showed me how blurry the line is between those who are considered handicapped and those who are not. I spent hours learning the language of her eyes and touch, discovering in these the treasure and beauty of Edith as a person, a child of God.

At times, when the challenge to love unconditionally became too great, I went to visit an older woman in the L'Arche community. She poured tea, listened to my woes, and dried my tears. She was

Jean Vanier's mother, Madame Pauline Vanier, who in her retirement years had assumed the role of grandmother in her son's community, a simple loving presence for handicapped and assistants alike. I knew nothing of her former life as the wife of Canadian Governor General Georges Vanier. She was just a wonderful grandma to all who lived at L'Arche. She listened to my pain without lecturing me, steering me gently in Jesus' direction. Like Siddhartha, I was still trying to pursue fullness of life as an object outside of me rather than an inner stance of peace in the midst of the outside turmoil. The day-to-day challenges of living with mentally handicapped sisters and brothers brought me face to face with the illusion of pursuing fulfillment as an object. It would never work. With Pauline's help, I was thrown back into the arms of God where I cried tears of sheer despair and joy, both at the same time.

There was Gary, a Jesuit priest from the States who spent a few months at L'Arche in France. Pauline Vanier sent me to see him. I had long and deep conversations with him, mostly trying to figure out where God was calling me. Gary always challenged me to place my whole trust and my entire life in God through Christ Jesus – and oh, did I hesitate, for the need to remain in charge was deeply entrenched. He saw the tug of war: my soul yearning to surrender while my ego insisted on running the show. It was my first experience of spiritual direction, and the first time I felt the tension between the ego and the self. Gary guided, affirmed and challenged, and always he prayed, calling to me on God's behalf. The success of my year at L'Arche depended on my ability to "let go and let God" – another conversion in my ongoing journey with God.

Once I was married and living in Canada, I worked as a counsellor at a shelter for battered women and children. The hours I spent listening to the women were a revelation, and I often felt I received much more than I gave them. I learned the hard way about solidarity, about unconditional love, about courage that knows no bounds, about terror and abuse, about the energy required just to survive the next day. Listening to stories of pain and exploitation stretched my faith in uncomfortable ways. I reappropriated death and resurrection in dramatically new ways as I witnessed how the love and care a woman received at the shelter could help her rise from the ashes of destruction and make a new start for herself and her children.

Next in my "litany of saints" are the cherished mentors and teachers at the Lutheran Theological Seminary. They showed me an unexpected array of possibilities while expressing unwavering confidence in my gifts and abilities. I will never forget them: Bill, who watched and guided my growing and learning over my seven years of studies and who delighted in what God was doing in me; Gertrude, who graciously allowed me to be her student, friend and client, and with her quiet manner made the impossible sound possible; Jann, who became the vehicle through which God called me to preaching as a way of being true to myself. When I graduated at age 41, again the sky became the limit. That this felt infinitely more threatening to my need for stable institutional belonging than did the dreaming in my teen years ought not to come as a surprise.

Then, last but not least, my husband, Jim, the prairie farmer who embodies an attractive combination of Catholic spirituality, commitment to the environment and concern for social justice. He is my life partner, and even though we are incredibly different from each other (which can make for genuinely hard times), our common values and beliefs, and the sacrament of our marriage grounded in Jesus Christ, carry us through each time. In him, with him and through him, I am learning to see each day as a new start, to tap God's forgiveness and mercy so as to be free from one another's destructive and hurtful actions. Acknowledging that our ultimate fulfillment lies in God alone, we are learning day by day to free each other from unrealistic, "idol-istic" demands. There is no better place for working out my salvation, for laying down my life for the world, and for growing a new healthy generation, than in the sacrament of marriage.

And so emerges a personal litany of saints – mentors, teachers, fellow pilgrims and guides who have shaped the person I have become over time. They are my sisters and brothers on the journey of life. Our needs colour such encounters. Some persons are significant for me because of their solidarity and common ground with me, others because of their ability to guide, inspire and encourage me, still others because of their willingness to carry me in times of distress.

Private devotions to specific saints are also coloured by our own need and our own (sometimes unconscious) belief system. In her book *Friends of God and Prophets*, Elizabeth A. Johnson gives a remarkably clear and historical explanation of the two quite distinct approaches to the "communion of saints": the patronage model, with saints as intercessors before God, and the cloud-of-witnesses model, with saints as sisters and brothers in the faith standing in solidarity with the suffering faith community, infusing new hope and courage.

> [In the patronage model] the saint became the good patron whose intercessions were successful, whose power was exercised benevolently, and in whose name the church's [spiritual] wealth was at the disposal of the whole community....
> Gone now was the mutuality and reciprocity of early Christian experience in which the living and the dead were filled with the Spirit and joined in a community of codiscipleship. In its place was the patron-client relationship whereby saints became powerful intercessors for needy petitioners before the distant throne of God, and thus were elite "friends of God" in a higher sense than the rest of the community.[26]

Johnson helped me finally to understand why a "patronage" type of devotion to the saints simply never appealed to me. According to Johnson, this model seems on its way out of the lives of modern-day Catholics, thus making room, she claims, for the old companionship model to be rediscovered and renewed. Listening to sermons on Mary or on the saints, at Mass or on retreats, often left me feeling like Elisabeth Schüssler Fiorenza, who describes her reactions to high school retreats:

> Our images of ourselves, our problems as young women, and our goals for life were totally different from the images of female saints that were preached to us. The lives of the saints presented more of a hindrance than a help in finding our own self-identity. These stories stressed suffering, sexual purity, submission, outmoded piety, and total obedience. They were anti-intellectual and anti-erotic; they told about nuns and widows and some queens, but rarely did they speak about ordinary women. While we desired our own independence and love, the glorification of the saints demanded humble feminine submission and fostered sexual neuroses.[27]

This patronage model was indeed on its way out in my child-hood years in the Dutch Roman Catholic Church. I did not grow up with popular devotions and the viewing of saints as elevated intercessors before God. However, settling in rural Saskatchewan, I discovered this private and collective veneration of the saints (which Johnson calls the patronage model) to be alive and well. In a strange way I envied those with strong devotions to Mary, or to any other particular saint. I tried to imitate this devotional spirituality, but it felt artificial. Praying this way felt foreign to who I was; it failed to satisfy my hunger for God. For a while I even felt deprived, because God did not grant me the security of this kind of faith. Thinking that this patronage model was the only way to relate to Mary and the saints, I finally gave up trying.

In recent years I rediscovered the great store of saints as the "cloud of witnesses" in our Christian tradition – Johnson's second model. In order to find support, courage and role models in my journey with God in the Church, I turned more intentionally to the memory and the stories of Christian holy women in particular. As I got to know them, I was taken aback by the similarities between my relationships with God and the Church, and theirs. As Mary Malone says of the first holy women:

> In the Christian communities of the first four centuries, there was continued tension between the immediacy of contact with God experienced by the martyrs and the hier-archically ordered life of the community. This was true for all lay people, but it was particularly so in the case of women…. A woman's life and spirituality was so circum-scribed by her subordinate position […] that often the only avenue for spiritual growth was to transcend the hierarchi-cal Church and experience direct contact with God.[28]

I began to read about the lives of women: Perpetua, Paula, Clare of Assisi, Teresa of Avila, Hildegard of Bingen, Catherine of Siena, Joan of Arc, Mary Ward and Thérèse of Lisieux. Unfortunately, mar-ried women with equal fame in the Church are difficult to find. Yet, whether they were married, single or religious, the intensity and intimacy of their relationship to God fascinated me, creating strong points of connection with my own experience. Several common golden threads emerged from these women's lives of faith. Each one demonstrated a remarkable capacity for self-determination, often in societies and in a church where their roles and positions were strictly controlled. Each one embodied the experience of liberation as a deeply religious one despite all the institutional restrictions. For each woman the original inspiration, the context and the way of living out the vision was different. But for each, the source of her vision and her mission was the all-encompassing will of a loving God who claimed her, intimately and totally, without prior assurance of success.

In light of my years of seminary formation, connecting with these women was a monumental event in my spiritual life and in helping me to redefine my relationship to the institutional Church.

> Several times my eyes fill with tears as I read *The Story of a Soul*, the autobiography of St. Thérèse of Lisieux. Shocks of recognition roll through me as I read of Thérèse's burning for God, her quiet trust in and faithfulness to God's call despite the obstacles, her courage and sheer audacity to pursue her call and claim its authenticity. Everyone discouraged this child who wanted to enter Carmel. Thérèse, at 14, went all the way to the pope to get permission to enter, but to no avail. The pain she endured in her soul because of the refusals! It all sounds so shockingly close to home... And even her humble insights into her own spiritual experiences with God: the greatest fulfillment lies in living out of the visions instead of speaking about them. In other words, let the spiritual blessings do their work in moulding the soul into God's own loving heart. Only then can the fruits of such blessings spread far beyond ourselves. If, on the other hand, we speak often of spiritual blessings, experiences and visions (like some people who witnessed Marian apparitions), their potency to mould the soul can be diminished, especially if this speaking is manipulated by our ego – a never-ending temptation. (Journal entry)

I found deep reassurance and companionship in befriending these women saints. I now feel at peace knowing that my experience of God fits right into a long and rich tradition of women claiming God's call in the diversity of their social, cultural and religious contexts. What feels so unusual and new for me is really quite old and profound. I sit at the feet of Thérèse, Catherine, Clare and all others – religious, single or married – who surrendered their lives to God without clinging to the outcome of their self-giving. I am merely the instrument; God brings about my surrender and draws out my best efforts to live what God has called me to:

> If you wish to rise above a life of imperfection, you must, like the apostles, prepare yourself for the coming of the Holy Spirit. Remain watchful and persevere in humble and continual prayer. When you are ready, my Spirit will come to you as he did to the apostles waiting in expectant faith in the upper room. You will be given the courage to leave your safe house of prayer and fearlessly announce to the world what you have come to know of my truth and my love, not fearing pain and rejection, but seeing the glory of whatever comes to you. I will give you a fire of charity strong enough to overcome your fears, your love of comfort and all the temptations of the Devil. Having the taste of my charity in your soul you can arise and give birth to it in your neighbours. For you cannot love me without loving your neighbour, nor can you love your neighbour and not love me.[29]

Homiletic Reflection for All Saints' Day in My Home Parish

Matthew 5:1-11

One afternoon a mother went into a church with her little boy. She took time out of a very busy day because she needed space for prayer and reflection. This was the first time the little boy had been in a church. With amazement he looked around, and was especially taken by the beautiful stained-glass windows. He tugged on his mother's coat and asked her what these windows were. With her mind elsewhere, she replied that those windows were the saints. The little boy was quiet for a while, mulling over his mother's words. Then he tugged on her coat again: "Mom! Mom!" With some irritation in her voice, she asked: "What is it this time?" Her son exclaimed with great excitement, like someone who has just found a treasure: "I know what saints are for! They let the light come in!"

Yes, saints let the light come in, warming our cold world with their lives of hope and faith. On this feast day of All Saints we remember them, we give thanks to God for these servants, and we commit ourselves anew to emulate them. But who or what are these saints, really? Many of us may think they are rather extraordinary people, the family of women and men who are officially recognized by the Church as saints. Just last month, for example, Pope John Paul canonized Edith Stein, a Jewish woman who became a Catholic Carmelite nun and who was subsequently killed by the Nazis in World War II because she was Jewish. What is it that singles out certain people as role models of faith? Are they miracle workers, or strict ascetical people, praying and fasting all day long? Do they have unusual gifts? Are they somehow "less ordinary" than most of us?

The answer to each of these questions is no. Jesus' words in Matthew's Gospel today confirm this, telling us what to expect from a saint. What's more, Jesus puts before all of us – not just a select, extraordinary few – the invitation to live a saintly life. One of the Fathers of the Church once said that the glory of God is the human being fully alive. The glory of God lies in the fullness of our own humanness. Being fully human does not mean shying away from our weaknesses, our hurts, our feelings. Reading about the lives of the saints, we learn very quickly that they too faced problems, struggled with failures and often showed deep wounds in their hearts. By embracing those human parts of themselves they discovered their own poverty, their own meekness, their own sorrow, their own hunger for justice and peace. It is in embracing poverty, sorrow, meekness that we find ourselves deeply blessed by God – "Blessed are the pure in heart."

Take St. Francis. He spent agonizing hours and days wondering what our Lord meant by these words: "Blessed are the poor in spirit." He quietly hoped that it would not mean he'd have to meet a leper, because they were the most despised type of people in his day. Well, God knew that Francis' way to blessedness was through embracing what he most despised. This is what Francis himself has to say about that:

> Whenever I imagined that I might meet a leper some day, I banished the thought right away. But I met one anyway. And the street was so narrow that I practically had to bump into him – unless I had run away. I certainly felt like doing that. Oh, how I felt like it. But the memory of Christ on the cross blocked my escape. I froze in the middle of the street. The leper was coming toward me, very slowly, all in tatters. He held his hands clasped toward me, and fixed me with a look of sweetness and sorrowful humility. It seemed to me that the eyes of Jesus on the crucifix were the same eyes that were now looking at me. Then I do not really know what came over me. I leapt forward and embraced the leper, and kissed him on the mouth. He began to weep, and so did I with him. I pulled out everything I had in my pockets and gave it to him. But it was nothing compared to what he had given to me. It was nothing compared to what he had made me see in that moment, and in that kiss. I had seen in him the eyes of Christ Jesus himself. I touched in that kiss the lips of our Lord himself....[30]

God knows that our road to blessedness involves embracing what we most despise in ourselves, and in others. The invitation to a saintly life presents itself when our own daughter or son embraces a lifestyle that flies in the face of all our own values and beliefs. The invitation to a saintly life comes in a diagnosis of AIDS, or cancer, or Alzheimer's. The invitation to a saintly life bursts forth in the fierce fight to preserve the family farm, or to protect nearby forests and lakes from pollution. The invitation to a saintly life comes in the painful task of rebuilding an indigenous culture that has been trampled by European colonialism. In the eyes of the world, there is nothing heroic about such demands, nothing noteworthy about such invitations. Many of the saints were not seen as heroic or noteworthy in their own day, but as we look back, they show us a life lived in solidarity with God's poor and simple ones. They show us a life completely grounded in Jesus Christ. In turn, they invite us to graft our lives onto Jesus in every respect. To be a saint is to let God mould our hearts with mercy and to pursue true justice, which cares not only about rights but also about needs. To be a saint is to labour according to God's mercy for reconciliation and peace, and to do all these things in the daily situations of our places of work, at school, in our homes.

To be a saint means allowing God's love to set us on fire, feeling inwardly seduced by God, and letting the Spirit transform our thoughts, feelings and actions. To live such a saintly life is the ultimate calling of all those who are baptized in Jesus. We are fortunate to be part of such a large family with memories and stories to inspire us, and to feed the flame of God's love in us. This family includes Dorothy Day, Jean Vanier, the three nuns and one lay missionary killed in El Salvador, Kateri Tekakwitha, Oscar Romero, Mother Teresa, Thomas Merton, Edith Stein – to name just a few who were recognized in the twentieth century. It is not just the job of a few unusual people to "let the light come in" – as our little boy said to his mother. It is your job and my job, the job of God's ordinary men, women and children, to take our place with all the saints, and to let God's light come in through the ordinariness of our daily lives, so that the world will become a better place for all. Blessed are they who embrace God's promises, who let God's love set their hearts on fire, for they shall see God. Amen.

CHAPTER 6

Preach What You Practise

And God blessed them, and said to them:
"Be fruitful and multiply,
and fill the earth and subdue it."
(Genesis 1:28)

The beauty and attraction of idealism comes through at most weddings. Even in the face of high divorce rates, women and men keep making the radical choice of a lifetime commitment in matrimony. Some call it holy; some call it foolish. I surely had big portions of both when I walked down the aisle in my Dutch hometown at the age of 23.

Getting married was not the only major decision linked to our wedding day. Marrying a man from far, far away, from a place no one knew, evoked feelings of adventure in my friends and worry in my parents. In marrying Jim, I married a country, a culture and a lifestyle. The excitement of new beginnings was electric. We were going to make a difference in the world – as a married couple, as Catholic Christians, as Saskatchewan farmers.

We were not comfortable adopting unquestioned middle-class, materialistic values in our self-identity and lifestyle, nor did we think of farming as agribusiness. The rebel in each of us pushed us into countercultural choices. We did not want to become enslaved. The prison of modern living looked more suffocating than the time-consuming and labour-intensive activities of hauling water from the lake, growing and preserving our own food, and chopping wood for cooking and heating. William McNamara's spirituality became real for us:

I share the secret of the child, of the saints and sages, as well as of clowns and fools when I realize how wondrous and marvellous it is to carry fuel and draw water. Once the spiritual significance of such ordinary earthy acts dawns on me, I can skip the yoga and the koans, the mantras and the novenas.[31]

We gardened organically and sold vegetables at the local farmers' market. I learned all about preserving our winter supply of food and about baking bread in the wood stove, things that were not part of my upbringing. My parents' goal in life was to get away from this type of "deprived" life in order to offer their children more comfort and affluence. They have never understood the strange kind of freedom and independence that comes with choosing this simple back-to-the-land existence. They could not see why I resisted embracing empty promises of happiness in career-oriented living and material comforts; neither did they have patience for my cries for social justice on behalf of those who are ignored and trampled. My lifestyle choices caused a rift in my relationship with my parents that never quite healed. Even though a scar has formed over the wound, and I have stopped trying to convince them, these misunderstandings remain my steady companion in the form of a deep sense of regret and loss.

Jim and I agreed on the big picture in our married life (our religious values and countercultural commitments), but we always struggled with vast differences in temperament, in approach to relationships, in ways of organization and routines, and in parenting styles. Our family backgrounds undoubtedly contributed to these differences, in particular regarding how relationships were formed and fostered. My parents expressed their love and affection for one another quite openly in the presence of their five children. They modelled togetherness in a most literal sense of the word: treating one another as equal business partners in their joint commercial ventures, working hard to give their children what they themselves never had. My parents were teenagers in occupied Netherlands during World War II, which prevented them from pursuing their own career dreams. As a result, they worked hard to ensure that their children would have opportunities that they themselves had lacked.

Jim's parents grew up with the pioneering legacy of rural Saskatch-ewan, which included very hard times caused by the severe drought of the 1930s. Their upbringing was marked by harsh living condi-tions (far worse than my parents') and with little expression of affec-tion at home. Since they hadn't grown up with such signs of affec-tion, they found it hard to express love to their children. The love in Jim's home was harder to detect than in mine. Our childhood mes-sages about love affected deeply the adults we became. Jim is struck by my natural caring capacity: on good days he experiences it as a gift not to be taken for granted, on bad days he calls it my compul-sion to serve people too much.

Our 23 years of marriage have been marked by blessings and pain. Taking charge of our health through lifestyle choices paid off in many ways. We shared a deep, underlying freedom and a sense of creative accomplishment knowing that we did not need the electri-cal gadgets and ready-made foods of a fast-paced consumer society. Our home became a nest with rich, wholesome food for body and soul where we raised three beautiful children whom God entrusted to us. As three- and four-year-olds, our children took visitors through Jim's garden, identifying plants by their Latin names. One day our eldest son came in, glowing, as if he just discovered a great treasure: "I know where God lives now," he said, "underground, busy push-ing the plants out of the earth." Now a young adult, our son is carefully exploring, mostly through his expanding world of rela-tionships beyond his family, whether God lives anywhere else, whether God goes by any other name, and whether God does anything more than push plants out of the earth.

Mixed in with these abundant blessings was a certain amount of hardship for Jim and I. The greatest source of pain continued to be our own personalities, which pushed us periodically to a relational abyss. Given our vast differences in communication styles, our mar-riage was work from day one. Marital love grew over time only as a result of forging careful, slow understandings about one another and about ourselves, resulting in an almost begrudging mutual respect. Every time a new communication crisis loomed, we both feared the worst. Abuse, addictions or ill will were never the problem – we simply continued wondering who we were to one another and how to make this marriage work. We felt the need both to share our joys with others and to reach out for support and guidance. Especially in the early years, our attempts to seek this kind of support had mixed results. Our budding coupleness felt additional strain as several family members experienced real marital difficulties; one of these marriages ended around this time. Finding people with whom to share our joys was easy; finding a listening ear for the problems and tensions we suffered was another matter. Even those whom we had met at our marriage preparation course fell out of touch; we had to find our own way. Those early years were marked by feelings of being rather alone and unsupported; we often wondered how to make this sacrament of marriage work.

I remember vividly one winter four years into our marriage. We spent three months living in Montreal as part of the L'Arche community, with our two-year-old and seven-week-old sons. We immersed ourselves in community life and drank deeply from the love and care surrounding us. Acknowledging marital strain, we saw a counsellor while in Montreal. When the time came to return to Saskatchewan and the train pulled out of Montreal's Victoria Station, tears streamed down my face. I did not want to go back. Our farm home felt like a wasteland with so little to nourish us both church-wise and friends-wise. How was this "one-flesh" stuff supposed to work? We did not want to approach our marriage as merely a private affair. It took several years of creating a social network of friends before we started feeling a sense of local community support.

Our couple involvement with Serena, the Canadian organization promoting and teaching Natural Family Planning, has extended throughout our married life, enriching us beyond measure. Besides offering us a rich social network and allowing us to teach both individual couples as well as groups, the relational demands of using Natural Family Planning deepened our personal and couple development in the areas of communication, self-esteem, self- and mutual respect and freedom, and confidence in our ability to learn and grow. Besides, our choice for a chemical-free method of family planning mirrored the non-chemical, organic approach to working the land. Jim always said: "I don't believe in putting chemicals on the land; why would we chemical our bodies to render them infertile?"

The healthiest and strongest support for our coupleness came through our work with Serena. For a long time, Serena's teacher-couples were the only friends with whom we felt safe sharing, and even joking, about the difficult relational and sexual aspects of our marriage. Throughout the twenty-some years of our involvement in Serena, we took our turn serving on provincial and national boards, making presentations at marriage preparation courses and teaching individual couples how to use the sympto-thermal method. Each time these talks brought us back to our basic marital commitment; our relationship needed the talks as much as those who listened to us did.

Marriage vows are declared once, but they need reviewing and reinterpreting many, many times. Whenever the going got rough and we failed miserably to understand each other, I was haunted by the question of whether we could stick it out. For a long time I feared that the mere presence of the question spelled the end of the marriage. We both had difficulty with compromise. I compromised easily and quickly for the sake of peace but at the expense of my own needs. When I ignored my needs too much, I exploded into emotional blackmail, as in "You don't love me if you don't do this or that." Jim, on the other hand, regarded any demand for compromise as an abandoning of his cherished principles. His first answer to any new proposal was always "no." We felt so stuck so often. What I did too much of, he did not enough of, or so it felt.

> Intimacy often demands compromise – a willingness to come to agreement through changes on both sides. But to the purist, compromise sounds like surrender, giving in without a fight, failing to stand up for what one believes….When is compromise a gesture of generosity and when is it a failure to meet an important challenge? How do we stay open to significant change without selling ourselves out?[32]

Because our marriage, our lifestyle and our farm home location were one intricate package, it was hard at times to sift out which parts of our commitment were in question. When I found my first job away from the farm, I felt as if I was betraying the marriage promise of living off the land together. However much I loved living off the land, I had to face that in terms of my temperament and my interest level, I was not cut out to work the land, whether on a big or on a small scale. While Jim was passionate about plants and fiddling with seeds, I was passionate about people, their problems, their spirituality and their stories. As our children grew older, I became interested in going to school. I battled deep fears in acknowledging this interest and this deep desire to learn and grow. My biggest fear was of not having a marriage left once I moved through university studies. Following my own dreams and aspirations threatened what I understood as my contribution to our togetherness. After I graduated, I took the position of magazine editor, with other ministry commitments on the side. The children were no longer attending the small rural elementary school but took the bus to the city high school. Before long our two boys added jobs to their school schedule. The commuting was wearing us all out. In order to accommodate both my needs and interests as well as those of our three teenagers, we took the big step of acquiring a second home in the nearby city for the children and myself while Jim spent most of his time on the farm. I sweated enormously over this decision: thoughts and fears of separation haunted me again. Where we will end up? Divorced after all? Not necessarily. We discovered that every move, every decision, every new direction, put before us a choice: we could use the situation to review and deepen our relationship, or we could let ourselves grow apart.

It is at those moments at the crossroads that marriage vows and the sacramental dimension of matrimony really come alive, sustaining and challenging us to grow deeper and deeper. At this stage in our married life we feel in a solid and grateful space. We continue to learn how to allow the other to become fully himself or herself while regarding our oneness as the foundation of everything we are and do. We continue to draw our spiritual water from the rich well of our Catholic tradition. We have three wonderful teenagers who obviously did not turn out that way in a vacuum. We cherish some unique family traditions (such as our live-in family Easters at Queen's House Retreat Centre in Saskatoon along with a hundred other people: parents, teens and children). Even though some of the gifts we passed on to our children seem to have gone underground in their adolescent years, we see the best of one another in each of them. Jim gave them his passion for growing things, his utter respect for creation, his love for knowledge in the broadest sense of that word, his capacity for critical thinking. I recognize in each of our children a capacity for warmth, compassion and generosity in relation to their friends. I see reflected in them my commitment to honesty and depth, tempered with trust and discretion.

Jim has been the stabilizing force in my life. I grow through a lot of emotional ups and downs in order to find an inner equilibrium. Jim's emotional stability allowed me to risk exploring new and uncharted terrain in my own life and in the life of the Church. I have always known that Jim is with me for the long haul. But even excellent qualities can turn into great sources of frustration. On bad days I experience Jim's stability as an enormous stumbling block that holds back the changes that I so deeply need at times. My emotional turmoil and doubt may have more to do with my own anxiety and my own capacity to live the sacrament of marriage as faithfully as he does than with any fear of losing him.

Jim's relationship to the land remains a mystery and a challenge to me. The land is part of Jim's soul, but I must admit my great ambivalence to the land. When I was growing up, we lived above our parents' fabric store, with a paved street in the front and a paved alley in the back, and not one square inch of dirt or garden. It is almost impossible to catch up to someone whose roots go down deep in the soil and have done so from childhood. Even more than twenty years on the land with Jim has not created in me an intimate relationship with God's creation, a relationship that sustains Jim deeply and independently of his spousal relationship to me. I go through myriad emotions regarding Jim's closeness to the land. Some days it feels as if he is married to two wives, and I am overtaken by jealousy, thinking that if only he invested as much into me as he does into the land and all that grows, I would not feel so needy and abandoned. Other days I am flooded with gratitude that I share life with a man who exudes the simplicity and peace for which our society cries out, and who reminds me that the most important things in life are very basic.

I never see myself leaving my marriage in search of greener pastures, or choosing to live life alone. Rather, I often feel as if I risk the entire marriage every time I allow tensions and questions to surface. We are so deeply conditioned to believe that good marriages are easy marriages – Hollywood has done its job well. My experience – the effort required to communicate – was difficult to harmonize with the simplistic images of romantic movies. My experience of the work involved in making two become one flesh was also hard to square with the Gospel imperative that "what God has joined let no one separate." It took years to understand that God joins us over time and through a lot of ups and downs, not simply on the day we said yes to one another. I was finally reassured that as long as the challenge of marriage kept drawing us in rather than pushing us away from one another (and yes, part of that is our free choice), I knew God to be present, and I knew that God is not finished with us yet.

As I grew more at peace with who I am in God, I discovered an increasing freedom to allow Jim to be who is he with God and with me. I grew more responsible for my own needs, and learned to withdraw false and unrealistic expectations. I also gave myself permission to discover who I am apart from my role as wife and mother, which in turn opened up new avenues of satisfaction and inspiration. No longer "needing" Jim to make up for my shortcomings or for my unrealized dreams helped me to appreciate him for who he is, rather than complain about who he is not. This realization was not a static piece of knowledge. Rather, I stumbled into those moments of insights, often accidentally and for only a split second. Preparing the sermon below, for example, caught me at a bad time. I was – again – in the throes of wondering where Jim and I were going together, if anywhere:

> Jim has left for Ontario till next Wednesday. A few days ago we started seeing someone for counselling. I do hope that involving a third person will help shift the way Jim and I hear one another… It is a mixed experience to have him gone from home. I soak in the solitude (except for when the kids are home), and in the freedom to schedule my own time. Yet I miss Jim in a strange sort of way. This is very much his farm. I live among his plants and seeds – odd not to have him here in this setting. And I don't like being alone at night here on the farm, although I could probably get used to it. It is not easy living with Jim, but it is probably no

easier living without him. What ironic coincidence that I should be called to preach this Sunday on the creation of Eve and on Jesus' teaching on divorce – my own ambivalence is being challenged. (Journal entry)

Honestly writing out such thoughts became an integral part of my inner preparation for preaching. Preparing the reflection was not easy, for both public and private reasons: public, in the sense that divorce has become common in our society. Given that fact, I agonized over how I could preach on this text in ways that would address the reality of broken relationships that is so much a part of all our lives. Privately, I felt God's irony that I should preach on the topic of marriage and divorce at this time of my own husband's absence, when I was plagued by my own turmoil and uncertainty – again – about the reasons for staying married to this man.

Wrestling with God's Word in full view of my own pain and questions, however, turned out to be a crucible of creative energy and vision. Not denying but facing my own inability to live up to this "one flesh" calling which is holy matrimony protected me from putting myself anywhere above my listeners. Again, the praying and preparing trimmed and pruned me, as it had so many times before, cutting my ego down to size and thus making room for God's Spirit to provide the words. God's Spirit worked not through the denying of my humanity, but precisely through my willingness to embrace fully my humanity with all its sinfulness, shortcomings, hurts and questions. Even though I had been through this movement several times, the risk felt new and enormous every time. How could I get used to this all-consuming call to surrender? Some days the demands of this call were simply too much.

Maybe the power of good preaching lies exactly in making a thorough examination of conscience the primary basis of preparation. In voicing my own sinfulness, I give voice to the sinfulness of the community. Experiencing in that act of confession God's own forgiveness and healing, I offer the same to the community. If the Word of God did not first seize me in the preparation, then I cannot expect the community to be seized and changed by that same word, no matter how eloquent the preaching. As David Buttrick says, any attitude and reality not first acknowledged in ourselves cannot be conveyed authentically in our preaching.[33]

Homiletic Reflection in My Home Parish

Mark 10:2-16

It was not easy to prepare this reflection. I attended two Bible studies and read a number of commentaries on today's readings. The Gospel especially seemed to provoke a whole gamut of responses and opinions. They went something like this: "It is important to speak strongly about the Church's teaching on divorce." "How can we uphold church teaching when divorce is so prevalent around us?" "Do not use the text as a whip to punish divorced people." "These texts have been used to keep victims in abusive marriages, so preacher beware." These thoughts, and more, probably go through our heads too as we hear Jesus' words today. In the midst of this world, our world, full of broken relationships, we take time to hear Good News in these words of Jesus.

Divorce. The very mention of the word wrings our hearts and wrenches our stomachs. The breaking up of what God intends to be "one flesh" rips through all of our lives. We have all seen and touched the pain – if not in our own situation, then in loved ones whose lives seem permanently scarred by marriage break-up. The private experience of divorce between two people affects the whole community. Because divorce is more than just a marriage break-up.

Divorce is merely the public recognition of a private reality that precedes it. Behind the legal process lies the alienation and separation of a woman and a man. Behind the legal term lies the pain of having lost confidence, dignity and respect.

Sometimes unhealthy behaviours of abuse, power and control violate marriage vows long before divorce is pending. Sometimes people grow apart over time, driven by over-focusing on individual self-fulfillment or just plain boredom. We stop loving, and the "one flesh" is hard to find. Even if we never seek divorce, every marriage risks falling prey to a daily flatness and drudgery... far from the "one flesh" union that spells fulfillment for each partner. Even for people who enjoy a healthy, loving marriage, chances are we experience the pain of break-up in other ways with those close to us.

Whether we call it divorce or break-up, we may all get burned in relationships at times. We invest ourselves in another, giving and receiving closeness and friendship. But even the best of friendships is tainted with the pain of separation, rejection, alienation. Husband or wife, parent or child, friend or neighbour: none of us is safe. Within our parish community, within our own selves and even with God, separation hurts and scars. It is not good for us to live alone. It is not good for us to live cut off from the human community, cut off even from God.

It is that reality, the sin of human alienation, that Jesus addresses here. It is that reality, more than the law on divorce, that is judged as not being part of God's intent at creation. The Pharisees come to Jesus, asking him a question to test him. We too are all ears to hear the answer. Like the Pharisees, we get caught up in living our religion, and our relationships, as if we are keeping a balance sheet. If we keep the religious laws, we will earn God's grace. If we keep the minimum rules of getting along, our marriage will last. Jesus does not buy into that system. Jesus confronts us with both the sinfulness of all separation and with the glorious grace of God's reconciliation. Legalizing divorce does not take away its sinful character, nor does it alter God's original intent of joining man and woman into one flesh. Legalizing divorce does not make any broken relationship right, nor does it take away God's forgiving and healing action towards us. We suffer from hardness of heart, but God is still the God of forgiving and healing love.

It is not our job to pass judgment on others, or to bury ourselves in guilt and shame over our sin. It is our job to face our own hardness of heart. We try to be God, in our own life or in someone else's life – and our heart hardens. We presume, with the Pharisees, that we can earn our way into heaven by keeping religious laws – and our heart cuts itself off from compassion and understanding. We seek only our own gain – and our heart grows cold to the pain we inflict on others. We are obsessed with hiding our woundedness – and our heart buries itself in the illusion of perfection and false humility. We help sustain a culture that promotes individualism and self-gratification – we help grow the collective hardness of heart. We help sustain religious attitudes and practices that exclude the sense of community – we collude with the sin of not supporting one another when our marriage feels like it has been set adrift. Marriage is such a private affair, we think. Before we know it, our "non-interfering" and our inability to seek help grows hardness of heart wherever we turn. We may not call every break in relationship a divorce. But every time we find ourselves alone, without support, cut off from our partner, alienated from community, we experience the pain of divorce. That is why it is not good for us to be alone.

Jesus levels the playing field. As men and women we are equally free to enter relationships. Once committed, we are equally responsible to grow in God's love towards one another. Jesus urges us to take the sanctity of relationships, especially marriage, very seriously. Creation may be broken and fallen from God's original intent. Our culture may not know how to support lasting relationships. But these are not reasons for despair, or for ignoring Jesus' answer. Jesus asks us to be responsible for the quality of every relationship in which we find ourselves. As a community of faith we are called to account for the measure of support we offer one another. Far beyond quarrelling over the permission to divorce, we are called to change our behaviour – to show more compassion than criticism, to listen more than we talk, to relate to one another as equals before God. Jesus condemns all separation and brokenness as sin. On this level playing field, we all fall short. Before God, we are reminded of the purpose and goodness of creation. Before God, we are all called to become "one flesh" – in the community of marriage, in our parish community, in the world.

In the daily routine of living, it is not good to be alone. As followers of Jesus, it is not good for any of us to be alone.

Children know that it is not good to be alone. Children do not hide their need for love. Children are ready to forgive and reconcile, often long before adults are. Children reach out without shame. In the middle of his serious conversation with the Pharisees, Jesus takes the child onto his lap.

In a society where children had no rights or social status, Jesus models before our eyes God's kingdom of right relation. No matter how painful the separation, or how big the fight, continue to reach out and ask to be held in loving care. No matter how foolish our questions, how fearful our doubts, how great our shame, God gently reaches out to us and nudges us towards right relation with one another.

Despite the sinfulness of separation, as God's children we may experience the reconciling love of God in Jesus Christ. Held by Jesus, not stopped by anyone, we come to see all our relationships as holy places where God's own presence and power are at work. That loving power of God in and through Jesus is infinitely greater than any of our sinful separations can ever be.

Jesus draws attention to this realization by welcoming children. Following the lead of today's Gospel, we too will end this reflection with a story about children. This story is about a girl in elementary school who had to do a project for science class. She decided to build a model of the world. So she took a rubber ball for her globe, carefully cut construction paper in the shape of all the continents, and glued them onto the ball. When she finished, she set the project on the table and went outside to play. A few minutes later, her little sister Sally came in and began to play with the globe. She took Africa and tore it off; she began to chew on China; and she took a crayon and coloured all over Europe. Just then, her older sister came back in. When she saw what had happened, she screamed at the little girl: "Sally, look what you've done! You've ruined everything. I hate you!" Sally was crushed. She ran away in tears. But when her sister realized what she had done, she found Sally, threw her arms around her and hugged her close, saying: "Sally, you've messed up my world, but I still love you."

You mess up my world, and you mess up relationships, but I still love you, and I continue to create you in my image, male and female, called into one flesh…says the Lord our God. Amen.

Many were stunned and speechless that Sunday, and from the pulpit I noticed some tears. I breathed a sigh of relief. It looked like God's Spirit indeed softened hardness of heart and brought healing to broken hearts. I gave thanks and praise, and felt deeply humbled to be God's vehicle. I still did not understand how all this happened, yet happen it did. There was a part of the whole experience that lay completely beyond my control, yet the features of the Spirit's control were unmistakable. Mixed in with all the post-preaching musings, the temptation of the evil one was not far off. In light of all the praise, I was plagued by fear and flattery:

> I give thanks while acknowledging deep personal fear. "Are you aware of the power of your own words?" asked a friend some years back. It is not my power, it is God's power speaking the words through me and in me... And the temptations are all around me, lying in wait to ambush me: either let the fear take over and paralyze me to the point of stifling the gift, or take the compliments, seize them as my personal possession, and use the gift to flatter my own ego... No, I do not revel in or despise God's activity. I cannot. Rather, I give thanks even more and I feel pulled to surrender ever deeper and ever more fully. It is the only way I can be worthy to be God's servant. (Journal entry)

As my husband, Jim messes up my world. As the one calling me to preach, God messes up my world. And I am far from living a perfect life myself. I will continue to be plagued by doubts, temptations, vanity, arrogance. Yet in and through the messiness and the sinfulness, God loves. In and through the tensions and the doubts God helps me to love, and to keep loving, my spouse. That is why marriage is indeed a mystery, God's own sacrament of love between a woman and a man. Maybe someday my love for Jim may start to resemble God's love for this same man.

CHAPTER 7

I Will Be with You Always

Then Jesus led them out as far as Bethany, and,
lifting up his hands, he blessed them.
While he was blessing them,
he withdrew from them
and was carried up into heaven.

(Luke 24:50-51)

One day our two sons announced that they did not want to go to church anymore. Without sounding antagonistic, and knowing we respect honesty and integrity, they simply admitted that this religion stuff does not mean anything in their young lives. They did, however, leave open the possibility that, once they were done being young and enjoying life, they might go back to it. Their candidness was touching, even though their decision was not my preference. I was thankful for the Catholic school where they still participated in school liturgies. If it were not for the school, they would soon forget what Mass was like, since both boys worked on Sunday morning. Even though their father was less accepting than I, we both admitted that our sons' forthrightness could be the fruit of raising our children to be independent yet thoughtful. We were merely getting a piece of our own medicine.

A number of my dear Catholic friends did not approve of my willingness to accept our sons' decision without a fight. To some, accepting a 16- and 15-year-old's decision to stop attending church meant losing the battle for their souls, throwing in the towel, and a few less polite expressions. To others, my position merely made me like the rest of society, encouraging permissiveness and a selfishly motivated freedom in our youngsters. They accused me of washing my hands of my children's spiritual formation. Maybe these were valid points, and some days I felt guilty of them all. How could I explain my position? I searched my faith, wanting to take seriously Jesus' promise to be with us always. My faith challenged me to consider greater possibilities.

I remember my own Catholic upbringing: the fights on Sunday morning over what to wear to church, about feeling forced to go without hearing valid reasons, about proper behaviour in the pews, about worrying what the neighbours said. Much of our religious practice seemed focused externally, with little attention paid to the state of the heart before God. Today, of the five children in my family, I am the only one who has continued an adult faith commitment as a Catholic Christian. With the exception of the youth group in my parish, most of the elements leading to this choice came from experiences that came after childhood: the Christian youth rallies, my frequent visits to Taizé, my stay at L'Arche. It remains a mystery why I chose to embrace Catholic Christianity while my brothers walked away from their childhood religious home, away even from any conventional avenues for their spiritual growth.

Keeping in mind the road I took as a young adult helps me to trust that my children will have their own share of growing to do in order to find their way. Our children are not afraid to speak their mind, but sometimes I regret having helped them develop such strong identities. It is easier to live with children who do what their parents tell them. However, when transferring a blind allegiance from parents to peer group, teenagers who never learned to listen to and express their own voice can find themselves in trouble. If truth and authenticity are their own reward, our primary task as parents was to foster that spirit of truth and authenticity in our children. Instead of reading into teenage rebellion a lack of faith, we learned to recognize and call forth in the differentiation of our children an ability to stand on their own two feet, with all the responsibility and thoughtfulness this demands. Every generation faces challenges on the road to adulthood, and this millennium era is no different. In a society where the pressure to conform is steadily increasing, and with a church that can no longer legislate unquestioning obedience from its members, it becomes paramount to instill in the younger generation a capacity for critical thinking in a spirit of honesty, respect and compassion.

I do not want our children to remain in the Church because *we* say so, but because their own yearning for God leads them there. My wish is that they choose their community of faith out of their own capacity to respond to their need for belonging in faith to both God and to one another. Even though our children seem uninterested in church and faith issues right now, and despite our share of problems, arguments and worries, I see Christ reflected in their very way of being. Christ promised he would be with us always; truth and integrity in self-identity and in relationships attest to this reality. But this promise does not imply an easy ride. At 15, our son Daniel had a circle of friends who seemed less than desirable. He chose to spend time and energy with kids whom others judged as losers, who had problems with divorced parents and got tossed from one to the other. He associated with kids who already showed signs of alcohol abuse and who lacked the inner strength to stand up for themselves. Fights, trouble with the law and suicide attempts were regular occurrences for his friends, yet Daniel insisted on being a positive presence in their lives. He was vulnerable in such a crowd: he is more a follower than a leader, and needs people to like him. I spent many a night worrying about him being pulled down with the problems, temptations and conflicts surrounding him. I tried to forbid him to be with certain people and to go certain places, until one day, Daniel looked me straight in the eye and said: "These kids need a friend, too, and I am it."

I was put in my place. My faith, both in Jesus and in my own son, was on trial.

> When the scribes and the Pharisees saw that Jesus was eating with sinners and tax collectors, they said to his disciples: "Why does he eat with tax collectors and sinners?" When Jesus heard this, he said to them, "Those who are well have no need of a physician, but those who are sick do; I have come to call not the righteous but the sinners." (Mark 2:16-17)

Until this moment of reckoning, it had not occurred to me that peer influence could also work the other way. I had been consumed by fear that the misfortune of Daniel's friends would rub off on him and my son would end up in some sorry state. Instead, Daniel trod the minefields carefully (most of the time!), and tried to focus on God's goodness in his friends, even if this goodness was covered with thick layers of pain and struggle. Even while enjoying the smell of risk, he displayed a crazy faith that his own strength, faithfulness and care would help his friends restore some hope and reason to live – much like Jesus, who chose to eat with sinners and tax collectors. This choice to love those who lack love made Daniel most vulnerable to the cost of love. He worried excessively when one of his friends ran away from home. He felt helpless when another cut her wrist again and again. He cried at his friends' resistance to seeking help, watching them push away those who could offer care and support. He always talked to us, his parents, sharing his concerns and his friends' little victories of overcoming the pain – sometimes. One day he told us about being the only kid in that group who came from a relatively normal, alcohol-free, non-violent, intact two-parent family, and who successfully held down a job on top of his school commitments. This assessment did not put me at ease!

Daniel did not attend church at that time, but Christ's own demands of a virtuous life stared him in the face at every turn. With trepidation in our hearts, we nevertheless supported him, granting him a listening ear, while at the same time asking him the one important question: "How will you protect yourself from getting into the same mess? Because if you do get in trouble, you lose the capacity to offer your strength and encouragement, since you cannot give what you haven't got inside yourself." He heard this question, and his actions showed that he kept those words before him, to guide and protect himself. Six months later, Daniel's perseverance overcame the darkness at least for a few people, and at least for a short time. Two of his friends came to live with us, desperately wanting to turn their lives around, grateful for a safe place to stay. In the end, these few months may have taught my children more than it taught the boys who moved in. My children experienced firsthand the annoyance and frustration caused when certain members of a household do not respect the rules that run the household. The boys eventually drifted away, unsure of how to function in a loving environment. Our own family was left with renewed appreciation for one another even while feeling great disappointment at not having been able to help these boys more effectively.

When Jesus promised to be with us, he meant this in a concrete, incarnational way. As St. Teresa of Avila once said, we become Christ's hands, heart, mouth, ears and feet in this world. To the extent that we image Christ in our parental love for our children, we bring them Christ in the fullest sense possible. In his book *Seeking Spirituality*, Father Ron Rolheiser talks about our capacity to bind and loose in relation to the love we hold for one another:

> If a child, brother or sister or a loved one strays from the Church in terms of faith practice and morality, as long as you continue to love that person, and hold him or her in union and forgiveness, he or she is touching the hem of the garment, is held to the body of Christ, and is forgiven by God, irrespective of his or her official external relationship to the Church and Christian morality. When you love someone, unless that someone actively rejects your love and forgiveness, she or he is sustained in salvation.[34]

These words are not meant to lead to cheap grace or to laissez-faire parenting. They are the most logical consequence of a faith that takes seriously Jesus' promise to be with us always. We underestimate the extent of that promise. I underestimate it when I wish that my children would attend church dutifully instead of wrestling with their faith in the blood, sweat and tears of their friendships. It is not that one is better than the other. Rather, their presence in church takes its meaning from their attempts to love and hold their friends in faith. They know that peace that the world cannot give by the steadfastness and loyalty with which they stand up for one another: "He's my friend; don't touch him."

And so I keep loving, forgiving, challenging and supporting our children. In these very acts I live out the belief that Jesus himself visits their hearts each time my love and care touch them. Yet I let myself get carried away by worry and fear about my children. I bring my concerns to God in prayer, offering my sons and daughter into God's care daily. Sometimes even that does not feel like it's enough. One day, coming home from a meeting two hours away, I stopped in a nearby church and, my children on my mind again, sat with Jesus in the pew:

> My daughter offered me Jesus Christ once again... I sit in the coolness of the church and gaze upon the cross, seeing there both Christ and my daughter... tears spring up in me

and I cry – cry at the realization that Christ Jesus has already claimed her for himself, for the sake of the Church and the world. Rachelle offers Jesus in all that she is: her generosity, compassion, sense of justice, joy, prayerfulness – all abundantly overflow with Jesus, and she freely offers him through herself to others… David [our eldest] reflects Christ in his thoughtfulness, his honesty, and his unbeatable positive attitude towards whatever comes his way.

He does not show interest in organized religion at this time, but I am reassured: Christ has imprinted himself on his very being, and the Christian life is still the avenue for him to be fully himself. He just doesn't call it Christian at this time, but Jesus is with him always… I gaze at the cross, and feel embraced by Love itself through that cross. (Journal entry)

I cannot protect my children from harm. They will get hurt in life because of events beyond their control, because life is not fair, and because they love so fiercely. As adults weighed down by the hurts, disappointments and loss of our own dreams, we have no right to rob our young people prematurely of their passion, their boundless energy, and their capacity to love intensely. So many adults, individually and collectively, seem to have lost faith in the younger generation because of the prevalence of violence, family breakdown, abuse and moral disintegration in their ranks. Some use the image of Sodom and Gomorrah as everyday language to describe the doomed future that belongs to our children. Others wander aimlessly in the world of meaning, joining the young people in rejecting organized religion, leaving both themselves and their children unequipped to still their spiritual hungers.

Sometimes the support and guidance we try to offer our children reveals itself in surprising ways. Our eldest child, David, displays an infectious enthusiasm for work and people. He spends enormous amounts of energy trying to figure out what makes people tick. He treats every customer in the video store as a friend. He laments how few people truly enjoy their jobs, and he dreams ambitious dreams. I am no *Star Wars* fan, but David is. As a matter of fact, his main culture at this point in his life seems to come from movies. At 19, working at a video rental store was therefore like hitting the jackpot. He saw a lot of movies I would and could never watch –the extent of the violence, sex and immorality disturb me. While I'm not a heavy-handed disciplinary parent, I watched this development with trepidation, consoling myself with the wild hope that the values we instilled while he was too young to object would now carry him through this minefield of temptations. Adolescence is not the time to introduce new values, but rather a testing time for the values given earlier in life.

David's favourite pastime with his dad was to watch movies. His choice of what to watch with Dad reflected an uncanny insight and respect for what his "old-fashioned" parents value. In the discussions following a movie, we sometimes noted his ability for keen observation and critical evaluation – he had no use for movies that are all noise or that lack story, message or meaning. We challenged him to develop critical thinking skills while immersed in the world of films and entertainment. Not showing up at church did not exempt him from Christ's demands. Jesus is indeed with us always, specifically in the places of our lives where our values are seriously at risk. Jesus may be there as a reassuring presence, or he may be there as the one asking the disturbing questions when we least want to hear them, even though we know they are important. As parents we embody that presence of Christ with our children in the very way we walk with them in the issues affecting their lives.

Sometimes we parents hit a jackpot of our own, as was the case when we went to see the remake of the movie *Titanic* a few years ago. David went back to see it many times. The cheap and romantic love story that had been added to the factual account of the *Titanic's* disastrous voyage had more layers of meaning than appeared at first glance. Watching the movie with the eyes of faith revealed deep sacramental movements: of the need for forgiveness and mercy in our moments of dying, for letting go and for the possibility of new life even at a ripe old age, for resurrection and ascension even in the most desperate moments. Without being explicitly Christian, the story was packed with the elements of Christ's promise to be with us always. I tried to explain to my son what "church" looked like in *Titanic*. At first he was unsure, blaming it on his mother's need to make everything look "Christian."

When preparing the following reflection, conversations with my son formed the main ingredients. I desired very much to break open a contemporary image in order to reveal the presence of the risen Jesus. *Titanic* allowed me to bring home the deep movements of letting go and Easter living.

Homiletic Reflection in My Home Parish

John 14:23-29

Many of you have probably seen the movie *Titanic* by now. As I reflected on today's Gospel this past week, a scene from that movie came to mind. It is the one where Jack and Rose, our heroes in love, find themselves hanging on to life in the icy water, surrounded by drowned and drowning bodies: a gripping sight, showing the ugliness and ruthlessness of death. Jack is talking to Rose, his whole body shivering from the cold. He pushes her into a promise to him: "Promise me, Rose, that you'll never give up in life. I'll be with you always, Rose. Promise, promise..." Rose panics, fearing Jack will die. She says she wants to die too. Jack says no, and makes her promise that she will not give up.

Like Jack, who knows he is drowning in the frigid water, Jesus sees in his mind's eye the shadow of the cross, death waiting to swallow him. Jesus knows the time with his friends is up. Jesus knows that soon pain and loss will rip them apart. Soon the disciples will experience fear and anxiety at a level they have never encountered before. Jesus tries to prepare them and to strengthen them, before the blow of his death hits them.

"...the Advocate, the Holy Spirit, will teach you everything.... Peace I leave with you, my peace I give you...." Words of encouragement in the face of an ugly death. Words of love and guidance in the face of the greatest loss the world has ever experienced....These words are for us too, each one of us: words of love and encouragement in the face of our loss, in the face of our death...

For if there is anything that is certain for those who love generously, it is the reality of the losses we suffer in our lives. In reflecting on Jesus' words I couldn't help but think of the recent losses right in our own communities: the horrible explosion in Delmas, which resulted in the death of one man who was a son, a husband, a father, and a friend to many; the family in Vawn who lost their house in a fire; the man in Glaslyn who suffered a severe farming accident last winter; the young boy in Edam whose mother died suddenly, only weeks before his confirmation.

And then there are all the other losses, the subtle and invisible ones, the blunt and the slow ones: like losing a job, or not being able to find one; or losing a driver's licence because of ill health or old age; or losing our innocence, our hope, our self-confidence... At those times we too can feel the deadening chill of the icy water, like our two heroes in *Titanic*. At those times we too can be swallowed up by fear and despair, like the disciples were after Jesus died.

"Peace I leave with you, my peace I give you..." In the face of the losses that are part of our living, what do these words mean? In the face of Jesus' crucifixion and death, what is this peace that the world cannot give? And how does the Holy Spirit "teach us every-thing"? Often, the answers to these questions are not clear until a crisis hits us and we are faced with the urgent choice between life and death, in whatever form this takes in our lives.

In *Titanic*, Rose was asked that question only seconds after Jack dies. Her heart is breaking as she shivers in the freezing water. The question comes to her in the form of the rescue boat that floats by at some distance. The men call out in the eerie quiet of this floating cemetery, throwing a bright light across the water as they look for survivors. At first Rose does not want to be found, and the tension mounts. Then she remembers Jack's last words, his last wish. She remembers the promise she made to him, and the Spirit of peace and understanding floods her heart. She rips a whistle off a dead body, and blows it with every ounce of strength she can muster. Rose is found, and eventually starts a new life in America. With Jack's spirit living in her, her heart goes on, as Céline Dion sings in the *Titanic* theme song.

Rose did not understand what Jack asked of her, or her re-sponse, until much later. Likewise, the disciples did not really under-stand Jesus' words immediately. Insight grew only after Jesus died and they encountered him as the risen Lord.

The disciples did not fully take to heart Jesus' farewell speech until they were faced with the challenge to proclaim the Good News of Jesus' resurrection.

Once their hearts were filled with that Spirit of peace and understanding, the disciples were even able to deal with crises and dissent in their own ranks, as the first reading tells us today. Once they were filled with the Spirit, they had a foretaste of the new world to come, as John shares with us in Revelation today. Once we are filled with the Spirit, we become bearers of God's love and light even in the darkest places.

Jesus' heart goes on, too, after he has died, in the form of the Spirit of peace and understanding – a peace that the world indeed cannot give – that makes its home in us. Jesus' promise of peace does not mean an absence of hostility and pain, nor does it mean no more losses. Jesus' peace allows us to find joy in the midst of the struggle, like the oasis in the desert, or like the quiet at the bottom of the ocean, while the storm rages on the surface. The peace Jesus gives is the hope in time of despair, the desire to rebuild in time of destruction, the calm haven in a time of turmoil. The Spirit of peace breaks through every time we love, every time we reach out, every time that love moves us to tears, that love hurts. A peace that the world cannot give. There is no greater love than to lay down one's life for one's friends…. Jesus' voluntary death out of love for us unleashed the greatest Spirit of all: the Holy Spirit.

Let us rejoice and believe, living our life soaked in the peace of God's own Holy Spirit. Amen.

After the service, David, who had graced us with his presence that morning, commented with his usual charming smile:"That was cool, Mom, and it made sense." I was pleased that he had listened, and grateful that he offered his feedback. Because it came from my son, these words were the greatest compliment I had received in a long time. God is truly with us, always.

CHAPTER 8

The Word Made Flesh

In the beginning was the Word
and the Word was with God,
and the Word was God.
The Word became flesh
and dwelt among us.
We saw his glory…
from him all kindness and truth of God
have come down to us.
(John 1:1, 14)

My daughter Rachelle moved her body gracefully, vigorously and creatively. She was part of a gymnastics club, she played team sports, and she learned to dance. But Rachelle's motivation to join in these activities had little to do with excelling or winning. For a long time she was not slender enough or driven enough to compete. Observing her closely revealed her deep inner satisfaction in learning the particular moves of a dance and in the experience of her physical capabilities. More than once I saw my daughter's face radiate sheer delight just from experiencing the fullness of living in her body.

I envied her untainted and unscarred way of living in her body. She was only 12. By the time most of us women reach adulthood, we have picked up all kinds of cultural taboos, religious judgments, and experiences of physical or sexual violations. With such heavy baggage it becomes an arduous task to recover a sense of the goodness of our bodies, let alone maintain throughout our life a God-given fullness of living in the flesh. Growing into a deeper awareness of the role my body played in my relationships – with God, others, creation and myself – did not involve dealing with memories of abuse or physical violations. However, the taboos and judgments collected and internalized over the years are still hard to uncover and dismantle. Deep, unexamined messages, hiding under many layers, can play havoc with psychological, sexual and spiritual wholeness. The notion that God's own Word took on flesh, and dwelt among us in the flesh, is a strong invitation to shed unneeded layers and to grow into the fullness of what living in our body can bring to the world. And in this case, women are in a particular position of privilege and responsibility to offer the world the fullness of living in the flesh. However, because of that particular position, women are also very vulnerable in the relationship to their bodies:

> Becoming incarnate, becoming wholly immersed in the flesh is not the result of a simple choice. It is a process that is mystery. It is a mystery intimate with grace, the admirable intercourse with divine life. While the desire for personal wholeness [...] is characteristic of many who have known the devastation of being shattered within their personal life experience, the technological milieu of the late twentieth century proves a constant challenge to personal [body] wholeness.[35]

Because we were committed to the land, and refrained from manipulating its fertility and polluting it with chemicals, as a married couple we adopted the same approach to our combined human fertility.[36] Roman Catholic Church teaching on family planning, the validity of which became clear only over time, fitted with our choice. I was ignorant about the inner workings of my reproductive system until I learned to observe my body symptoms with the help of Natural Family Planning (NFP). I became greatly intrigued with the realization that so much of my bodily functions occurred without my interference or knowledge. I developed a sense of awe, and grew into an intimate relationship with my body through observing the signs of its cycles. I regarded my fertility as a gift to cherish and work with, rather than a liability or a burden to get rid of:

The fundamental difference [with men] is that a woman does not *have* a womb or breasts or ovaries; a woman *lives* a body that may ovulate, lactate, or burgeon with an indwelling child. Every moment of (her) existence is touched by the subtle interplay of hormones (or their induced silence).... For a woman who is attuned to her basic rhythms, the menstrual cycle is not an infirmity or "curse" but a gift, enabling her to participate in the vital intercourse of daily life with greater understanding.[37]

Living in harmony with my natural body rhythms reaped its own rewards. The challenge to discipline our sexual activity according to our combined fertility – wishing to achieve or to avoid pregnancy – brought deep, long-lasting experiences of mutual respect, commitment and maturing marital love as it required us to communicate and collaborate in both the times of sexual availability and the times of abstinence. In turn, developing communication skills and fostering mutual respect of our bodies regarding family planning helped us to weather relational storms over the years. We experienced a growing into one's body as mystery and as the place of God's own Holy Spirit: "Surely you know that your body is the temple of the Holy Spirit. The Spirit is in you and is a gift from God. You are no longer your own. God paid a great price for you. So use your body to honour God" (1 Corinthians 6:19-20).

Now, it is one thing to grow a deeper awareness and appreciation of one's body according to God's plan. It is quite another to use this awareness to judge those who cannot see their body as gift. I secretly, and at times not so secretly, felt disdain for those who did not seem to be able to live a debt-free, back-to-the-land lifestyle. In the same way, I sometimes looked down on people, especially women, who had been deeply wounded in their bodies.

Working as a counsellor at Interval House challenged me to submit to the pain of other women, pain that was securely lodged in their bodies as a way of knowing beyond words. Listening to their stories of sexual and physical abuse threw me into inner turmoil, making me wonder how a woman could be assertive and self-confident in successfully using a natural form of family planning when she lived in a destructive relationship.

Without knowing it, I headed out to confront some of the greatest obstacles to compassion and spiritual growth: the sophisticated illusions in which we carefully bury ourselves, hiding from God in the most ingenious ways. One of mine was a self-righteousness in heart and mind combined with a strange ignorance of the inner and outer pain in so many relationships. I fooled myself into doing everything "right" for God, including and especially our commitment to natural family planning. Listening to the stories of abuse and exploitation at Interval House was hard, but on the way home I consoled myself that I was spared such ordeals. At first I worked hard to keep at bay questions about how natural family planning could work when your husband or boyfriend beat you into having sex when he wanted, how you could choose to carry a child to term in a violent home, and how you would find the inner resources to cherish the goodness of your body if the only message in your head was that you are filthy.

Over time, working with abused women forced me to re-evaluate what I considered to be permanent and universal values. In order to grow in respect and compassion for those broken lives, I slowly learned to recognize that I too shared in women's personal and collective experience of being exploited, controlled and defined by men:

> I think of the women at Interval House, and I am starting to realize that I am not immune to their experience of pain and control. I am coming to the place of deep recognition: I share the pain, the fear, because I am woman. I share the effects of being controlled by a man, even in my own husband, who has a passive/aggressive way of exercising his will. I thought for so long that I was different from most women at the shelter, that restricting cultural and religious norms (some good, some not good) had not invaded my relationship to my body, to men and to other women. How wrong of me to think that, and how painful to let the solidarity occur… In a strange way I am starting to feel closer to the women at Interval House, and it hurts. (Journal entry)

My initial ignorance and reluctance to feel compassion and solidarity (trying to maintain a mental division between "them" and "us") seriously inhibited my ability to live a full body-spirituality, in spite of my saying all the right words and doing all the right things. Then God decided that enough was enough. The sexual applecart got upset, accelerating my mid-life chaos as I questioned all the choices I had ever made. Combined with my renewed sense of call and mission in the Church that emerged so clearly in the years at seminary, it took a woman with a man's name (an old practice in religious life) to increase my understanding of the connection be-tween my body and ministry. I was more than fertile ground for the words of Timothy Prokes SSND in her book *Women's Challenge: Min-istry in the Flesh*. Even though she wrote twenty years before I picked up the book, her words shed beams of light on what I was experi-encing in both my psychosexual and my spiritual journey:

> Ministry is touched by uniqueness of bodily expression. A
> woman receives and ministers to another differently than a
> man because she expresses in a body-person with capacities
> that he does not have. Since woman has been so wounded
> because of cyclicity, vagina, breasts, womb and ovaries – it
> has bearing on the redemption of all the universe whether
> she assumes or rejects what has been so wounded when she
> comes to the ministry of healing in Christ. What is meant
> for women to minister out of this awareness is only at a
> breakthrough point, a threshold of potentiality. Here and
> there such ministry begins to take flesh....[38]

Before the quickening of a call to ministry was felt, I undertook a long, arduous journey into my sexuality as woman. Each and every part of my intimate sexual reality was called into the light of aware-ness and consequently touched with the hot kiss of God's own lov-ing embrace and desire. Once healing and wholeness became acces-sible to my sexual reality, the foundation was laid for God's call into ministry:

> That Christ's ministry touched concrete daily life, especially
> at disintegration points, has immense significance for those
> who extend that ministry, searching for effective expres-
> sions of it. Whoever flees the human condition departs from
> Christ's ministry. Whatever remains unreceived of one's own
> human condition, or that of others, is an obstacle to minis-
> try. What has not been assumed has not been redeemed.[39]

Cultural conditioning, with the abundant presence of distorted images of sexuality in the media, makes our capacity to develop a healthy understanding of sexuality almost impossible. At best it is fraught with many internal tensions and contradictions. I was brought face to face with these tensions in my own efforts to unravel what lay beneath the surface of my own sexual identity.

My heart was terror-stricken when, seemingly out of the blue, sexual dreams and fantasies involving other women emerged from somewhere inside me. My first reaction was a strong urge to shut down these disturbing messages from my unconscious so as not to upset who I understood myself to be as a sexual being. I took an enormous risk when I chose to interact with these sexual dreams and fantasies, many of which involved images and scenes that at first sight seemed to violate every moral norm I based my sexual identity on. It was difficult to see what God was doing, and whether God was behind this at all. Over time, with some professional help and carried by my own commitments to honesty, courage and prayer, I discovered that these dreams and fantasies were the means that my unconsciousness used to befriend and integrate deep centres of female energy, both sexual and spiritual in nature. Giving birth to previously unknown, suppressed, and deeply feared parts of myself, brought me face to face with both pain and promise, terror and excitement, death and resurrection, much like the cervix opening and closing in the painful intensity and mystery of childbirth. What happened to the audacity and confidence with which I took every other new turn in the road of my life? Where was my courage when I most needed it? The butterflies in my stomach seemed impossible to control. Slowly, I learned to hold off interpreting and judging the images, letting them first speak their truth to me, in order to see deep into myself and, consequently, into God. By doing so, I found a truth that far surpassed any superficial interpretation of sexuality and of spirituality.

Reclaiming my female sexuality, my bodily integrity and wisdom as a woman revealed strong dualistic understandings (surprise!), understandings that had been deeply internalized from cultural, social and religious conditioning. I felt the power of perversion and temptation, of sin and evil, in my own bones. But I was in for an even greater revelation. Sin and evil were not, as St. Augustine had us believe, intrinsic characteristics of my sexual drives and passions. As I risked getting close to these centres of powerful energy, I also tapped into the incredible potential for creativity and vision, for passion and compassion, for boldness and courage, for deeper intimacy and love, for right relation and inner authority – all fuelled by this same sexual energy. And so, wrestling with my sexual angel, the choice was once again mine to make: "I call heaven and earth to witness against you today that I have set before you life and death, blessings and curses. Choose life so that you and your descendants may live…" (Deuteronomy 30:19).

From the heart of that sexual fire, God spoke, and put before me the choice of life and death. I came to understand that life in Christ was to consume, to absorb all of me, with my sexuality at the centre. In a very tangible way God communicated that my body, and every human body, is the holy ground where God dwells. The separation between sexuality and spirituality became increasingly blurred and arbitrary. The place of deepest sexual passion burst with the promise of the deepest intimacy with God. The wound of dualistic thinking, after dominating Christianity for twenty centuries as a result of Greek philosophy and St. Augustine, was slowly being healed in my own flesh and bones.

I understood anew why God came to us in the flesh: in Christ Jesus, God assumed our human condition totally in order to redeem humanity once and for all. The coming of Jesus in this world was to forever mend the separation of mind and body, of sexuality and prayer, of women and men, of human beings and creation, of earth and our bodies. This is Incarnation: the Word becoming flesh, healing all divisions, including the human-divine and the life-death division. It is a miracle that, in all the twenty centuries of Christianity oppressed by the weight of dualistic thinking, this fundamental and radical act of God remains intact, simply waiting to be reclaimed in all its power. In Jesus, God chose the human body as the medium of divine-human union. How did we miss something so unique and so potent of salvation? Incarnation is waiting to be claimed deep inside each human being, and therefore keeps happening over and over and over:

> To know myself as profoundly relational is to know myself
> as body. All our relationships are mediated through our

bodies. In our emotions we interact with the world. In our sexual, sensuous selves our sense of relatedness is grounded. It is our sense of bodily integrity that grounds our power to be with others and our capacity for vulnerability with them. When I sense the holiness of my own body, I begin to sense the holiness of every other body.[40]

Incarnation, living holiness in our bodies, is therefore a prerequisite for all ministry in the name of Jesus. This is especially important for women who carry so many personal, cultural and religious wounds in their bodies. Once my own hidden pockets of sexual and spiritual woundedness were exposed to the incarnational light of redemption, the road to God's call became less shrouded in mist.

> I am aware that my female presence in the pulpit breaks the listener open into a new experience, one that a male priest cannot offer. I heed the potential power and intensity of such an experience. I yield and submit body-mind-soul while knowing myself centre-stage and God's instrument. I make every move, speak every word, make every gesture and make eye contact deliberately and in a spirit of service, knowing myself at that time to be mediator, healer and teacher by my total communication of self in the name of the Gospel. (Journal entry)

Sr. Timothy Prokes helped me see – in hindsight – the reasons for the psychological and spiritual journey into my sexuality in terms of ministry. The many years of involvement with natural family planning helped internalize the notion that my cyclical fertility is a blessing, not a curse. This inner and outer stance through living with natural family planning minimized the temptation to buy into the contemporary culture's contraceptive thinking and quick-fix mentality towards anything physical. I looked back over all the reflection and the struggle sparked by our commitment to natural family planning. Now I saw these forming a crucible, out of which the blessing of a holy sexual identity became possible. Other aspects of my life were brought into this new configuration, somehow setting me apart from mainstream culture, indirectly preparing a more explicit experience of call to ministry. The many years of living off the land in a somewhat self-sufficient lifestyle continually reminded me that beauty and lasting fulfillment lie in utter simplicity. Now these things worked together to form an even greater picture of God's prophetic, pastoral and priestly call: "I have need of you in the world. Do not fear; I am sending you...."

In the weeks of reading and reflecting with Sr. Timothy Prokes' words, I prepared to preach once again. This time I became acutely aware of the role my body played in the process:

> Where in my body does energy gather? In my womb, the place where new life is conceived and grows in darkness, until the time for birthing has come. In my womb, the sexual centre of my being from which flows the most intense passion, arousal, vision and compassion I am capable of. In my heart, where God fuels the fire of love for the Church and for the world. In my heart, where the flowers of Eden once again wait to open and be embraced by the warm, nurturing sun. In my soul, where longing for union with God is mixed with the pain of the world, thus forming the crucible of divine love. In my soul, where the desire for self-giving burns fiercely, luring me into the true freedom of God alone. In my breasts, bursting with divine milk to feed the hungry. In my breasts, which risk overflowing if I do not suckle God's little ones. (Journal entry)

Preparing to preach for the second Sunday of Easter, I found myself in the company of two close friends. The first one was Marian, to whom I spoke over the phone and whom I had gone to see a few weeks earlier. It seemed that Marian's body utterly betrayed her, becoming sick, leaving her and the doctors at a loss for a diagnosis. I struggled to see meaning in Marian's suffering. I saw her anger and frustration. I heard the exhaustion and the yearning for wholeness in her voice. Marian was beginning to consider the possibility that her body carried deep scars of childhood betrayal, and that part of her physical healing had to involve a touching of those wounds in order to offer them to God for redemption. She expressed apprehension (for none of us go there willingly) and a need for prayer.

The other friend keeping me company was dear doubting Thomas in the Gospel for that Sunday. Jesus invites Thomas to touch his wounds; no matter how often I heard that Gospel, Jesus' invitation burst with new meaning in light of my reflections on incarnational, body-centred ministry and the woundedness of women in their bodies. I went about my business of daily housework, baking bread, caring for children, all in the company of Marian's struggle with her body and Jesus' invitation to "touch his wounds." I felt the energy gather:

> I put on the text of both Gospel and homiletic reflection (which I wrote yesterday) like a diving suit – fitting snugly, featuring every little contour and angle of who I am in my totality. I am preparing for eucharistic self-offering in preaching. I yearn for the consummative union of Eucharist, Christ's own most intense form of self-giving....But tomorrow there is only Christ's self-giving in the Word proclaimed and preached, and in the assembly gathered to pray. This ought to carry us over until the fullness of Eucharist is once again available, presided over by our priest in the Mass. I burn with God's call to break bread and feed God's people. (Journal entry)

The "Word made flesh" took on a whole new meaning as I faced the faith community, a community including many whose bodies knew betrayal, brokenness and bruises.

Homiletic Reflection in My Home Parish

John 20:19-31

A small town in British Columbia has one claim to fame: their mountain, Mount Crawley, towers over the town like a monument to eternity. Most of the time, however, the mountain is hiding in the clouds. On the few clear days in the valley, you can hear people say to one another, "The mountain is out!"

Now, even when it cannot be seen, the mountain is there. If you follow the directions on the road map, there is no doubt that you will bump into Mount Crawley. It is a long drive around, and it is a difficult climb up that mountain. Many tourists come to visit that small town, hoping to catch a glimpse of this piece of natural beauty. Many are there on the grey and cloudy days; they do not make the effort to find the mountain hiding in the mist. Many leave the town, not believing that Mount Crawley is really there, because if they cannot see it, chances are that the mountain does not exist at all…

Unless I can see for myself, I may doubt the existence of whatever it is. Unless I can see for myself, I may not believe. Unless I can see for myself, I may live in fear that God may not be real. All we know for sure are the wounds and the bruises we collect over time. No wonder Thomas demanded to touch the wounds of Christ – just for proof. We do not argue with suffering and death: they are as real as the clouds around Mount Crawley.

My friend Marian knows about the thick clouds around the mountain. Not that she has ever been to that town in B.C. – she hasn't. As a matter of fact, she has been so sick in the past year that she has not gone much farther than a ten-minute walk in the forest around her house. Visits to the doctors in the city are so tiring, she needs days in bed afterwards just to recover from the trip. Marian is young – in her mid-forties – and is blessed with a caring husband and two young children. But Marian's life has been seriously curtailed by illness, as if her body has suddenly betrayed her. Doctors grasp at a diagnosis: thyroid cancer, chronic fatigue syndrome, mercury poisoning from dental fillings, damaged immune system from radiation treatments are a few of their inconclusive findings. It is becoming a bit like Russian roulette. Meanwhile, Marian fights to maintain a sense of God in the midst of the pain and the fatigue. Like the disciples on that first day of the week, fear grips Marian's heart and settles in like the thick clouds around the mountain, locking the doors of her soul. Marian screams silently in the lonely hours in bed, day and night, saying with Thomas: I cannot believe in you Lord, unless you heal me…

Marian is Thomas' twin, and so are we all. Not only do we want proof to show that Jesus is risen; we dismiss any proof that comes our way. We who profess Jesus as Lord, we who have been baptized into his death and resurrection, cannot hide behind the excuse of ignorance. We are not among those who do not see and yet believe – we are among those who do see Jesus, who have received Jesus' Spirit of peace and still do not believe, locking the doors with our fear. We offer and receive comfort — Jesus is there, clear as day. We welcome a stranger, visit a prisoner — Jesus is there, clear as day. We forgive and receive forgiveness — Jesus is there, clear as day. We hear God's Word and take part in the Eucharist — Jesus is there, clear as day. But more often than we would like to admit, fear holds us back from one another, and from God, keeping us from seeing Jesus. Fear is our biggest enemy, just as it was the biggest enemy of the disciples. Fear moved them to lock themselves in that upper room, not realizing that the "enemy" was not outside the room, but right in their own hearts. Fear is the thick cloud around the mountain, hiding from view the new life promised in the Risen One of God.

Earlier this week I asked Marian to reflect with me on today's Gospel and to share what Easter means to her this year. She gave me permission to share her thoughts with you. Lent was particularly trying for Marian. Panic struck every little bit of faith she had left. "I now realize," she says, "that my deepest problem was not my health, but fear. Like a persistent underground current, fear undermined every effort at healing. I feared constantly that God may not want me to get better."

It was only when Marian unmasked the enemy in her own soul that God's healing power could move in. Jesus touched Marian's wounds with the Love that moves right through locked doors. "Never before have I felt the power of the resurrection so tangibly in my body," says Marian, overjoyed that she made it to church on Easter morning. Slowly, Marian is healing. The road will continue to be rocky, and there will be setbacks. Now she knows that the wounds in her mind and body are touched, are soaked, in Love, and everything else will take its cue from there. Jesus breathed on her, blowing away the clouds around the mountain, bringing peace and a clear sight of him who is steadfast Love and Mercy.

The Healer of our wounds, our illness, our brokenness bore our wounds in his death. The Healer of wounds lives, and dwells among us. With Thomas, and with Marian, we are invited to touch the wounds of Christ in one another. The wounds of the world are the wounds of Christ on the cross. The pain in our own lives is the birthplace of resurrection faith: "Put your finger here and see my hands. Reach out your hand and put it in my side. Do not doubt but believe" (John 20:27). The peace of the risen Lord blows away the thick clouds around the mountain. We bump into Jesus as we wind our way up that mountain, the joy of his resurrection.

Baptized in Christ, we are an Easter people. Sharing in his resurrection, we have been given the gift and power of God to heal, to forgive, to comfort, to bring peace. Jesus stands among us today, dispelling fear and disbelief, inviting us to be his guiding and healing presence in our broken world. Let us rejoice, knowing ourselves loved and redeemed. In Christ, we are worthy bearers of God's gifts to our broken and beloved world. Amen.

Walking back to the pew I felt depleted. I needed space and silence to recentre, to reorient, but the rest of the service rolled right along. I surrendered, I offered, I fed – "eat and drink" – in the task of preaching. Experiencing preaching this way was not new, but with all my reading and reflecting about ministry in the flesh I was much more conscious of my own emotional, physical and mental processes. I gave birth to something that grew in secret, and saw it scattered like grain for the fields, planting itself in fertile soil of souls. The words were no longer mine – and maybe never were. I felt like Mary, in whose body grew the Son of God. God's Word grew in me, stretching and using every particle of my being like a seed in gestation, only to be broken open and scattered as food for the world. I awoke to a passion deep and all encompassing, capable of remembering and loving into wholeness the many fragmented bodies and souls.

PART III

Feeding off the Crumbs

Woman with the Hemorrhage

Bleeding woman
spending timeless years
seeing, feeling, smelling
life flowing out of her,
draining her
of most vital elements
of body and spirit
holding on to empty
cures and promises.
In agony she rolls
on the ground
utterly despised by all...
bleeding woman
in my soul
thirsting for healing
aching to be
touched by
Loving Power –
running here and there
hurt and scarred by
failure and rejection
nothing left to lose
Jesus...
I touch merely the
edge of his being, for
fear
my blood may
stain him too...
but no, instead
his love stains
me
stops the bleeding
healing and
rebirth
life death life

CHAPTER 9

I Am the Bread of Life

While they were eating,
He took a loaf of bread,
and after blessing it he broke it,
gave it to them, and said,
"Take; this is my body."
(Mark 14:22)

Most insights do not strike like a single lightning bolt. Instead, they emerge as if out of a dense mist that sometimes lasts too long and leads us to fear that we will lose our way. Opportunities for preaching opened up and new needs – although they were not easy to articulate – surfaced in the faith community. The shortage of ordained ministers felt acute in our rural parishes, where one priest served six faith communities. The process of finding new ways to worship and to offer pastoral ministry was, and continues to be, fraught with both fear and tunnel vision. Used to celebrating Mass and having a priest available at all times, many Catholics still find it difficult to imagine liturgy and ministry without Eucharist and without a priest. When I began to sense keenly God's call to embrace a new model of ministry and leadership as manifested in preaching, I too was at a loss. As our local church had trouble conceiving of new forms of liturgy and ministry, I too felt seriously hampered in naming the range of possible interpretations of what I was experiencing.

Being a relational extrovert and therefore needing to talk through my own thought processes did not help matters. The more I tried to speak of God, the less I felt understood. The more I tried to name my experience of God using existing categories, the less adequate the words seemed. There was something totally irrational yet logical, informal yet official, personal yet public about this dance with God. The gifts found on this journey were both blessing and curse, treasure and liability. From these paradoxical dynamics my spiritual director nevertheless helped distill the authentic presence and activity of God. Gently but firmly God led me into the one place where such activity can be most fully heard and discerned: the prayerful silence and solitude of my own soul, where I was totally alone with God. I had great difficulty entering that place, not to mention feeling at home there. I was more comfortable looking for external "signs" of God's guidance outside myself in events and people. This trek into solitude became a most trying part of my discernment process:

> The creative writing and the inner movements desiring to be named stay locked up inside if I do not allow solitude and silence in my days. When I let the dazzling flurry of activity rule my life, the musings of my soul barely reach the surface of consciousness. I am realizing more and more that the greatest creativity is born out of deepest solitude. And how difficult it remains to cultivate this solitude, physically and otherwise. The task of preaching requires much, much solitude. What irony – the place where fullness of life originates and emanates from is now the most difficult to get to. Having lived in the relational mode for so long, I find it difficult to stay in the solitude with God for any length of time. God is pulling me into this place of intimate presence with him, yet I fear going there, and I fear losing the sense of belonging in human relationships. (Journal entry)

As happened to Peter, someone else put a belt around my waist, taking me where I would rather not go (John 21:18), both in the Church and in my own spiritual journey. At times I distrusted my experience, partly because it seemed to fall outside of all existing and officially allowed categories, and partly because I feared losing control over my life. Every time I returned to the Scriptures, only to find there God's own confirmation of the dance with my soul, with my life: "See, I am about to do a new thing; now it springs forth, do you not yet perceive it?" (Isaiah 43:19).

These dynamics within my personal faith experience have their counterpart in the larger church. Taking a historical view of the development and understanding of lay ministry in the church, Kenan Osborne OFM points out:

> In the many reform movements from 1000 to 1600, it was the reading and rereading of the enscriptured word which nourished (in the laity) the longing for gospel discipleship. Such a reality is taking place today in many new forms, and there results a new reformation both of life and of person. Gospel discipleship has become, once again, a powerful spiritual magnet.... This enfleshing anew of the enscriptured word is a major form of today's Pentecost....[41]

Reading and rereading Scripture was like examining familiar clothes for new features. I felt a newness I had never noticed before. The Spirit of God does blow where it will and this same Spirit will help the Church find new ways of ministry and liturgy. Celebrating Eucharist on a Sunday is the high point of our Catholic Christian identity. It was not our choice not to do so. We were being deprived of the fullest expression of our faith, and this at a time when Pope John Paul II emphasized frequently that we are a eucharistic people and urged us to seize this reality with all the faith and courage we can muster. Making sense of the pope's words on Eucharist in light of the decreasing frequency of Mass in my area required me to open myself to new ways of understanding Christ's words at the Last Supper.

Preaching became one way of "feeding" Christ to the faith community. After all, I preached when our parish priest was not with us and we participated in a Sunday Celebration of the Word with Communion. At non-eucharistic liturgies, the Word of God proclaimed becomes the food for the soul, which we "eat" through the preaching. Thus Christ's body and blood is given through the Good News proclaimed and preached. We receive communion (reserved sacrament from a previous Mass) at such a service, but this is not the eucharistic action of Mass. Preparing the homiletic reflection became much like finding the right ingredients to serve the message of the Gospel in meaningful ways. I do not always get this delicate mix quite right, and sometimes my homiletic reflections are as dense as the ones back in the preaching class:

I delivered my latest homily in our preaching group at LTS. Even after taking several courses, I totally bombed. It was too long, too dense, too theological, and too much content. My professor called it being too smart for my own good, as if trying to feed the hearer one indigestible mass of the richest dessert. This is a humbling experience; will I ever get it? (Journal entry)

Since preaching was still sporadic, I unconsciously felt an urgency to "say it all" in the one chance I got. Using the occasion of preaching to meet my own need, however, turned out to be counterproductive. I needed ongoing vigilance, disciplining my thought processes ruthlessly and yielding to God, while anchoring the task solidly in prayer. Preaching feeds the Word of God to the hearers in bite-size pieces without choking them and without allowing them to be passive receivers (no baby food for adult believers). While non-eucharistic liturgies were not considered the full celebration of our faith, I still considered preaching serious food for the soul, in expectation of the next time we celebrated Eucharist once again in our parish.

My preaching thus occurred in a eucharistic vacuum of sorts; yet for me it overflowed with Christ's promise to be for us the "Bread of Life" (John 6:48). If the Eucharist is about offering both the beauty and the pain of the world as summed up in Christ's total offering of self, I found parallels in proclamation and preaching. Humanity's strength and beauty, mingled with our crucified and dying reality of life, are lifted up through the proclamation of God's Word and the preaching of Good News, much in the same way the bread and the cup are held up in priestly blessing. The bread, fruit of the wheat that has died to itself to become bread, and the cup, filled with the dead and crushed grapes turned into wine, feed us Christ's own body and blood in the Eucharist. Equally, in the mingling of Christ and humanity through proclamation and preaching, a eucharistic offering is made to all: take and eat this divine Word, take and drink this living water.

That summer our parish celebrated non-eucharistic Sunday liturgy once every three weeks. Even if our need was for Eucharist, it was important to do our best at the ministry entrusted to us. As a team we worked hard to prepare our hearts and minds for the tasks before us. Our normal eucharistic celebrations included active lay participation in the various ministries, but somehow the lay-led liturgies felt more a product of our joint efforts. New and nervous, we quickly learned the ropes as we celebrated these liturgical services more frequently. Before the start of the liturgy, while preparing in the sacristy, we looked at one another in nervous expectation. At the end of the service we truly shared the joy of a job well done. This liturgical experience formed us into community in a new way, as we became aware of the presence of God in one another.

While the newness of the experience was a source of fulfillment and joy for some, other parishioners preferred to attend Mass in another community. I respected their decision, but I felt sad that we were not all equally comfortable with new things. Their overriding concern was to get to Mass. My perceived call was to feed the people with God's Word. I cannot feed them if they do not come. I needed the congregation to be present to hear and actively receive the preached Word. I invested a lot of time and effort preparing, and I placed great importance on the role of the community in "authorizing" my preaching through its act of listening and receiving.

One Sunday, the readings were filled with eucharistic images. I struggled to draw out their meaning for a faith community gathered without the Eucharist; at about the same time, I interviewed a number of ordained and non-ordained women working in a wide variety of ministries in different traditions. These interviews formed the basis of a newspaper article I was asked to write. Mingling the eucharistic elements of the readings with the witness of women living out a call from God to serve the Church was potent:

> Preaching involves feeding the Word of God to the people in bite-size pieces, in a way that they can chew it for the week without getting indigestion. The women I am interviewing are sharing with me the many ways they feed the community of faith. Feeding the multitudes has always been one of women's strengths. I felt the trembling of my own soul as Amanda spoke of her call, her discernment process, her love for the Church and the Eucharist, her desire to feed Christ to the community, her understanding of her priesthood. My soul trembled because I heard in so many ways my own story. I am not merely an objective reporter.

Through the stories of these women I seek to articulate my own, and to find my rightful place in this beloved church, a church that is hungry for Christ's body and blood. (Journal entry)

Feeding and caring for others was always an integral part of my nature. It was not hard, therefore, to make the leap in understanding from feeding my own biological children and caring for loved ones to feeding the faith community with the food from heaven. God's Word proclaimed and preached took on eucharistic significance for me. There was an element of sacrifice in this kind of feeding. Besides offering Christ in the preached word as food for the soul, I offered my own experience of God's call as a sacrifice. I prepared to feed the congregation, yet I felt acutely and painfully that the fullness of that feeding as in the Mass could not happen through my preaching alone. Under the restricted circumstances I gave all I could, knowing it was incomplete. I also lived with the constant realization that I could be dismissed or ignored at any time.

On a particular Sunday, with readings full of eucharistic food, I was indeed ignored and dismissed. As our lay leadership team prepared the Sunday service without Eucharist, a holidaying priest showed up at the rectory on Saturday night, offering to say Mass the next day. Our pastor and several parishioners rejoiced that the lay leadership team was no longer needed. I experienced conflicting reactions. I was happy to celebrate the Eucharist, but I still felt abandoned and rejected. I had worked hard to write my homiletic reflection, and thus had prepared a meal, albeit with an incomplete list of ingredients. Now my meal was not needed, since we had access to more substantial food, i.e., Eucharist. What was I to do with the food I had prepared with so much love, commitment and creativity? Was no one coming to eat at the table I believed the Lord had prepared in, through and with me?

My parish priest used parts of my reflection in his own homily, which he preached in the neighbouring parishes. My Lutheran friend preached that same Sunday in his church on the same readings and borrowed my ideas. Thus my thoughts, distilled and gathered into one meal, were scattered, and crumbs were fed to others. The priest in our parish that day was a stranger and unfamiliar with our rural congregation. He preached as if he were teaching his students. There seemed to be little connection between his exposition of the Scriptures and the local lives of those gathered. Yet we had Eucharist, we rejoiced because we had, as one parishioner called it, "the real thing." It was a strange experience, and I was taken aback by the extent of my own sadness:

> I was supposed to have preached today. I worked hard to prepare the homiletic reflection, breaking open God's Word to feed the faith community. But last night I heard that a visiting priest is coming to say Mass – thank you for the effort, but your reflection is no longer needed. I feel strangely sad. We still have such a long ways to go as church. No one seems to think of those who are being displaced in this magical appearing of an ordained priest. Fr. Tony affirmed my reflection, and Kris is borrowing heavily from my ideas – a bittersweet consolation. Being "parked" at the last minute would not hurt so much were it not for the fact that the pulpit feels more and more like my new home in the Church. This is a surprise… it is so far from anything I had planned or anticipated, or even aspired to. Does this witness to God's own participation in this surprising development? And if so, is the faith community denying itself God's gift because of our rules on who can be ordained, and because of our deeply embedded and cherished habits, beliefs and attitudes that limit the field of possibilities that God is putting before us? (Journal entry)

I tried to respond to Jesus' call to be "the light of the world" (Matthew 5:14). Being replaced by a priest at the last minute felt much like someone covering the light I was about to let shine. Yet, rather than locking myself in bitterness and anger, I felt the kind of movement of soul that was so characteristic of St. Thérèse of Lisieux when she faced rejection. Drawing on the spiritual nourishment of God's call, another image from Scripture pressed itself on my heart:

> Do not fear those who kill the body but cannot kill the soul; rather fear him who can destroy both soul and body in hell. Are not two sparrows sold for a penny? Yet not one of them will fall to the ground apart from your Father. And even the hairs on your head are all counted. So do not be

afraid; you are of more value than many sparrows. (Matthew 10:28-31)

God was looking after me, gently reminding me that this preaching business was God's work and not mine, and that for God, nothing is wasted. Like St. Thérèse, who lived her "Little Way" with gusto, I took hold of God in the midst of this sadness. Nothing, not even my sadness at being sidelined, escaped God's eye. Somehow God would keep calling me, would cherish the words that remained unspoken, and would take note of my painful invisibility as a woman in the Church who was longing to feed the faith community. This sense of God still being in charge infused my entire being, preventing anger, criticism, judgment, frustration and bitterness from finding their home in my soul. Instead, St. Thérèse took me by the hand and led me to Mary, the mother of God. With my homiletic reflection in hand, I looked up at the angel, and asked: How will this come to be?

Three years later I pondered the same Scripture readings. This time I was asked to preach at a United church in a nearby town. With surprise and awe at God's tenacity, I reworked my original text into a sermon for my Protestant sisters and brothers. Nothing is ever wasted: my meal, God's meal, prepared with such love, dedication and faithfulness, was served after all − and all ate heartily, leaving twelve baskets of leftovers.

Sermon at the United Church

Genesis 32:22-31, Romans 9:1-5, Matthew 14:13-21

Judging from the Gospel stories, Jesus sure eats with people a lot. He eats with Pharisees and scribes, with tax collectors and prostitutes. He eats with his disciples and close friends. And today we witness the most miraculous potluck meal ever recorded in the Scriptures; a meal that fed so many because Jesus invited all to share the little they had.

Potluck meals always amaze me. (Remember the last one you attended?) The spread of dishes surprises even the best of cooks. The food is much more diverse than any of us could ever prepare alone. Potluck meals are not magic events, but they are miraculous. They are miraculous not only in the quantity of food prepared, but also in the sharing by so many in the preparing and the eating. Lives are put on hold, attention is focused – all to make this shared meal a success.

It is this kind of shared meal that needs the input of every person, however little she or he brings. When we share the little we have, God blesses our gift abundantly. Miraculous feedings of the multitudes, like at potluck meals, like in today's Gospel, happen because Jesus blesses our sharing.

That sharing seems easy at potluck meals. Yet in other areas of our lives this sharing is not so forthcoming. We live in a world where two-thirds of the human family lives in economic poverty, while the other third suffers from spiritual emptiness. We live in a world that produces enough food for everyone, yet the multitudes go hungry because of a lack of sharing. We live in an environment that is rapidly being destroyed, because we fail to render to the earth the care and respect it is due. Here in the Western world we live in freedom while entire countries cry out for liberation and justice.

In our zeal to make it in this world, we forget how to share. In our rush to buy our way to comfort, we can forget the importance of the human qualities of care and dignity – qualities that cannot be bought and sold. Seeing the evils of the world on television, we are discouraged. Hearing about the strife and suffering of others, we feel weighed down and want to close our eyes as we think, Please let me keep my world small – I have enough worries of my own. Another fundraising campaign knocks on our door, and we pretend not to be home. We feel worn out, and want someone else to take care of all these needy "others." Echoing the disciples, we want to say: "Tell them to go away, for we have nothing to give." But Jesus tells us, like he tells the disciples: "They need not go away; you give them something to eat." Contrary to what we might think, our problem is not a lack of resources or solutions.

Even though we ourselves are just as hungry and broken, we can always find something to offer to another. Even though we may only have one little dish to bring to the potluck, like the boy with the five loaves and two fish, the power of sharing that little bit will fill our hungry stomachs. The real problem is more often a lack of faith: it is not believing that our little bit matters; it is not believing that God can take our little bit and feed the multitudes, no matter whether our hunger is physical, emotional or spiritual. In our zeal to make it in our modern world, we can lose faith in the power of sharing our lives.

Jesus takes the loaves and the fish, blesses them, breaks the bread, and gives them to the disciples to distribute to the crowd. God works miracles with the ordinary stuff that we offer out of our daily lives: bread and time, fish and caring, wine and compassion.

God blesses our little bit of offering abundantly, with twelve baskets left over. This is the miracle. This is the food that Jesus offers, the food that will still all hungers. This miracle still happens here and now: in you and me, in our homes and cities, in our worship and service. In Prince Albert we find an example of this feeding of multitudes with a few loaves and fish.

Pat and Waltera are two ordinary women who, some ten years ago, opened their home to the Native community in Prince Albert. With the little bit they had – big hearts and a burning desire to serve God in God's people – they set out to befriend those who have been forgotten and ignored by our church, our society, and sometimes even their own kin. Waltera and Pat provide physical, psychological and spiritual help. Their place of ministry, called Kateri House, includes a food bank, a clothing depot, and a safe place to cry, to talk and to pray. They help people deal with the justice system, and cry along with them at the prejudice many Native people face. They journey with women and men in their personal and cultural healing, and feel the pain of the ruptures and divisions in Native culture. In sharing the fullness of both the pains and joys of Native people, these two women form a bridge for those who are estranged from the Church, and for those seeking cross-cultural reconciliation. Associates have formed around them to help in their ministry. Pat and Waltera also know about structural suspicion and judgment: they themselves are subject to scrutiny and ridicule, often from the very people who claim to follow Jesus.

These women break bread daily with the hungry, in the form of breaking open their lives in compassion and solidarity. Jesus takes their lives, blesses and breaks their gift of self, and feeds the multitudes.

God still performs these miracles, right before our very eyes. The miracle is that God uses the ordinary stuff in our daily lives to feed the multitudes. The miracle is that Jesus Christ cares enough to satisfy that deep human hunger – the hunger to belong fully in God. To that purpose, Christ has broken his own life on the cross, becoming the bread that feeds the world. Thus, all creation has a place at the banquet of the Lord. When we celebrate Holy Communion, we offer everyone a place at the table. In Holy Communion, Jesus offers his very self as bread from heaven and says to us: "Here, feed the world," and the world takes its place at table. In the ordinary elements of bread and wine lies the protest against the sins of greed and selfishness: a protest against the unjust distribution of the earth's abundant gifts, gifts meant to feed the multitudes.

Christ's body was broken for the life of the whole beloved world, not just for those who happen to live in the better part of town. In Holy Communion, Jesus provides the little bit he has to give, his own life and his own faithfulness to God. With this, Jesus tells us: "Do something, for the hungry need not go away." Jesus calls for the breaking of our lives in compassion and solidarity with those in need. Compassion, faithfulness and solidarity form the basket in which we bring our loaves and fish to Jesus. Jesus takes this little offering, blesses it and breaks it open, in order for it to be shared. Jesus asks us – his disciples – to feed the hungry with care, love, commitment and deep respect. Whenever we offer deep compassion out of caring hearts, God still performs miracles.

The world indeed still needs such miracles, the kind that fed the five thousand, the kind that hung on the cross and died for us. The good news is that Jesus' life has been blessed, broken and poured out for us. The good news is that God has abundantly blessed this ultimate gift of self by raising Jesus from the dead. The good news is that the boundless grace of God does provide for all. God's miracle of feeding the multitudes happens each time we feed the hungry, no matter what form that takes: when we comfort the mourning, even if all we can do is to cry with them; shelter the homeless, even if we have to overcome our own reluctance; visit the sick, even if we have no promise of a cure. God's miracle happens every time we share our very selves with our neighbour in need. Amen.

CHAPTER 10

Prepare the Way of the Lord

What does the Lord require of you but to do justice,
and to love kindness,
and to walk humbly with your God?
(Micah 6:8)

Fr. Anthony de Mello tells of a miser's prayer:

"If the Almighty, may his holy name be blessed, would give me a hundred thousand dollars, I would give ten thousand to the poor. I promise I would. And if the Almighty, may he be glorified, were not to trust me, let him deduct the ten thousand in advance and just send me the balance."[42]

Writing, like preaching, is never easy. Some pieces write themselves, others are born of anguish and distress. This chapter falls in the latter category. I felt uneasy and unsure, and sensed the judge and the coward in me watching over my shoulder. As the years roll by, I recognize the miser's attitude more and more, both in myself and in others around me. Despite the desire to keep the miser, the judge and the coward from scrutiny, my commitment to honesty nevertheless spurred some soul-searching. Some incidents with my kids, and reading the chapter on social justice in Fr. Ron Rolheiser's *Seeking Spirituality,* finally gave me the courage to trust that God was with me in the thoughts that came. I claim to have based many of my life's choices on the noble motives of social justice, care for the earth and world peace. Despite my best intentions, however, I stand as guilty as anyone of hypocrisy, discouragement and a plaguing helplessness. Any noble motivation, any zeal I can muster for God's "little ones," is part of a bag containing a deadly mix: the holy anger over injustice, the self-sacrifice and the no-strings-attached love dished out is seasoned with varying amounts of selfishness, arrogance and pride.

The greatest obstacle to speaking and writing on the honourable causes of ecology, social justice and world peace is belonging to the educated middle-class culture. I am immersed in cultural privileges to the extent that I cannot see them any more than a fish notices water. This statement startles even myself: I always had a special bent towards social justice activism and a commitment to caring for the earth. As a teenager I got fired up about helping the less fortunate, sometimes in ways that caused disputes with my parents, like the few Christmases I chose to work at a special day-long celebration for seniors who had no family. The dream of a better world haunted me, fuelling a fire in my heart. I was involved in anti-nuclear protests, Amnesty International, promoting healthy sexuality through teaching natural family planning, to helping seniors and handicapped people, adopting a Third World family and raising money for the pro-life cause. Now seasoned by mid-life reflection, I see how the very privilege of being free to choose these involvements sets me apart from the people who receive my charity or who suffer oppression at the hands of my consumer society. My ability to give of myself was heavily determined by my having economic security, educational opportunities, emotional and mental well-being – the riches that the miser in de Mello's story wanted to be sure of.

Over the years of living on the farm we embraced voluntary simplicity in our land-based lifestyle. We chose to heat and cook with wood, hauled water with pails instead of installing a full plumbing system, walked to the outhouse in summer and used an indoor portable toilet in winter. On bath day, when the children were young, I filled the big boiler with water and stoked up the fire, and we had baths as in the "olden days," from youngest to oldest. Baking bread and canning fruit were day-long activities that filled the house with warmth and enticing smells. We lived happily without television, without a microwave, and for many years without a computer (we did have power for lights, stereo, fridge and freezer). Using wood for heat got us outside and would heat us twice: once as we gathered it on crisp winter days, and the second time as it burned cheerfully in the stove and heater. My primary rationale for these lifestyle choices was to express solidarity with the majority of the world population that lives without running water because it is not available. I now know that there is an enormous difference between voluntary simplicity of lifestyle and structural poverty. Renunciation as an act of free will can reveal God in a most immediate way, but externally enforced deprivation reveals sin and evil. Exercising the freedom and the power to choose is a luxury that the poor rarely enjoy. Even in the simplicity of a back-to-the-land existence, my middle-class culture caught up with me.

The struggle for justice is a daily seeking, says Gerald Vandezande in *Justice, Not Just Us.*[43] The task is to be God's image in action in a suffering world. If I cannot be conscious about how our economic and cultural position in society affects what I see as justice and what I am blind to, I cannot be an effective bearer of Good News. "The pursuit of justice is a human struggle engaged in every day through prayerful reflections, communal deliberations, and social and political actions, all done in the liberating power of the Spirit."[44] Many of our lifestyle choices have been consistent over the years, even the recent decision to embrace city life in order to meet family needs. What has changed most significantly is the motivation and the kind of energy employed to maintain the commitment to justice and simplicity. For a long time my "preferential option" for simplicity was fuelled by a defiant attitude. I wanted to prove that I did not need whatever the media wanted me to desire. Despite my defiant spirit, my good intentions and my social justice involvements, my understanding of following Christ remained ego-centred. My prayer resembled that of the Pharisee giving God his surplus and beating his chest in righteousness, thanking God that he was not like the tax collector.

After all was said and done, I could not explain why I still felt empty and wanting inside. I stumbled my way through the Gospel, the one place to which I kept returning for guidance and answers. With the caring and prayerful help of a skilled spiritual director, I learned to become more honest: there was still a lot of looking in the wrong places. The reality of my own broken humanity – jealousy, pride, arrogance, self-pity, resentment, self-righteousness, bitterness – started to meet me at every corner. I was not as good as I thought, and I did not have it all together, like I wanted so much to believe. I now started to understand the words of Thomas Merton, who naively thought that entering the monastery would wash him clean of all his sins. Instead, he realized that "all my bad habits, disinfected, it is true, of formal sin, had sneaked into the monastery with me and had received the religious vesture along with me."[45] Slowly I began to feel like an inside outsider standing in the midst of a society marked painfully by cultural deprivation, economic hardship and spiritual emptiness – feeling that my own brokenness hindered me from making any meaningful difference. I became aware of unspoken yet powerful belief systems that not only drive the economy and consumer demand, but also artificially create "needs" in people and even determine what "reality" looks like. The greatest challenge in remaining apart from the consumer mentality was to move from an energy fuelled by arrogance, disdain and anger to an energy fuelled by love, compassion and caring.

My work as a counsellor at Interval House opened a new world, and became the school of unconditional love where God taught me. Until my involvement there I had no experience, understanding or contact with those who live with abuse, violence and addictions. I was taken aback by the extent and the depth of the pain the women at the shelter shared with me: their lives were ugly, dirty and often hopeless. I ached for them, prayed desperately for them to be healed and made whole. My compulsion to help was severely put to the test. I could not take away the pain, and I could do nothing to prevent the abuse from happening again. All there was left was to love these women for the time they lived at the shelter and to model with them a healthy way of relating. It was hard to accept that this ought to be sufficient; it was hard to accept that the women needed to be given the freedom and dignity to make their own choices, even if those choices were life-destroying ones. The "them and us" divide between the women and me started to melt into "one and all," because as long as one of God's little ones is hurting, we are all in pain, whether we are oppressor, oppressed or bystander. The experience at the shelter gave me a glimpse into the heart of God: forever loving us and alluring us, while leaving us free to make our own choices. I felt pain when women returned to destructive relationships, and I realized that God must feel pain when we turn away from Love eternal.

> What we are coming to realize is that one of the reasons why the world is not responding more to our challenge to justice is that our actions for justice themselves often mimic

the very violence, injustice, hardness, and egoism they are trying to challenge. Our moral indignation very often leads to the replication of the behaviour that aroused the indignation....The anger, crass egoism, bitterness, hardness, and aggression of so many [...] can never serve as the basis for a new world order.[46]

Rolheiser helped formulate the reasons for my own nagging discomfort with many who fight literal fights to make the world take note of injustices, whether these are towards creation and the environment, towards the unborn and children in poverty, or towards violence, abuse and war. I shied away from pro-life activities because I was not comfortable with militant tones that provoked confrontation, judgment and division. I discovered that I feel more comfortable connecting with people than with disembodied issues that can get used as political footballs. Instead of carrying banners down the street, I engaged with individuals and their concrete stories. I preferred the concrete one-on-one (or two-on-two) involvement with couples, empowering them to be in charge of their combined fertility through teaching them natural methods of family planning. Instead of joining women's advocacy groups, I worked with abused women and children, supporting them in their pain and giving them hope. Besides being a critical consumer, I tried to model a full and happy life, growing and preserving our own food with few modern conveniences.

Our back-to-the-land existence brought us into contact with many who tried to make similar choices. At first I shared the anger and disdain some displayed as the driving force behind their decision to turn their back on the over-technological, over-consuming, power-hungry and greedy Western world. Over time, however, I realized that this kind of negative energy could not sustain countercultural choices in a life-giving way. Rather, I saw a bitterness and intolerance towards mainstream society like Rolheiser describes as being self-destructive and counterproductive. This made relationships and even mere conversations extremely difficult:

> It is hard to handle the outbursts of anger and militant criticism of some of my friends. Whether it is about consumer society, about the school system, about gays and lesbians, or

about the Church, letting these things fuel an ongoing stream of anger seems to work against the desire to offer a life-giving alternative to the existing order. I do not see structures as "them and us." I choose to function within structures in a life-sustaining way. I see a face behind every issue. I also admit that the faults we see outside of us can first and foremost be found inside ourselves. I tend to be gentle with criticism, patient with institutions and loving towards those who are victimized and who fall between the cracks of any system. Maybe this is a cop-out on my part, but I see the spewing of anger as a destructive force – destructive of relationships and destructive of effective attempts to live a new world order within one's own soul. Some anger at injustice is indeed justified, but if overall anger and suspicion become a way of life, I question their effectiveness and I feel obstructed in developing friendships. (Journal entry)

Despite Rolheiser's well-founded criticism that a lot of peace and justice activism in the Church fails to be effective if it lacks a radical foundation in love and non-violence, I continue to see the best possibilities, as does Rolheiser, for a lasting alternative in Christianity. Nothing calls to account my hypocrisy so lovingly and firmly as does my Christian faith. Trying to empty myself of arrogance and judgments of systems and people, I put my trust in a God who can purify even the most ambivalent of motives and transform even the ugliest of injustices. "Blessed are they who hunger and thirst for righteousness, for they will be filled" (Matthew 5:6).

Effective social justice makes charity unnecessary. The way to get there involves developing deeper solidarity between the "haves" and the "have-nots." I tried to grow a big heart, and allowed my narrow world to be broken open by the pain of others, thus helping to break the deadly isolation which so many feel every day. I watched my son, the one who at 15 stubbornly kept company with the "unwanted" in town. He was driven as much by the smell of risk and adventure as by a wild faith that he could show them the road to a hopeful future. As he pursued his friendships with a tenacity and fortitude that made adults feel embarrassed, I was once again going through a "poor me" phase in my own life:

The holiday season is hard in certain ways. This time of year somehow sharpens my own aching loneliness and not-belonging… in solidarity with most of the world, I suppose. Why should I feel sorry for myself? Is my pain still self-centred rather than God-centred pain? Yes, most of the time. Yet even this pain is relative, taking on different features and varying in intensity with each changing context. A big part of the world is starving, oppressed and at war, exploited – and my major concern is that I live in a vocational vacuum in the Church. While my son keeps hanging out with the wrong crowd in an effort to save them from self-destructive behaviours, I let my selfish aching get so big that it overshadows the riches I do have. I take it all for granted so easily. When the pain takes over, all I can see is the lack… Lord, have mercy. (Journal entry)

Having a home where teenagers feel welcome came with a price tag. Hospitality was not always extended on my terms. My children's friends hung out at our place with great appreciation and, for the most part, with respect for both property and elders. There were unspoken trade-offs: lunches eaten at our house were "paid for" by the regular gifts of homemade sausage and the odd case of Kraft Dinner. I earned their trust by refraining from lecturing on their failures, and by holding off giving advice until asked. One year on Mother's Day, which also happened to be our son's graduation weekend, I found an army of teens in my kitchen, busy cooking "Mom" brunch. Being involved in their lives gave me a glimpse of the pain that too many endured in their home situations. Many tried to grow up in one piece while dealing with family conflicts, divorce, volatile and violent behaviours, and the fear of parental abandonment through alcohol and drugs. A couple of the boys who, six months earlier, I had feared would drag my son down into their misery, ended up living with us for a time, desperately needing support to turn their lives around. One of them commented one day: "It is so easy not to swear in this house." His joy over that realization spoke volumes about his childhood. When one mother shared her feelings of total isolation and loneliness while trying to help her son, I felt embarrassed about ever feeling alone and abandoned. Here was someone who had every right to support and encouragement, and yet these seemed impossible for her to find in our modern society. As a member of a society that sends people to the moon and communicates globally by simply pressing buttons, I stood accused. Where was the justice, where was the compassion and caring for this mother and for each human being who is in need and in pain?

Jesus came to set the captives free, to bind up the broken-hearted, and to give sight to the blind (Luke 4:18-20). I admit that I find it hard to sustain the kind of social justice activism that set my heart ablaze in my younger years. As I become more nuanced in my thinking and more reflective in my understanding of God, self and others, I also encounter, reluctantly yet honestly, my human limitations. Knowing that I cannot possibly save everyone from the claws of our communal sinfulness, I am moving more into a faithful "abiding with," a quality of presence to one individual at a time. I am learning the value of Mother Teresa's words: "We are not called to be successful, we are called to be faithful." This does not mean that we can abdicate our social and political responsibility to work for a just world order. But I can put up with one hurting teen sleeping in my living room. I can offer listening time to an anxious parent. I can stuff Christmas hampers. I can offer to be an advocate for that one kid who fights prejudice and discrimination. I have come to see that the most important gift to another is first and foremost sharing the pain and making God's light shine on it. Hidden pain has destructive power; pain shared in love has redeeming power – the power to turn an entire world upside down, or maybe right side up in God's plan. I make my feeble attempts at contributing to the coming of God's reign, that new world order for which we all hunger, and which starts in our hearts and minds. I can realistically handle one human encounter of love at a time, all the while knowing that what is important in God's eyes is faithfulness, endurance, patience, joy, forgiveness, gratitude.

> All of our actions for peace must be rooted in the power of love and the power of truth and must be done for the purpose of making that power known and not for making ourselves known. Our motivation must always be to open people to the truth and not to show ourselves as right and them as wrong. Our best actions are those which admit our com-

plicity and are marked by a spirit of genuine repentance and humility. Our worst actions are those that seek to demonstrate our own righteousness, our purity, and our moral distance from the violence we are protesting.[47]

Homiletic Reflection in My Home Parish

Isaiah 40:1-11, Luke 3:1-9, Second Sunday of Advent

Story #1:
Maria and her children live in the Philippines. She works in a factory, assembling clothes for export. She starts work at 7 a.m. Often she does not leave for home until 6 p.m. Even working such long days, Maria does not earn enough money to feed her children adequately. When Maria returns home she is so tired that it feels like her feet are going to explode. Her boss harasses her and makes fun of her fatigue. He says that tired women are more compliant. And Maria fears for her health – the fumes in the factory nauseate her…

"…every valley shall be filled…"

Story #2:
Joan and Lyle live in rural Manitoba. They are hard-working farmers. They broke ties with the Church many years ago – all because of conflict over the fact that Joan, a Roman Catholic, married Lyle, a Baptist. They feel bitter and resentful, even after all these years. They are good people, doing their best at making a living and raising their family. They carry life's burdens on their shoulders – they pride themselves on handling things without the Church. But lately, their struggles do not quite fit on their shoulders anymore. They feel more alone and isolated – it is hard to deal with their delinquent son. And their daughter's burden is tearing their own hearts to pieces. For their daughter's little boy, *their* grandson, contracted AIDS through a blood transfusion. And now, no preschool will welcome him – no one wants to have a kid with AIDS around.

"…and every mountain and hill shall be made low…"

Story #3:

Joao lives in Brazil. He has been cutting sugar cane and picking vegetables since he was seven years old. Joao loves his wife and children, and he dreams of a better future. He dreams of owning land, maybe – someday. Right now he wakes at 4 a.m. to get on the truck that takes the workers out to the fields. He returns at 9 p.m.

He earns $1 per day. He does not eat properly – his children come first. Joao is only 35, but he looks like he is 60.

"…and all flesh shall see the salvation of God…"

These stories are us. Most of our stories do not hit the evening news, but they are the stuff that life is made of. And listening to our stories, we see that pain and despair become the great equalizers. We hurt, and we recognize Maria as our sister. We despair, and Joan and Lyle become our neighbours. We dream, and Joao is our brother… We feel alone and without hope, and we lament with the dispersed people of Israel: has God – and the world – abandoned us?

Interspersed through the stories of our life, God's Word breaks in, like the voice of one crying out in the wilderness. In the darkness of night, in the cold of winter, lightning pierces the sky:

Take off the garment of your sorrow and affliction – prepare the way of the Lord.

God will not have us mired in the mud of our daily troubles. While the world insists on being turned in on itself, God cries out to us through the prophet, through John the Baptist, through Jesus. Almost despite the world, despite our hopelessness, God breaks through with the urgent voice of a messenger who cannot contain the fire in his or her soul. In the face of Maria's oppression and harassment, God insists on her human dignity. God's righteousness cries out to be heard. Joan and Lyle hear it in the whispers of a caring invitation from the local church. Joao bumps into God's desire for him in the images of his dream…

Joao has joined other landless peasants in the Sem Terra movement. He now works diligently for land reform, and no longer feels alone. Life is still harsh, but now he belongs and feels cared for. And he is starting to believe in his own dignity again – maybe he *will* own land some day… Take off your garment of sorrow, Joao. Maria has joined other women in a similar movement. She is discovering the power of solidarity. Together the women lobby for better working conditions and fair wages. Together they fight for their children's welfare, and for their children's future. In sharing their struggles with others, Joao and Maria discover that God does remember them and their children: "Put on the robe of righteousness that comes from God, and see your children gather…"

The struggle for land reform is slow. The task to improve working conditions and attain fair wages is hard and frustrating. But Joao and Maria already find new purpose and meaning. They are learning to claim their dignity as God's children. They are no longer afraid to share their pain with the world. For pain and suffering do not define who they are… "Put on forever the beauty of the glory from God…"

Joan and Lyle are cautiously finding their way back to the faith community. The local Catholic parish is enrolled in a diocesan renewal process and has invited Joan and Lyle to join a small Christian community. They accepted, out of a stubborn hope for healing and belonging. In the small group Joan and Lyle learn to reflect on their lives in light of the Scriptures. Together with the other group members they face attitudes of pride, judgment and denial – making straight the crooked ways to prepare for the Lord's coming. Slowly, people in the group share their stories. Slowly, baptism takes on new meaning – filling every valley and making every mountain low. In community, Joan and Lyle learn to care deeply and to share without fear. In community, they find healing and love for who they are. God is bringing them back – to their own sense of dignity shared with others in solidarity, a dignity and solidarity grounded in the Lord Jesus Christ.

God's Advent cry reaches us here in our rural parishes dotting the Saskatchewan landscape. Alongside the stories of Maria, of Joan and Lyle, of Joao, we place our story – as individuals and as a faith community. We are invited to prepare the way of the Lord. We are invited into greater solidarity with one another. Like anywhere else, there is much pain among us. Like anywhere else, there is much denying and judging among us – many crooked turns in the road.

Yet God will not have us give up on one another, or on ourselves, or on Him: "the crooked shall be made straight, and the rough ways be made smooth…" The Lord is coming: prepare his way. Pope John Paul II's move to declare the year 2000 a time of Jubilee was a call to prepare the Lord's way right here in our own communities. Many twists and turns lead us to sin, oppression and alienation from one another. The Advent cry breaks into our world: straighten out your attitudes and behaviours, to prepare for the Lord's coming.

Advent invites us to wait vigilantly and in hope. Pray that we learn to care more deeply in this Advent time; in this we claim the mercy and righteousness that comes from God. Pray that we learn to love more passionately this Advent, and every valley will be filled. Pray that we learn to share our pain in a community of love, and God will clothe us with glory. The light of Christ is coming. Our baptism calls us into this light – a light that cannot be extinguished. The dark of night, the cold of winter, the agony of human suffering – none of these have the final word, because the Lord our God will not let that happen. May our prayer for one another this Advent reflect Paul's words to the Philippians: that our love will overflow more and more with compassion, knowledge and full insight to help us grow pure and blameless before God. Come, Lord Jesus, come… Amen.

CHAPTER 11

Claiming the Scraps

She came and knelt before him, saying
"Lord, help me."
"Even the dogs eat the crumbs that fall
from the master's table."
(Matthew 15:25, 26)

Graduation was both exhilarating and terrifying. Exhilarating, because it was time to celebrate the accomplishment of years of arduous, committed learning. The spirit of joy permeated those graduating, drunk as we were with this incredible feeling of having arrived at the finish line. Each of us had had our share of obstacles and doubts along the way, and some of us knew many a time of tearful discouragement. Graduation swept us away in elation. God had brought us here, and God had seen us through, and now we were ready to be sent out into the Church and the world to do God's work. But though I felt exhilarated, I was also terrified.

Bringing closure to my life as a student felt like jumping into a big black hole of nothingness. While fellow graduates announced with joy their first pastoral appointment or place of ministry, I was left grappling with air. It was not clear that God called me anywhere. It was not clear even whether my church was willing to make room for a woman with theological formation. While that realization sparked fear, the graduation fever nevertheless fed a wild trust:

Three more sleeps and the most important weekend of the year is upon me. Besides preaching the graduation sermon, I am now also preaching two days later, at the Sunday Celebration of the Word in my own parish. This is a most striking co-incidence: to preach in this place of learning which

I am leaving behind and in my local church where my future lies, and where my call to serve is to bear fruit. My future as a trained layperson is so uncertain – at least I do not see clearly at all. But for now I just go with whatever is offered, without pushing too hard, and with my soul-eyes and ears wide open and vigilant. And despite my nervousness about the coming weekend and about the future, there is also a quiet abiding in God – in full trust that God is with me, guiding me through the coming events, the coming months and years. There is a fullness about my present feelings that is hard to explain. Even the pain of closure and the anxiety about the future are real feelings and full feelings, and I welcome them as good rather than as a threat to my sense of equilibrium. Lord God, I quiet my spirit and rest in your love, the only place worth calling home, my home. (Journal entry)

There was no job waiting for me after graduation. I was not upset, for I was in dire need of plain recovery time; the commute had taken its physical, emotional and psychological toll. The empty time stretching out before me beckoned as a generous gift from God – time to rest, and rest some more. I soaked up the beauty of that summer on our farm by the lake. I could not think of a better place to re-centre on just being and taking care of the tasks of being a mom, a wife and a homemaker – nothing more, for the first time in seven years. Looking back at the journey I had just completed, I was baffled. How in the world had I managed it? What wild desire pushed me into the car week after week, for seven long years, and made me drive the 180 kilometres each way twice a week to and from class, balancing precarious family schedules and braving winter road conditions?

Throughout my studies, I felt sustained by God's own hand to be faithful and to succeed. God's grace fed my husband's intellectual support, his interest and sharing in my learning. God's loving presence ensured that my children did not feel neglected all those years when my studies took priority over them. In fact, having a mom in school brought home to them the value and importance of studying. They saw the effort and commitment it took to see a course through. They shared my victories when I brought marks home.

My heart overflowed with gratitude and awe that whole summer long. Eventually, along with the rest and recovery space my soul craved, came the nagging question of where God would take me next. Sometimes the question made me anxious and impatient, but most often I sensed God's invitation to anchor ever more deeply the knowledge received and the gifts awakened. Growing deep roots at this time was prime preparation for the flowering season. I found fulfillment in simply remaining faithful to the movements of my heart, in writing my journal and spending time in solitary prayer. The realization that nothing is wasted for God took hold in a new way. Even if nothing else came from this incredible journey, that was enough. Again I connected with St. Thérèse of Lisieux:

> Now I wish for only one thing – to love Jesus even unto folly. Love alone attracts me. […] My only guide is self-abandonment. I no longer know how to ask passionately for anything except that the will of God shall be perfectly accomplished in my soul.[48]

Like Mary Magdalene after she met the risen Jesus in the garden, I too felt that I had indeed seen the Lord. Nothing else mattered anymore. In the years of seminary formation I experienced beyond my wildest dreams the power of God's hand directing my life. I felt the pain of an ego dying to itself, followed by the resurrection into new life in Christ in ways that I did not understand, yet that plunged me into a fullness of life never tasted before. And all this was enough. None of it could ever be taken from me. In the company of St. Thérèse, I knew that if I was to live God's call in hiding, I was bound to do that with all the passionate love, creativity and faithfulness I could muster. Nothingness and invisibility in the eyes of the world (and the Church) now started to overflow with God's own fullness of life.

Reading a book on discerning vocations proved helpful; it affirmed my growing inner stance of acceptance:

> In relation to Christ and our participation in the mediative aspects of his priesthood, mediation is more fundamentally a way of being and becoming. It thus pertains to self-identity and vocational lifestyle…. Jesus as priest was victim in his own sacrifice…. He did not offer something; he offered

himself.... Being mediator and victim in one's own sacrifice thus constitutes the quintessence of priestly life.... God
calls certain persons to make self-oblation the core of their
life. The Lord moves them to accentuate consciously, willingly and radically the priestly dimension of their baptismal
and confirmational commitment....The accent falls on how
they become themselves for God and for others.[49]

I became more securely anchored in the value of "being" over
"doing." The challenge was, first and foremost, to remain true to
myself in God and with others, and only secondarily, to express this
in some external form of ministry. Yet as fall approached and my
children resumed school and I did not, questions resurfaced about a
role in church ministry. I felt the bishop's support and prayers when
I met with him after graduation, but this support was not yet trans-
lating into a placement in pastoral ministry. I recalled vividly Father
Leonard's words at graduation time: "Sit tight. Do not expend energy by worrying about closed doors – merely walk through the
ones that are open. And remember: if Jesus is truly involved in this,
the risen Lord was not stopped by closed doors. Whatever you do in
church ministry, do not become another lone ranger – we have too
many of those. Remain connected to the Body of Christ, the Church,
and you'll be all right." These words became my guide and support
for the year ahead.

I took a few small yet significant actions. I listed various ministries on a business card. I put together a proposal to offer spiritual
direction through the parishes and presented this at the local dean-
ery meeting (monthly gathering of Catholic clergy and pastoral
workers). I approached the local ministerial association and was
granted associate membership. I was invited to join a Bible study
with local Protestant clergy to share on the Lectionary readings for
the following Sunday as a way to help one another prepare for preaching. This weekly hour with the pastors from Anglican, Lutheran,
Presbyterian, United and Pentecostal churches and the Worldwide
Church of God became a place of fellowship and friendship with
those who, because of my theological formation, regarded me as
their peer.

As the year went on, my visibility in the local Roman Catholic
and ecumenical community increased. Besides preaching in my own

parish on Sundays when our priest was absent, I spoke at a couple of local Catholic Women's League conventions. I joined the chaplaincy team at the local psychiatric hospital. I offered workshops on liturgy-related topics. I wrote articles for the weekly Catholic newspaper. I was brought in as guest preacher in other churches, and I accompanied several people in their faith journey as their spiritual director. I moved with great care, knowing well the importance of gaining the faith community's trust slowly and carefully. Taking nothing for granted, and having no automatic status or mandate to exercise pastoral ministry, I continued to foster in my prayer life an attitude of total abandonment to God. Faithfulness to God required that I make no claim to anything other than to be filled with God's own abundant love for the Church and for the world. How this abundance of love would find expression was to be revealed only in God's time, not mine. In learning to expect nothing and be filled with nothing but God, every little opportunity to bring the Gospel to others became pure gift.

Despite the various opportunities for ministry in that first year, there was something odd about my experience. It felt as if I was going at this ministry business in a freelance way. It was only several years later that I learned about nineteenth-century women perceiving a divine call to preach and to ministry. They were often itinerant freelance speakers, not affiliated with or sanctioned by an established church.[50] In contrast to their understanding, which did not consider the church connection important, I saw such a call as linked to the Church. A call to ministry originates in God, but for me was to be firmly connected to and confirmed by the faith community. I was concerned that my freelance ministry could be viewed as my personal thing. The faith community seemed insufficiently aware of its responsibility in calling forth the minister and her ministry. The local church did not take enough ownership of what I did on its behalf. I was experiencing what Kenan Osborne describes:

> Lay ministry [...] is an ecclesial entity, with its own grace-given vocation, with its own role within a *communio*, and with its own mission, which is ecclesial, even though it includes an extra ecclesial mission and ministry as well. It is a "vocation *in ecclesia*" and must be honored as such. As with every vocation, every ministry and every mission (in the

church), it has its roots in the call and commission to the *tria munera* (threefold baptismal anointing) by the Lord himself; it also has its communal role within the Christian community, a role which includes the discernment process by the community and a validation by the community through some liturgical service.[51]

Living in the realization that ultimately the faith community had the power to call forth or to ignore what I offered out of God's overflowing love in my heart was a double-edged sword. I never felt that ministry was my possession to push around or manipulate; this created a delicate balancing act. Historically and theologically, we come out of a long era of relying on ordained ministers – bishops and priests – for our every spiritual and pastoral need. The fact that ordained ministers are becoming older and more scarce does not necessarily force a change in the old expectations and attitudes. More than once I heard versions of the following: "Yes, we know you are quite competent and trustworthy to do this workshop/that talk, but it would be received so much better if a priest does it."

The Canaanite woman in Matthew's Gospel became my unexpected companion in that first year of cautious exploration. I truly got the scraps that fell from the ministry table. If a priest was not available, I was allowed to preach. If a priest could not lead a given workshop, I was asked to fill in. If a priest was unavailable to be the Roman Catholic presence with psychiatric patients, I was welcomed into the circle of chaplains who took turns visiting the patients on the wards. A priest's familiarity with and support of my ministry activities greatly affected my credibility and the extent of successful implementation. Gaining the trust of ordained clergy, Roman Catholic and Protestant, required patience, gentleness and a lot of "wasting time" together, the kind that allows friendships to grow. Accepting the importance of this relational process and finding the patience to let it happen was deeply rooted in my spirituality:

> I am at peace today, even though my immediate professional future is still so up in the air. Rather than feeding off outer relationships and events, this peace feeds off the quiet abiding trust in God that fills the solitude in my soul, making it spill over. I am squarely in the world and in the Church,

but my food and drink originate in God, sustaining me as the Source that never runs out, that never deceives, that never rejects, refuses, abandons…. Faithfulness to being has become as essential as physical food, shelter and clothing. Since God's call to ministry pertains first to a fullness of being, I am becoming less anxious about doing. Lord, do with me what you will – You alone are enough. (Journal entry)

Writing down my experience became vital. I journalled profusely, strengthened by the fact that if all else failed I could at least entrust to paper what the journey was like and leave my journal as a gift to the Church. To my surprise I heard these words echoed in St. Thérèse of Lisieux's autobiography. She firmly believed it was important to share with the world and with the Church her own intimate experience of God, but she also had a strong intuition that most of what she had to say would only be truly understood and appreciated after her death. I found in St. Thérèse an unexpected companion on the journey, as I began to realize similar things:

God's call is solidly located in my being – not my doing – so all I need to do is to be fully me. My private, inner life with God far exceeds my personal life and defies any church definition/explanation. Success is not based on any visible or measurable results, but on the quality and perseverance of my faithfulness to God. My inner reality and my interpretation of that reality are firmly rooted in Jesus Christ, our risen Lord. My fullest calling is to fix my gaze upon the One who loved right through death. What fills the pages of this journal cannot be shared for the most part. What I do sense, and deeply hope, is that even what occurs in the privacy of my soul not only *affects* the world and the Church, but also both affirms and challenges them. I have a strong sense that most of these written reflections will bear fruit after my death. Let these words be offered to heal and break open the hearts of many into the heart of God. (Journal entry)

Sermon at St. Andrew's Presbyterian Church

Matthew 15:21-28

There is tension in the Gospel today. Who is Jesus' ministry for? Do foreigners and outcasts have a right to lay claim to God's grace and healing? Just like in our time, there were strong cultural ideas in Jesus' time about who was acceptable and who was not: clean and unclean people, they called them back then. So it is no wonder that even Jesus hesitates to grant the Canaanite woman her request. The Canaanites were deeply despised by the Israelites, especially because fertility rites were part of their religious practices. Jesus experiences tension and the reality of human limitations. The Canaanite woman issues a bold challenge: even if Jesus' mission is initially meant for the Jews, is he nevertheless willing to respond to genuine faith no matter whose it is? Who knows what this woman is about? Better safe than sorry; better not throw the message of God's kingdom to the dogs.

We'd rather be safe than sorry ourselves. Most of us have made up our minds about what is important in our lives. We can be quite clear about how to live our commitment to faith and the Church. We stick to our priorities with honourable loyalty and a principled sense of duty. So principled and so loyal are we that nothing can divert us from our goal to serve God. Until someone rattles our cage, like the Canaanite woman does today. Several years ago my friend Bob was asked by a social worker to become a buddy to a man who had AIDS. Bob started to visit Jerry regularly, and the two men, who were around the same age, became friends. Bob learned about Jerry's struggle with his homosexuality, about his marriage, which ended in divorce, and about his feeling that the Church had rejected him. Yet, despite feeling judged and not wanted, Jerry had maintained an unfailing trust in God. Now, in the final stages of the disease, Jerry had come home to his family to die. Bob contacted the pastor of Jerry's church to request a reconnecting and a reconciliation.

The pastor was afraid to visit Jerry. Even when he did come, months later, he remained too fearful to make it past the door of Jerry's hospital room. Meanwhile, Jerry and Bob talked about everything, and prayed about everything. When Bob offered to bring Jerry Holy Communion, Jerry replied: "The Church has made it clear that I am not wanted. But thank you anyway." When Jerry died just after Easter, the pastor came to the funeral. Better safe than sorry…

Sure, Jesus' mission is intended for God's chosen people. But who are God's chosen people? My friend's experience reflects today's Gospel. Both accounts hold up the mirror. We see ourselves. We are the disciples who tell Jesus to send the woman away, for she keeps shouting at us. We are the pastor who is afraid to enter into relationship with the gay man dying of AIDS.

Leaving the beaten track to respond to a cry for help always, always upsets routines, goals and priorities. Jesus feels that, and we feel that most of the time. We fear engaging with Canaanite women, with contemporary outcasts. When we engage with the least desirable among us, we come face to face with ourselves. How many times, Lord, have we not recognized you because we were too busy with our own private interests? We can all be outraged when we hear news reports of the illegal immigrants who get smuggled onto our Canadian shores. We say that we should send them back because keeping them costs too much money. But our outrage is cheap and hollow. For we are the ones who have everything at the expense of people who are oppressed in their own country. We all help perpetuate the unjust distribution of the earth's wealth, a wealth given by God for all people. With the disciples we say – if not out loud, surely in our hearts – "Tell them to go away, for they keep shouting at us." Yes, Jesus' mission is intended for God's chosen people. But as Jesus himself discovers, God invites the Canaanite woman, invites the gay man dying of AIDS, invites the smuggled immigrants to be part of God's chosen people. Even though we are limited by time and space, God's love has no limits and accepts no boundaries. In the risen Christ, all people are invited to become God's chosen people. Like the Canaanite woman, we are all invited to great faith. Relating to someone in need reveals our own need for God's healing and salvation. On this side of death, we are all saved and unsaved, saint and sinner, all at the same time. We all bear the status of foreigner in

God's kingdom. We are really not that different from the Canaanite woman, the gay man with AIDS, the smuggled and suffering illegal immigrants. We may not experience their particular illness or social rejection. But at times we have all felt rejected, unloved, ignored, denied, attacked and judged. None of us goes through life without collecting the deep scars that sin and evil inflict.

Engaging with someone in need will lead us to the scars in our own heart. Only when we let this happen can compassion be born and healing occur. In the end, we all stand together, hungry and thirsty before our God as God's chosen people. Only then will boundaries and distinctions fall away.

Like the Canaanite woman, we too can lay claim to God's grace and healing, no matter who we are. We do not have to belong to the right church or follow the right rules and obligations. She didn't, yet great was her faith. Sometimes established religious institutions become the obstacle instead of the vehicle for the Gospel.

It is that freedom of the Gospel, filled with the boundless grace of God, that makes Jesus exclaim: "Woman, great is your faith! Let it be done to you as you wish." Despite Jesus' initial reluctance, never once does he rebuke the woman, never does he silence her, and never does he send her away. Instead, Jesus engages her in dialogue. Jesus enters a relationship with her, binding both her and himself in dialogue. God's inclusiveness has nothing to do with cheap grace that makes no demands or has no expectations. It has everything to do with human dignity and the cost of entering into relationship. In and through Jesus Christ, God entered into relationship with all humanity. For God, there is no turning back, and neither is there for us. Like the Canaanite woman's faith, our faith in God's unfailing grace will bring us healing and lead us to God. Even if we feel like the dogs under the master's table, we are still entitled to the scraps that fall from that table.

Standing before God with bold faith, we can indeed claim God's grace and healing, no matter who we are and no matter what church, if any, we belong to. We cannot limit God or trivialize what God can do. To those of us who hang on to rules and regulations, Jesus says: "Risk dialogue and relationship, leave the beaten track, and be open to find faith in unexpected places." To those of us who downplay rules and commitment, Jesus says: "Put a face and a name on the one in need; enter into the demands of relationship, for your sake and for the sake of the other." And to all of us Jesus says: "Always remember both your own need for healing as well as your calling to bring God's healing to the world."

And so, the tension in today's Gospel is not resolved. Rather, we live the tension fully in the day-to-day challenges of our lives. For we are wounded healers, saints and sinners. As wounded healers God calls us in the service of the Gospel. Without limiting God, and without trivializing God's healing love, we are the hands and feet, and the heart, of Christ. "We" are all God has on this earth. Amen.

CHAPTER 12

Comfort the Mourning

*She came up behind him
and touched the fringe of his clothes....
Then Jesus asked,
"Who touched me?
Someone touched me;
for I noticed that power had gone out from me."*
(Luke 8:45–46)

My husband's godfather, Uncle Albert, died and was buried in Kamloops, British Columbia, just before Christmas. Since he lived for many years in our part of Saskatchewan, his daughter planned a memorial service in the nearby city where he used to lived. She asked Jim and me to plan and lead the service. Her only wish was that this be a non-denominational gathering, since they had already had the Catholic funeral Mass in B.C. She turned to me in particular and said: "And we want you to preach because Dad wanted that."

I was a bit taken aback by her request. Yet, these invitations were slowly becoming more regular. In the invitation the community – in this case, Albert's family – authorized my preaching; ultimately, the community takes the preached word and validates it as God's by its affirming and listening presence. Jesus, too, needed the community's faith in order to heal and teach with authority, and to be recognized as the one sent by God. This request to preach at Albert's memorial service was made in the same year that I lived off the scraps falling from the ministry table. I slowly got the message that God had not, as had been my worst fear, abandoned me at graduation. Instead, God used me in most unusual ways, with opportunities and requests that seemed to have no logical explanation or precedent.

The Presbyterian minister in town became my friend and confidante that year. She was an older single woman who quietly decided to take me along in her hospital chaplaincy work. She took me to visit the wards, and sometimes asked me to take her place leading the prayer service at the long-term care facility. She spent many hours simply listening to my experiences and my attempts to discern God's hand in it all. When I told her about this latest family request, she was not surprised. She helped me distill the elements revealing God's activity, saying, "None of this comes from you. Rather, it comes from the people. Listen to that, be open to that, and follow wherever each opportunity takes you. No more, and no less. It seems that it is time to make 'comforting the mourning' part of your ministry."

I had known Uncle Albert, one of the few active Catholics in his family. I knew his children, none of whom seemed to have retained ties with the Church. Somehow my position as a lay person trained in preaching and ministry made Albert's children, as well as friends and relatives who did not share his church affiliation, feel comfortable. Some harboured hard feelings towards organized religion. Some looked with suspicion on everything Catholic. I needed to trust the Spirit, taking into account the assembly to be addressed.

> After writing my reflection for Albert's memorial I went for a walk, mulling over what I had written, bearing in mind those who would be listening, in particular those who do not share Albert's love for Jesus. And I feel called to account, big time. My nice words on love are meant for me as well. I do not know how to love any more than do all those who will be gathered to remember how Albert loved. I do not know how to love even the ones close to me – I would sooner withdraw. I do not know how to love my church – I'd sooner pout, kick and scream. I do not know how to love my children – I'd sooner take the easy way out and placate them. I do not know how to love this place of natural beauty on the lake – I'd sooner curse the isolation. I do not know how to love this lifestyle – I'd sooner complain about its inconvenience…. So who am I to talk about love? The words are God's, meant for me too. I am at one and the same time preacher and listener, giver and receiver. (Journal entry)

Many different strands converged in this single event. The family told me to choose my own Scripture passage. I wondered if they gave this freedom as a courtesy, thinking it made my job easier. I did not feel free at all – quite the contrary. As the preacher I do not pick my pet passages from Scripture – the community hands the Scriptures, asking the preacher to break open that holy word of God. I appreciated anew the "freedom" of the three-year Lectionary cycle. I do not carry the burden of picking Scripture, running the risk of using only my own preferences. Through the Lectionary the universal Church chooses the readings. Various traditions use this cycle of readings, which shows its value. Sometimes this means wrestling with texts that make me uncomfortable and frustrated, forcing an ever deeper reliance on God's Spirit. Always it means surrendering to the chosen text with increased faith, expecting to be surprised. The Lectionary puts the responsibility where it belongs and respects the proper order of authority. My authority as preacher bears no weight if I do not subject this authority to both God's Word and to the community that chooses the Word.

It was the first time that I had preached to extended family, and to people who, for whatever reason, had turned their back on institutional religion. More often than we care to admit, people leave the Church not because of Jesus, but because of painful experiences with insensitive pastors, critical and self-righteous parishioners, and poor preaching. They often leave hurt and disgusted, and must find their own way to feed their hunger for God and for community. I ache for their leaving, not because I judge it to be wrong, but rather because I sadly recognize the possibility of such decisions. I, too, could have left many times, because of personal negative experiences of priests, of narrow-minded and judgmental fellow Christians, of poor and unsustaining liturgies and homilies, of rigid church rules and regulations that reward blind obedience while frowning on critical reflection. I wonder how the Gospel can be compromised by the very people who profess it so loudly – and who push many right out of the Church. Many such wounded people attended the memorial service: it was Albert who brought us together. Regardless of our position with the institutional Church, we came together in our need to remember Albert, to mourn his passing, and to celebrate his life.

Giving unwarranted praise of either the Church, which Albert loved so devoutly, or of Albert himself, whose failure to love was there for all to see, was not appropriate. There was nothing to gain by covering up the sinfulness of the institution or of Albert. My deepest desire was to preach the Gospel in an inclusive and life-giving way, especially for those whose wounds over the Church were still raw. My personal relationship with Jesus Christ had to be sufficient for guidance. Praying with my experience of Albert, and being asked to pick whatever passage I "liked," I asked God to guide me to the Scriptures. Matthew 7:21-27 came to mind with gentle insistence. At first I feared that passage, because it sounded so harsh. I became preoccupied with bending over backwards to sound inclusive in a nice way. But when I allowed Matthew's words to challenge and convert me too, I realized that these words were not for those outside the Church but also, and maybe especially, for those inside it. "It is not those who say 'Lord, Lord,' who will enter the kingdom of heaven, but those who do the will of my Father who is in heaven." Jesus' words reveal the sin of hypocrisy wherever it erodes community and faith in God. I took nothing for granted, and I knew that I could only say what I said because I was asked to say it on God's behalf.

Homiletic Reflection for Uncle Albert's Memorial Service

Matthew 7:21-27

I would like to think that when Albert knocked on heaven's door he was recognized and welcomed as the one who not only said "Lord, Lord," but also as the one who lived his life doing God's will. I would like to think that Albert was one of those people who built his house – which was his life – on solid rock. I don't just think that. The witness of Albert's life is indisputable. The fruits of one person doing God's will are here in this gathering of love and fellowship: no matter how long ago we saw Albert last, we chose to come together today. No matter how diverse our backgrounds are, remembering Albert brings us together today. Whether we share Albert's strong

Christian faith or not, all of us know too well that paying lip service to religion is the worst kind of idolatry. Jesus sounds harsh in this Gospel passage, and for very good reason. Doing God's will is so much more than saying the right words, and sometimes it has nothing to do with the "right" religious words. Rather, doing God's will invites us into a quality of loving. In that sense, Albert wore his faith on his sleeve the best way he knew how.

He loved people. He loved life. Albert could not help but love. Even when disagreeing, or feeling frustrated and impatient, Albert loved, however awkwardly and inadequately. In his last years, Albert's capacity to love brought the comfort of prayer and compassion to terminally ill patients, a ministry that earned him a special award in his community.

Thus grounded in love, our faith extends far beyond lip service. Touched by love, we overcome distrust and hurt. Growing in love we judge others less, and appreciate and accept them more. Miracles happen when love is dished out generously, for God's quality of love has the power to heal and to bring back to life.

A chiropractor once told the following story: One day a man in terrible shape walked into his office. Obviously he had not been looking after himself. He looked unkempt and dishevelled (he had not bathed in a while). The chiropractor felt horrified at the sight of this man. He cringed at the sight of the man's body, a body that was twisted with pain. But the chiropractor had one strong golden rule that a wise old colleague had taught him years before: Always find something lovable in each of your patients, no matter what it is. So the chiropractor looked the man over, searching for something he could appreciate. His eyes rested on the man's shoelaces: they looked surprisingly new, and neatly tied. So the chiropractor related to the man through his shoelaces, treating the man with love and respect. A few days later, the man came back to the office, this time clean, well dressed, and looking much better. The man explained that on the day of his previous visit he had actually been heading for the nearby bridge to commit suicide.

But first he had decided to give one more person a chance to change his mind. The man said: "The first place I saw was your office, and so I came to you. I must thank you for being so kind to me. I felt your acceptance and love. You encouraged me to go on living, Doctor, and I want you to know what a difference your kindness made."

I can imagine Albert being like the chiropractor, always looking for something lovable in the people he met. I can also imagine Albert in his time of need, like the hurting man in the story, aching to be touched by the love of another. For we all live a dynamic mixture of being the healer and being the one in need of healing. In solidarity with Jesus in his suffering, we all cry out for love, for healing, for meaning and purpose. In the blinding light of the risen Lord Jesus we learn, like Albert and the chiropractor learned, that love transforms everything.

We are not asked to be perfect lovers; Albert likely was not. Most of us probably fall short of the mark a lot of the time. We can be mired in guilt and self-judgment over our inadequacy to love. We can spend enormous energies judging others for their lack of love, for their shortcomings. No, rather than looking for or trying to be perfect lovers, we are merely asked to struggle faithfully with how to love until the end.

It is our struggle with love that forms the foundation of our house, which is our life. Jesus invites us to imitate his quality of loving. Jesus invites us to make our own his struggle with love. Jesus' own life, death and resurrection reveal the extent of Love's transforming power, transforming even death into life. Albert now shares in the fullness of this transforming power – and that is cause for celebration.

In remembering Albert, we rejoice in the quality of loving that he shared with us, a quality that was grounded in the person of Jesus, a foundation strong enough to hold firm in the storms of life: a gift from God, bursting with meaning and purpose. God desires nothing less.

God desires us to be all we can be. We build our house on this rock of love and we find ourselves in harmony with God, for God is love. Amen.

Did the words reach the hearts of those present? I will never know and I struggle with that. A pastor friend once said that preaching at funerals was so difficult for that exact reason: how do you know whether you say the "right" thing? I am still learning to let go of that worry. The Spirit moves different people's hearts in different ways.

Some months later, another elderly uncle died and once again I was asked to preach. His wife, who had died a few years earlier, was a devout Catholic, but he had not followed her in this practice. The family wanted a priest, but no funeral Mass, and insisted that the priest allow me to break open God's Word. Again I was called forth to preach comfort in the moment of sorrow. I wondered what people were looking for when they turned to someone like me. Did they have any idea how their requests affected me? Did finding my preaching voice, claiming the treasure, make people gravitate towards me? I had more questions than answers while the comforting continued.

About a year later, a woman I will call Claire approached me to help her explore the possibility of being baptized, at the ripe old age of 77. She also asked me to "do her funeral" when she died. Both these topics opened her up to share intimately about her childhood and private experience of faith. I was intrigued: why did she need to go through me instead of a recognized minister or priest? Our conversations revealed that Claire feared and distrusted institutions, and that she was very self-conscious, private and modest about her faith. The Anglican priest was invited into the circle only after Claire did considerable exploring on both topics with me, yet she stopped short of going through with the baptism. When she was near death six months later, the family called. In the presence of her children, Claire was baptized in the hospital with the Anglican priest and I sharing the rite in a moving witness of faith. She died the next day. The Anglican priest acknowledged that Claire and her family had turned to me as to a pastor. He coached and supported me while I did a delicate and painful balancing act between this calling and my own church's ambivalence towards women in such a role. The experience of this pastoral work, the baptism and involvement in the funeral was a privilege of the highest honour. My spirit soared while in another way my heart was ripped open in pain.

Requests came periodically for me to be involved in funerals. Sometimes I was called upon in a pastoral role; at other times the family asked me to lead the funeral service. Most of these requests came from people who, for whatever reason, considered themselves outside organized religion, yet sensed a need to "touch the hem of his garment" (Mark 5:28). Each call felt like a door opening, inviting me to walk through the particular experience of ministry that each opportunity offered. Each of these situations found me. I came to believe that such movement into ministry – from the community to me, and not the other way around – is one of the hallmarks of God's own guiding activity. When a door opens, I do not argue about how it opens or whether it is appropriate for it to open at all. As Father Leonard said to me several years earlier: "Do not worry about doors that are closed – merely walk through the ones that open. And remember that the risen Lord is not stopped by closed doors." Joan Chittister describes this phenomenon as "God creates, Jesus leads, and the Holy Spirit shows us ways that are not always in the book."[52]

> We buried Uncle Art today. Father Tony presided over the prayer service at the funeral home. He said he was proud of my preaching. …I felt the passion run through my veins. I felt the power of God's call in my soul as I prepared in fear and trembling (will God come through this time?), as I put on the text, while focusing the inner energy, in the hour prior to the service….And I know and see and hear, again, that what ends up reaching into people's hearts is so much more than spoken words. I am silent and in awe before such Holy Presence and Activity. I am left speechless. (Journal entry)

While I learned to trust the emerging invitations for ministry, I also faithfully attempted, and with an open heart, to understand what I was experiencing. Every now and then the question arose: does all of this have anything to do with a call to ordained ministry? Is this what men experience when they feel called to priesthood? Ministry becomes the fullest expression of all that is true and holy and creative within a person, with all the passion and compassion one is capable of. I lingered and resisted often, feeling caught between two worlds. Chittister's description of the sacrament of confirmation spoke volumes about my new reality:

> Confirmation, the sacrament of the Holy Spirit, thunders the arrival of courage and the recognition of gifts given to each of us […] for the good of the whole church. Confirmation, it seems, is a kind of ordination of the laity. A rite of

passage to full membership, full adulthood, full responsibility in the church that despite the theology of it [...] never
comes for women and only sometimes comes for men.[53]

I read books on baptism and priesthood, on discernment and
vocation, on spirituality and ministry. I did not understand why I
seemed privy to a priestly experience without having the option to
formally claim the experience in ordination. I also knew that this
call into ministry, especially the preaching ministry, was not something I went looking for or expected to find during my years of
studies. I did know it to be my duty to grow in faithfulness and
understanding, for my own sake as well as for the sake of the Church
as a whole. William D. Perri's book *A Radical Challenge to Priesthood
Today* shed some light on my experience and my questions:

> Many people who are ordained may or may not have re-
> ceived the indelible mark of priesthood. For that matter,
> many who are not ordained may actually participate in this
> archetypal vocation. The function of priesthood is much
> broader than any institution or organization. Perhaps the
> priesthood has, for too long, held a special place. This is not
> to say that a certain exceptional nature is not a part of this
> vocation. In fact, it is. But priests have abused this distinctive
> gift by turning the priesthood into an exclusive and some-
> what elitist hierarchy. Others who are not institutionally
> ordained have also experienced the true message of this
> vocation in their lives.[54]

If these words contained even a small amount of truth, there
was much reason to mourn and much need to comfort. For in the
end, by restricting and rigidly defining who is suited for ordained
priesthood, the Church misses out on the power and greatness of
God's calling activity, which manifests itself in the diversity of gifts
found among its members male and female. Sometimes powerful
bouts of pain washed over me, coming from deep within and from
far beyond. Not having experienced personal and direct exclusion
and discrimination at the hands of the Church until very recently, I
wondered what this pain could be about. Somehow, as I finally concluded through praying, reading and spiritual direction, this pain
was emerging out of the collective memory of women's pain and

intruded on my soul. That this collective memory exists and affects subsequent generations is evident in Pope John Paul II's own efforts and speeches on the need to heal the memory of the Church regarding the sins of history. The papal Jubilee celebration of confession and forgiveness in March 2000 included a prayer of contrition over the sins inflicted on women throughout the history of the Church:

> Let us pray for all those who have suffered offences against their human dignity and whose rights have been trampled; let us pray for women, who are all too often humiliated and marginated, and let us acknowledge the forms of acquiescence in these sins of which Christians too have been guilty.[55]

If God's call consisted of deeply mourning the many missed opportunities and the multitudes of gifts, mostly in women, that were unused and unappreciated in the course of history, then my response ought to flow out of the same desire for faithfulness and perseverance as when I mourn the passing of a beloved relative or friend. I may not understand why, but I need to trust that God knows what God is doing; in that security I am called to surrender my whole being to the mourning process.

Blessed are the poor in spirit, for theirs is the kingdom of heaven.
Blessed are those who mourn, for they will be comforted.
Blessed are the meek, for they will inherit the earth.
Blessed are those who hunger and thirst for righteousness, for they will be filled.
Blessed are the merciful, for they will receive mercy.
Blessed are the pure in heart, for they will see God.
Blessed are the peacemakers, for they will be called children of God.
Blessed are those who are persecuted for righteousness' sake, for theirs is the kingdom of heaven.
Blessed are you when people revile you and persecute you and utter all kinds of evil against you falsely on my account.
Rejoice and be glad, for your reward is great in heaven, for in the same way they persecuted the prophets before you.
(Matthew 5:3-12)

PART IV

That We May Be One

Dedication

Who are you that you
move me and intrude into
my soul uninvited
what is it in you that
rolls the stone away from
the tomb in my own being and
lets blinding new light and
life spring forth in
dazzling colours?
Is it the writer and poet in you
your love and play with words
making them come alive…
Is it the priest in you
your love affair with
Holy Things
your blessing of Bread and Wine…
Is it your profound humanness
your lack of self-confidence
your feeling of inadequacy
your sense of humour
your frustrations and limitations ..
Is it the woman in you
birthing and bathing and bleeding
mothering the world into life…
Is it the pain hiding in you
tainting all you touch – including me
the pain of loss, death, of loving
too much…
Is it the fire in your belly
swirling the Gospel all around
through your eyes and your words…
Is it your catholicity
your embrace of the Body of Christ
through us all and in all
creation…
Is it all of these and none of these
bursting me open into a
new reality never tasted
before…

CHAPTER 13

Together We Believe

For by grace you have been saved through faith,
and this is not your own doing;
it is the gift of God –
not the result of works.
(Ephesians 2:8-9)

Before entering theology studies my world was embarrassingly Catholic. Even though my world view and beliefs were steeped in the Catholic theology and spirituality of Vatican II, which helped me to be fairly open, I could not always recognize and articulate this. When it came to ecumenical savvy, I was downright sloppy. The language I and many other well-meaning Catholics used betrayed a certain ignorance. People in other Christian traditions were considered "separated from us" and referred to as "those of the other faith." I still encounter the use of the term "other faiths" when people simply mean Christians from other churches. Our faith is the same: the Christian faith. Those of "another faith" are Muslim, Hindu, Buddhist, Taoist, etc.

Being with students from at least five different Christian traditions brought about significant changes in my understanding of both Catholicism and other traditions. One of the biggest realizations was that Catholics do not have a monopoly on the theological schools of thought, or on liturgical and sacramental practices, or on a commitment to the truth of God as revealed in the person of Jesus Christ. At first I glossed over the differences, and revelled in the discovery of commonalities. The Lutheran-Catholic dialogue was particularly personal and intimate, since I had submitted myself as a Catholic to comprehensive formation in a Lutheran context. At one point I wondered whether it really made a difference whether I was Lutheran or Catholic:

> Lutherans sound suspiciously Catholic in all they believe. One student commented that most Lutherans do not know how Catholic they really are. A Lutheran professor told me she is really a closet Catholic. What does all this mean? Where do I fit? Does it matter where I belong? I have indeed taken my own tradition for granted. Is that being challenged right now? I have been comfortably Catholic, but have I ever examined what keeps me there? (Journal entry)

Interacting with the learning often tossed me to and fro. Getting a good dose of Lutheran theology made me see things in a different light. Then I mulled things over in the car while driving the two hours home. I sifted and sorted at a deep, intuitive level at first: What thoughts and beliefs could I harmonize with my Catholicism? Which ones jarred with my own beliefs? Then followed more questioning: How could I explain my Catholic position in a way that contributed constructively to the larger picture? What particular insight could I contribute that seemed missing in the Lutheran perspective? Sometimes I asked questions in reverse: What is missing in the Catholic view that the Lutheran perspective could add?

Our respective theologies of creation, or at least the strongest expression of these theologies that dominate our traditions, is a prime example of such a dialogue. Some Lutherans talked about the human state of total depravity so often that it literally risked pulling me into a depression. "Knowing I can do nothing to save myself is so freeing," one Lutheran friend said. Somehow, this emphasis on the corrupt nature of human beings sounded like a complete lack of acknowledgment of the goodness of creation: "God saw everything that he had made, and indeed, it was very good" (Genesis 1:31). To my ears the depressing Lutheran emphasis sounded vaguely familiar: when I listened to older Catholics speak of their church upbringing, they recalled some of pre-Vatican II theology that kept them bound in the same way, constantly reminding them of their sinfulness instead of focusing on the original blessing of creation. That same negating approach urged people to the sacrament of penance out of fear for divine punishment instead of as a celebration of God's mercy and reconciliation. Some Lutherans, though not all, sounded suspiciously like old-school Catholics who had been urged into a "works" mentality to set the record straight with God. Even though Lutherans adamantly claimed to be saved by faith alone through grace alone, I saw a certain irony. I learned that some strands of Lutheranism had developed a complicated system for living with an entire list of prohibitions: no dances, no parties, no drinking, all for religious reasons. The popular Catholic caricature was not necessarily better: Catholics could dance, party and drink all they wanted as long as they went to confession before Mass!

Intense discussion of the various denominational views caused creative tension, forming a crucible of sorts. When we dug deep enough, we bumped into mirror images of one another. The Lutheran emphasis on "justification by grace through faith alone" had produced some strains of Puritanism and quietism, with a risk of privatizing religion and abdicating social responsibility. Our Catholic overemphasis on sanctification had indeed encouraged a common belief that we could work our way into heaven. One Lutheran woman shared stories of her childhood, recalling Catholic conversations that included statements like this: "I have to do so many good deeds this week before I can show up at Mass." Such words merely added to her belief that Catholics earned heaven by doing good works.

I never subscribed to this kind of Catholicism, and much of these pre-Vatican II notions were on their way out as I grew up in the Netherlands. Yet hearing such understandings from some Lutherans forced me to examine the entirety of Catholic teaching on justification and sanctification. During my years at the seminary there was not yet an official common text like the *Joint Lutheran/Catholic Declaration on Justification by Faith* that was signed in October 1999. I struggled to formulate my discomfort with the Lutheran emphasis on justification divorced from sanctification. I knew that the extent to which we cooperate with God's grace is vitally important in our living out the grace we have received through faith. In discussions I challenged my Lutheran friends about our responsibility to share our being justified with the world through good works.

I was forced to articulate what is uniquely Catholic and how I carried that unique Catholic quality in my faith experience and expression. Eventually I realized that the sacramentality of Catholic theology, liturgy and spirituality is what anchors me in my tradition. A reading course on the Catholic sacraments, under the guidance of a Roman Catholic priest/professor, confirmed what I started to formulate for myself. The greatest gift we Catholics bring to ecumenical dialogue is our sacramental theology and practices. Moreover, such a deeply sacramental understanding of life protects us against a dominant negative view of creation and of humanity, without negating the reality of sin:

> Catholicism has never hesitated to affirm the "mysterious" dimension of all reality: the cosmos, nature, history, events, persons, objects, rituals, words. Everything is, in principle, capable of embodying and communicating the divine. There is no finite instrument that God cannot put to use. On the other hand, we humans have nothing else apart from finite instruments to express our own response to God's self-communication. Just as the divine reaches us through the finite, so we reach the divine through the finite. The point at which this "divine commerce" occurs is the point of *sacramental encounter*. For Christians, *the* point of a sacramental encounter with God is the *humanity* of Jesus Christ, the primordial, or primal, sacrament.[56]

Clarifying my own Catholic understanding of faith demanded vigilance, honesty and courage. It was not good enough to settle for the first possible answer. I became a keen observer of the practice of our Catholic sacraments and of my inner experience of these sacraments. I appreciated the richness of the sacramental life in new ways, but along with that, felt greatly cheated at times when these sacraments were not celebrated with engaging fullness. Five-minute baptisms with three drops of water, half-hour Masses, and two-minute assembly-line confessions could not possibly plunge the depth of sacramental experience. Knowing the potential power of good liturgy and how it can facilitate a deep experience of the sacraments made me more demanding of both priest and gathered assembly. That in itself was a mixed blessing, bringing both affirmation and frustration. In most parishes, we simply do not experience the fullness of what Catholic sacramental life can be. Yet at other times good liturgy affirmed my Catholic identity so deeply that my spirit soared:

> This morning I attended the funeral of a 15-year-old girl who went to the Catholic high school. This event moved me deeply for several reasons. First, I realized with acute urgency that this tragedy could have happened to any of our children. Being a parent made me realize anew the precious gift our children are – and how often we take one another for granted. Secondly, I was deeply aware and moved by the depth and meaning of this liturgical farewell: the ritual, symbols, prayers, readings, Eucharist were rich and pregnant with God's promises for God's people.... I recalled my own questioning about whether I'd ever leave the Catholic Church – and this morning I drank so deeply from the life-giving liturgy that it hurt... How could I not be in this church? These holy things, these symbols and prayers, are forever etched into the structure of my being. When I die, I want to be prayed for and sent off in and by this beloved church. I cannot ever conceive of life in another tradition, let alone in none. This morning the Church was fully true to itself: breaking us into the incarnation and resurrection of God in Jesus Christ, in the face of our pain, in the face of death itself. (Journal entry)

Thus, my time with Lutherans had nothing to do with becoming Lutheran. It had everything to do with becoming more fully Catholic. I was pushed ever deeper into the treasures of my own tradition. I learned to become more explicit and articulate about the specifically Catholic aspects of my Christian identity and mission, and to express these with pride, love and appreciation without needing to judge, minimize or criticize another tradition to do so. I became freer to encounter those in other churches on their own ground without feeling that my own position was threatened. Such anchoring became vital for any healthy and respectful ecumenical involvement.

As someone who felt the pain of division in the Christian body in her own flesh and bones, and as one who brought a Catholic heart and soul to a Lutheran theological understanding, I felt like a bridge between two traditions. My preaching ministry allowed me to experience forming such a bridge. Preaching in the Catholic Sunday service, I shared my Lutheran experience, and in the Lutheran pulpit I was intentionally Catholic in the words I spoke. I could do this because both sides, according to one Lutheran pastor, considered me "one of their own." One weekend I preached the same sermon on the same Scripture readings in both a Catholic and a Lutheran worship service. In both churches the Gospel was a section of Jesus' discourse on the Bread of Life from John's Gospel. Consequently I preached on Eucharist in the absence of Eucharist at both services. Only after leaving the Lutheran seminary did my dual denominational formation really start to bear fruit in opportunities like this.

A year after graduating, I attended a Catholic theological college for the first time. Whether it was coincidence or providence I will never know, but the course I took was on the writings of St. Paul. Any good Lutheran knows that it was primarily Martin Luther's interpretation of Paul's letters that led him to disagree with Rome on the doctrine of justification. Time and again in the class I found myself understanding the Lutheran position almost from the inside out. There was much discussion on the insights Martin Luther derived from Paul. By default I found myself the Lutheran "expert" in the class as I was most familiar with the Lutheran nuances, even more so than the professor. God does have a unique sense of humour! Through the discussions and through exploring Paul's theology I sensed a coming together of Catholic and Lutheran understandings, interpretations and emphases. The basis of the final exam in the course was the text of the *Joint Lutheran/Catholic Declaration on the Doctrine of Justification by Faith*.[57] It was the first time I had read this text. The text articulated what I experienced deep within me as a Catholic student among Lutherans. It is hard to describe what I felt. Here was an official text that caught the essence of my time with the Lutherans. Delight, affirmation, relief, joy and peace flooded me:

> Last year I remember feeling like I was in a denominational vacuum, as if I did not belong anywhere. Today the same reality is shifting meaning: I realize that I have grown into a denominational hybrid, belonging everywhere and carrying both the Roman Catholic strengths and the Lutheran

gifts into my Gospel ministry. From my Roman Catholic roots I bring a keen, embodied awareness of the sacramentality of human existence and the meaning of sacramental ritual. I bring the strong conviction that, having been saved by grace through faith, we are constantly called to live lives of holiness in order to appropriate that salvation in this life. I bring the strength and value of historical tradition, the strong belief in the Holy Spirit's ongoing activity of revelation in the Church, in the people of God who are the Body of Christ. I bring a theology of service and ministry that is drenched in the eucharistic and Paschal paradigms. And, last but not least, I bring from my Catholic roots a powerful intuitive understanding of Mary and her priestly role in God's plan of salvation. After all, not only is she the first disciple, she is also the first to give her body and blood to the world as she gave birth to Jesus and as she witnessed his death on the cross. (Journal entry)

From my Lutheran formation I bring a keen sense of the gratuitousness of God's grace for all people. I bring a deep insight into God's call to both men and women to church leadership and the awareness of the priesthood of all believers, expressed in the local church's taking ownership of calling forth its own leaders and in the quality of life among its own members. God calls, the church community confirms by calling forth both women and men who offer their gifts and their lives for the sake of God's reign. Also from my Lutheran formation I bring a new and forceful insight into the sacramental nature of the preached Word of God. It is in the daring act of preaching that the Word becomes flesh again here and now in our midst. (Journal entry)

Now it dawned on me why God placed me with the Lutherans all that time and what part of my call was now – to become a bridge for others to walk across in order to befriend one another after 500 years of strife. And even this continued in surprising ways.

The pastor of the local Lutheran congregation saw it fitting that I preach in his congregation on that famous Reformation Sunday, October 31, 1999, in conjunction with the *Joint Declaration* signing ceremony in Augsburg, Germany. I was struck by the awesomeness of the global event and of my small yet significant role on the local level. I informed my bishop of the part I would play and asked for his prayers and blessing; after all, even though the invitation was to me personally and the Lutheran pastor knew and trusted me, I was clearly invited to represent my tradition on this historic occasion. I approached the local Catholic clergy at their monthly meeting and informed them of the Lutheran invitation. For once, I had Rome on my side, when I asked them how this historic event would be marked in our Catholic parishes. I issued a clear request to my own clergy and pastoral workers that I be supported as I climbed into the Lutheran pulpit on Reformation Sunday. I felt again, as I had so many times, that this preaching ministry was not my own doing, and that it needed mandating and supporting by the local Church leadership. The signing of the *Joint Declaration* merely helped to legitimate my request.

This single request became the springboard for a larger conversation between the Catholic clergy and me about the preaching I did in other churches. It was my first opportunity to explain directly how I understood this ecumenical ministry, an opportunity that was long overdue. Every time I stood in the pulpit of another church, I engaged in a delicate balancing act. I knew I brought my Catholic identity with me every time, and I used it deliberately; yet I also knew that I had no ordained mandate to do what I was doing. I did not want to be doing my own thing, yet I had no church structure that endorsed this activity, protected it and took responsibility for it. My commitment to keep my local bishop informed was largely motivated by this desire to have my church take ownership of this unique ministry and by my need for protection. The conversation with clergy and parish workers clarified various issues and answered questions raised in the Catholic community about my ecumenical adventures (news travels fast in small towns, and not always accurately). At the end of our time together, recommendations of support and protection were expressed and agreed upon. I left the meeting feeling slightly overwhelmed – the mandate given and the support shown brought tears to my eyes, filling as it did my deep desire to be called and sent forth by the faith community. This was probably as close to a formal mandate as I would ever get.

I have always kept Fr. Leonard's advice before me: "Whatever you end up doing in church ministry, just make sure to stay connected to the Body of Christ, and you'll be fine." That is why this morning's meeting was so important. None of this ministry is my own doing. Rather, it is meant for the building up of the Church, the Body of Christ. It is so important to know that when I stand in the Lutheran pulpit next week, I do not stand there alone. Now it is clear that these preaching commitments fall under the protection and authority not only of my local bishop but also of the local Catholic leadership. Somehow this is incredibly important, and so very integral to the call. This work can only bear fruit when mandated and confirmed. My heart overflows with gratitude and praise. (Journal entry)

With great rejoicing, and knowing myself to be on solid ground with my church, I preached reconciliation and healing to the Lutherans on that famous Reformation Sunday, a day that went down in history as one of the most significant steps taken towards Christian unity in the past 500 years.

Sermon on Reformation Sunday (October 31, 1999) at Zion Lutheran Church

Jeremiah 31:31-34, Romans 3:19-28, John 8:31-36

I remember how honoured I felt when I preached from your pulpit last year. I remember it especially because of the trust you showed to me, a Catholic. Little did I know then that my next time in this place would be on Reformation Sunday 1999 – the day that we, Lutherans and Catholics together, are clearing at the highest church levels the biggest obstacle that has kept us divided from and suspicious of one another for nearly five centuries. Four hundred and eighty-two ago years to this day, Martin Luther nailed his 95 Theses to the Wittenberg church door. Today, in the city of Augsburg, Germany, where the Lutheran Confessions were written, eight representatives of the Lutheran World Federation (LWF) and two of the highest Vatican officials are now reversing, and making, history. They are officially signing the *Joint Declaration on the Doctrine of Justification by Faith*. Your Evangelical Lutheran Church in Canada has sent a petition of support with nearly 1400 signatures to the LWF, with your national Bishop Telmor Sartison saying: "We want to be there at Augsburg, at least in signature if not in person, to celebrate our life in Christ as marked by the history, old and new, that Augsburg will mark." Having studied and prayed as a Catholic in your Lutheran Seminary, I got a foretaste of this joint declaration that is now being signed. That is why this world event has deep personal significance for me. I cannot help but be overwhelmed by this powerful sign of the activity of God's Holy Spirit in the hearts and minds of Lutheran and Catholics alike – the only adequate response is one of praise and thanksgiving. The Lord is truly filling our hearts with love for one another, showing us the way to freedom, which the truth of our Lord Jesus Christ promises and effects in those who place their trust in him.

Things have not always been this hopeful, and in many places people's hearts are still imprisoned by fear, insecurity and suspicion. In talking with your pastor, I learned how the Lutheran kids in his hometown used to pick on the Catholics, throwing snowballs, provoking fights, all because they were "different." My own childhood environment was so Roman Catholic that I thought everyone was Roman Catholic. There was occasional talk in the town about that small group of Protestants who supposedly met in secret, but nobody really knew what they did at their gatherings. Now that I am actively involved in ecumenical work and ministry, I still encounter hardness of heart that is tainted with a personal need to be right. Some people have even gone to "complain" to my parish priest, saying: "What is she doing, hanging out with Protestants and preaching in their churches?" As editor of *Our Family* magazine, I have published articles sharing ecumenical questions and experiences. I have received letters from some readers accusing me of "denying" the Catholic faith by choosing to publish such articles. The other day I received the new issue of *Faith Today*, an independent evangelical Christian publication. Back in the spring, *Faith Today* ran feature articles on the new and cautious dialogue that is starting between evangelical Christians and Catholics. This month's issue of *Faith Today* carried letters to the editor, some applauding the thawing relations, others warning the Pentecostals with great fervour not to "sell out" to Catholics. Yes, the hardness of heart, the fears, suspicions and divisions are still alive and well.

No wonder Jeremiah's words have a freshness and an immediacy that cut right to the core. It is hard, it is so hard, to give up the old stereotypes. We are so fearful on both sides of letting go of our suspicions and prejudices. On our own we cannot find the courage in our hearts, so God decides to take radical action: "I will put my law within them," says the LORD through Jeremiah, "and I will write it on their hearts; and I will be their God, and they shall be my people." That will fix them: I'll scar their hearts with my love. The *Joint Declaration* is a powerful expression of what can happen when God scars our hearts with his love and grace. The fruit of 30 years of common listening with that love of God in our hearts, the Declaration echoes Paul's words to the Romans today and says: "The Lutheran churches and the Roman Catholic Church have together listened to the Good News proclaimed in the Holy Scriptures. This common listening has led to a shared understanding of justification. Together we now confess: By grace alone, through faith in Christ's saving work (his incarnation, death and resurrection) and not because of any merit on our part, we are accepted by God and receive the Holy Spirit, who renews our hearts while equipping and calling us to good works."[58]

The text goes on to explain how each of our traditions has used different words, has focused on different aspects, and has developed different theological strengths to elaborate on this basic doctrine. The result was that we did not recognize Christ in one another. For centuries we did not recognize in one another the One we have clung to as our Lord.

How has it been that we have failed to recognize each other as Christian? How is it that all this time we have professed our faith in the one Lord who sets us free, yet our hearts were not free and open to each other? Jesus says in John's Gospel: "If you continue in my word, you are truly my disciples; and you will know the truth, and the truth will make you free" (John 8:31-32). Both of our churches have been guilty of using these words of Christ as a weapon to hit others with, as a hammer of judgment – forgetting that the right to judge belongs to God alone. Forcing others into our way of thinking is hardly a fruit of the freedom of Christ.

Treating those in other churches with suspicion and disdain is hardly a sign of God's love in our hearts. The truth in Jesus Christ sets our hearts free in ways that nothing else in this life can: a radical reorientation in love makes everything look different.

With the freedom promised in Jesus Christ, those in other traditions are no longer considered a threat. Rather, they become God's own bearers of Good News, for God's love keeps offering us different gifts and insights. Grounded in God's love, ecumenical dialogue is not about selling out or settling for the lowest common denominator. Rather, ecumenical dialogue becomes a sharing of gifts at God's own banquet table, a banquet table that culminates in and is prefigured in the risen Lord, and comes to full expression in the Eucharist celebrated in his name.

My daughter once asked a Lutheran seminary friend of mine why there are different traditions like Lutheran and Catholic. My friend used the image of a family to explain: in a family we each have a first name and, generally, we all have the same last name. Parents and children belong to one another, yet each one is a unique individual. A healthy family-belonging is essential to the development of a healthy, balanced individual. Thus in traditions our first name is Lutheran or Catholic or Pentecostal, and our last name is Christian. It is our last name that we proudly profess together as a sign that we belong to one another in Christ, without taking away the unique gift that our first name is.

Just like in our family we need to belong in order to be psychologically healthy, the sense of belonging to the larger Body of Christ is essential to our developing a healthy, balanced and deep denominational faith. Each time I engage in ecumenical ministry I come away having grown in my Roman Catholic identity, my first name, and feel strengthened in my sense of belonging to the Christian family, my last name. This may sound like a simplistic analogy, but surprisingly, the image has stayed with me over the years. It makes a lot of sense and has deep meaning. Just as we do not give up our first name in our families, Christian unity is not about giving up our denominational name. As Konrad Raiser from the World Council of

Churches said: "Today marks the closing of a long and painful chapter in the history between Lutherans and Catholics." This joint declaration on justification shows that we have cleared the biggest hurdle. However, this does not mean that all differences collapse. We are not ready for joint Eucharist – not just yet.

We have a long way to go. We cannot ignore the fact that we have developed apart from one another for nearly 500 years, each with rich and different expressions and understandings in liturgy, theology, spirituality. But agreeing, after 500 years, that we are justified by God's grace through faith alone now gives us a clean slate. Based on that essential article of faith, we can now move into tackling other differences with hope and commitment that God's Spirit is with us, leading us to that unity that Christ died for.

It is in our own best interests as the Body of Christ to admit honestly the checkered history we have as Church. Many people today have written off the Church because we fight so much among ourselves; because we have so often robbed others of their dignity and freedom, supposedly in the name of God's freedom. But just like Jesus Christ himself died, hanging between two thieves, the Church, his Body on earth, will always hold within its family the thieves and the saints, the sinners and the heroes of the soul. To belong to the Christian family is to carry the mantle of the worst sin and strife, as well as to belong with the greatest sons and daughters of God.

Carlo Carretto, a great spiritual writer from the turn of the twentieth century, embraced the truth of Christ to such depth that he was set free to hold within his own heart both the sinfulness and the holiness of the Church. We fight, we argue, we accuse, we judge, yet God insists on using us as his instrument of grace in the world. As we listen to Carretto's words, we rejoice today that God's love and grace is triumphing in our churches, scarring our hearts with God's own law of love, despite the divisions and strife of the last five centuries between us:

> How much I criticize you, my church, and yet how much I love you. You have made me suffer more than anyone and yet I owe more to you than anyone. I should like to see you destroyed and yet I need your presence. You have given me much scandal and yet you alone have made me understand holiness. Never in this world I have seen anything more

compromised, more false, yet never have I touched anything more pure, more generous or more beautiful. Countless times I have felt like slamming the door of my soul in your face – and yet, every night, I have prayed that I might die in your sure arms. No, I cannot be free from you, for I am one with you, even if not completely you. Then too – where would I go? To build another church? But I could not build one without the same defects, for they are my defects. And again, if I were to build another church, it would be my church, not Christ's church. No. I am old enough. I know better.[59]

The Lord God says to us today through Jeremiah, "No longer shall you teach one another, or say to each other, 'Know the Lord,' for you shall all know me, from the least to the greatest; and I will forgive your iniquity, and remember your sin of division no more." Amen.

CHAPTER 14

Mirror, Mirror, on the Wall

Now in the following instructions I do not commend you,
because when you come together
it is not for the better but for the worse.
For, to begin with,
when you come together as a church,
I hear that there are divisions among you.

(1 Corinthians 11:17-18)

The professor teaching church history spoke about the events leading up to the Reformation. Being a good Lutheran, he loved this era in the life of the Church. Most of the time, he went to great lengths to present the Reformation issues from all perspectives: social, theological, economic and historical. The student body was diverse: Lutheran, Mennonite, Presbyterian, Anglican, United, and yes, three Roman Catholics. We listened alertly, eager to recognize in his words strands of our own particular theological and ecclesial perspective. Whenever this did not happen, the professor was "grilled." What about Menno Simons? What about the Counter-Reformation, Ignatius of Loyola and the Council of Trent? What about John Knox and Thomas Cranmer? On one occasion our questions frustrated him so much that he finally threw up his hands in exasperation and said, with a smile in his voice: "This class used to be easier to teach when it was all Lutherans!"

These words offered a crash course in ecumenism. His words startled me, opening up a larger Christian world than the one I knew. As if seeing everyone for the first time, I realized that we all cherished our beloved church traditions and wanted nothing more than to serve God in ministry in that church we each knew best.

And who was to say what was closer to the truth? If our faith is cradled only within the security of our own church walls, we easily assume that Gospel truth equals denominational truths. The seminary student body was made up of denominational camps, but was nevertheless a unique faith community discovering Gospel truth together. As we plunged into theological, ecclesial, historical and spiritual questions and discussions, we engaged in deep personal and denominational soul-searching. Each of us brought the perspectives characteristic of our denominational home, the cherished "stuff" we grew up with. Many of these were truly precious gifts that often threw fresh light on questions for those in other traditions. An over-emphasis on our denominational views risked not only deforming the Gospel itself, but also undermining our sisters and brothers from another tradition, thus producing "fruits" of disrespect, judgment and disharmony. Slowly we learned to hold our particular perspectives in full context of the view of others, with all the tensions and seeming contradictions this brings. Only by humbly submitting to the loving scrutiny of the other did the Gospel reveal itself more fully. Slowly but surely, we learned to love in diversity, experiencing in our relationships that unity that Christ has indeed won for us.

Sharing the same place of learning was both affirming and challenging by the simple fact that we were required to enter into relationships of trust, respect and love with one another. This filled us with hope for growing closer, personally and maybe someday as churches: "And hope does not disappoint, because God's love has been poured forth in our hearts through the Holy Spirit who has been given to us" (Romans 5:5). Slowly, and at times with great effort and strain, we learned to listen to one another, sharing those holy things of God living deep in our hearts.

Venturing into relationship presupposed an abiding respect, along with a commitment to learn about and honour our own and the other's traditions, teachings and disciplines. The ecumenical directory issued by the Pontifical Council for the Promotion of Christian Unity states that one of the objectives of dialogue "should be a greater mutual understanding of each other's discipline."[60] The ecumenical learning setting provided means to grow in this mutual understanding, and became foundational for everything that followed in my life and ministry, even though I did not know it then. Once in a while someone asked me why I, a Roman Catholic, was studying at a Lutheran seminary. The question forced me to examine my own heart and my faithfulness to my tradition as well as my understanding of Roman Catholicism.

The ecumenical learning forced me to dig deeper into my own tradition, its teachings and its liturgy, its spirituality and its history. Deepening my faith with my heart, mind and soul had a strong "opening" effect: the more I anchored my whole being with trust in my faith tradition, the freer my heart became to truly embrace those from other traditions on their own terms. Knowing where I belonged dispelled the fear of getting lost, thus making room in me to welcome those with different perspectives. Rooting my sense of being in Jesus made it impossible to see those in other traditions as threats to my spiritual and ecclesial security. So much of our experience of the other is determined by our own fears, biases, hurts and insecurities. As I slowly faced, healed and corrected these fears, a deep joy about being Catholic started to permeate me. By engaging with those of other traditions, I deepened my appreciation of and in many ways rediscovered the rich beauty of my own tradition.

With this deepening and opening, however, also came a good dose of humility and brutal honesty. Our church history is not blameless, as Pope John Paul admitted in the March 2000 service for reconciliation. In other churches, many still walk around with bruises and open wounds that go back centuries, wounds for which the Roman Catholic Church is partly responsible. Genuine faith does not need an exclusive and fearful defence; rather, it must be humble and contrite, desiring the healing of wounds with the greatest care and submission, to the point of setting aside its own agenda for the sake of the whole:

> [...] Besides the doctrinal differences needing to be resolved, Christians cannot underestimate the burden of long-standing misgivings inherited from the past, and of mutual misunderstandings and prejudices. Complacency, indifference and insufficient knowledge of one another often make the situation worse. Consequently, the commitment to ecumenism must be based upon the conversion of hearts and upon prayer, which will also lead to the necessary puri-

fication of past memories. With the grace of the Holy Spirit, the Lord's disciples, inspired by love, by the power of the truth and by a sincere desire for mutual forgiveness and reconciliation, are called to re-examine together their painful past and the hurt which that past regrettably continues to provoke even today.[61]

Very early on in my years of study, I preached in a nearby United church. At the time I still felt quite new in ecumenical matters, and wondered about the appropriateness of accepting such an invitation. Questions plagued me: Was I disowning my Roman Catholic faith by stepping into the pulpit of another church? Did God wish me to join another church? Was I doing something that was not allowed? At other times such ecumenical learning and involvement felt like a "leaving home" and a temporary drifting in order to find purpose and direction in a new way. For a long time I had no clear view of a specific ecumenical ministry, clouded as my learning was by major inner upheavals:

> I have rarely felt so far from home as in this stage of my life. And rarely has this drifting been so deeply interior, and thus hardly visible on the outside. So much is shifting and moving and changing. Foundational structures are shaking, undergoing needed rebuilding. While the tearing down feels painful, there is underneath all the rubble a new yet fragile home being built as in a new way of being.... Most of the time I acknowledge on a head level that this weaving is going on. But on many days my heart cannot see this yet. It feels ripped apart since there is no more belonging in the usual places. The old home is gone in many ways. (Journal entry)

Since the ecumenical dynamic was such an integral component of my formation, this, not surprisingly, eventually started to bear fruit locally. In time the muddy waters of transformation settled, and my ecumenical presence was welcomed and appreciated. Through my participation in the ministerial association I came to know the pastors from most Protestant churches. I spent time building relationships, while these pastors took their time, I learned later, wondering if they could trust me. Over coffee and in the sharing on

Scripture I learned about their various faith traditions, in particular the smaller evangelical churches, with whom I was less familiar. I remember vividly one such coffee hour, when the young Pentecostal pastor asked: "Why are you in the church you're in and what keeps you there?" One by one, going around the table, we shared what each of us held most dear about our specific churches and how we encountered Jesus in the diversity of ministries entrusted to us. We took the question seriously and personally; the extent of the sharing created a deep bond of fellowship that gave us a feeling of wonder. It was a graced moment filled with the presence of the risen Lord.

Slowly, the invitations to preach in other churches became a regular occurrence, at a rate of eight or more per year. One time I preached on three consecutive Sundays, each one in a different Protestant church. The preaching engagements brought me into those churches in a more formal way than if I had simply been a visitor in the pew. It became important, therefore, to exercise this unusual ministry with the utmost care and within the guidelines on ecumenism in the various churches, including those of my own Roman Catholic tradition. There was no precedent to follow, and I acutely sensed the delicate nature of the ecumenical challenges. The preaching invitations came to me personally, yet none of this felt like my freelance ministry and I brought my denominational colours with me wherever I went. All ministry arises out of the church body and is meant for the building up of the church body. But because there was no precedent, and because I had no official mandate through ordination to preach or to represent my tradition in another church, I often felt unprotected and unsupported in any formal way.

Again I went to see my bishop. Looking to him for direction, approval and protection, I explained my ecumenical involvements and asked for his input. He affirmed the validity of the call, however unique and unprecedented. He expressed trust in my ability to respond with faithfulness and integrity. Together we placed my ecumenical involvement before God, asking for guidance and protection. From that time on, I made a point of informing the bishop about my ecumenical work. I continue to send him the text of every sermon I preach outside of the Catholic Church. This small communication channel is significant in that it shares the responsibility of my individual church involvement with the local church ordinary, the bishop. In this way my contributions in ministry remain connected to the Body of Christ, the Church, as a form of protection and a place of support, albeit informal. The very nature of ministry revolts against any attempt to privatize and monopolize it either economically, theologically or otherwise.

> Today, in many parts of the world, under the influence of the grace of the Holy Spirit, many efforts are being made in prayer, word and action to attain that fullness of unity which Jesus Christ desires. The sacred Council exhorts, therefore, all the Catholic faithful to recognize the signs of the times and to take an active and intelligent part in the work of ecumenism…. Such actions, when they are carried out by the Catholic faithful with prudent patience and under the attentive guidance of their bishops, promote justice and truth, concord and collaboration, as well as the spirit of brotherly love and unity.[62]

Ecumenical ministry is about risking relationships of trust, taking seriously the notion that the presence of the risen Christ extends far beyond our own upbringing, our own understandings and our own churches. For me, relating to those in other churches has become a treasure of love and mercy.

As intimacy grows, so does the level of comfort with church humour. The respect and care shown to one another allows us, for example, to tease the young pastor of a small evangelical church about the fact that his church "used to have the truth." Bill shared during the ministerial Scripture study about the recent great doctrinal upheaval his church had undergone.[63] He was deeply moved by the welcome his local congregation received from the other ecclesial communities. Realizing that the truth of Christ is bigger than any one church, we looked to one another for support, guidance and admonishment. When *Dominus Iesus*[64] was published in 1999 by the Congregation for the Doctrine of the Faith under the leadership of Cardinal Ratzinger, our discussions became heated. Even though there was much in the document we all agreed on, several pastors felt hurt and insulted about not being considered true churches, and I felt awkward. These churches were not distant entities. These churches had faces and feelings and deep faith, and they were friends of Jesus' and friends of mine. In the end, mercy and patience towards Rome prevailed in my relationships with them. Pastor Bill, with his delightful sense of humour, put it succinctly: "It's okay. Our church used to think we were the only ones who had the truth, but we learned that was not so. Rome has a lot to learn yet."

However positive and enriching these relations are, the questions and challenges arising from ecumenical ministry were not always easy, and sometimes they are downright awkward, sad and painful.

The Roman Catholic presence at ministerial meetings consisted of only laity: three religious sisters, one religious brother and myself, a married woman with a theology degree. In the various topics discussed at these meetings, the Protestant community regarded us as speaking on behalf of our tradition – yet it was most difficult for us to do so. We felt sad that our own Roman Catholic priests were ecumenically absent. This is not the kind of ministry that can be delegated. When a team from the Billy Graham Crusade came to our community to explore whether we could host such an event (a unique opportunity for ecumenical collaboration), the Protestant clergy looked to the five of us to discover whether the Roman Catholics were willing to be involved. Once we established that our clergy were not interested, the ministerial association decided to hold off bringing the Crusade to town. When we discussed the worship schedule for the Week of Prayer for Christian Unity, we could not always commit to having a Roman Catholic parish host such a service. Some parish priests were unwilling to get involved ecumenically, others had not delegated us to speak for a given parish, and still others were unaware of the importance of such ecumenical initiatives. When negative experiences with Roman Catholics surfaced in conversations, we listened in humility and pain, asking forgiveness on behalf of our church without really knowing if our church wanted to ask for forgiveness. Many Catholics still do not feel the need to apologize for our arrogance and ignorance as a church. And so, being the Catholic lay presence with the other churches carried both the joys and the sorrows of ecumenical relations – and both are deep in more ways than one: "Every effort [is to be made] to avoid expressions, judgments and actions which do not represent the condition of our separated brethren with truth and fairness, and so make mutual relations with them more difficult."[65]

Sermon on Reformation Sunday
at St. Andrew's Presbyterian Church

Luke 18:9-14

"Mirror, mirror, on the wall, who's the fairest of them all?" Each day the queen would stand before her magical mirror and pose this question. And each day without fail the mirror would reply, "You are the fairest in the land." Then the queen would happily go about her business. But there came the day when the queen stood before the mirror and asked, as usual, "Mirror, mirror, on the wall, who's the fairest of them all?" This time, the magical mirror, which could only reflect the truth, answered, "Snow White, Snow White is the fairest of them all." The queen flew into a rage, unable to bear this truth and…well, you know the rest of the story.

The Pharisee went up to the Temple to pray. He stood by himself, and praying before the mirror of the Eternal he informed the mirror of his exceeding righteousness: "I am not like other people: thieves, rogues, adulterers, or even like this tax collector standing nearby. I fast twice a week; I give a tenth of all my income." The mirror of the Eternal, like the queen's magical mirror, reveals only the truth. But unlike the fairy-tale queen, the Pharisee never asked the Eternal mirror to verify his righteousness. To the Pharisee, it was self-evident. Why question it?

But the tax collector, standing at some distance, did not even look into the mirror of the Eternal. Instead, he beat his breast as a sign of contrition, and prayed, "God, be merciful to me, a sinner!" If the tax collector had dared to gaze into the Eternal mirror, he would have been astonished to see the loving face of God gazing back at him. "For all who exalt themselves will be humbled, but all who humble themselves will be exalted."

What do you see when you look into the bathroom mirror each morning? Do you see the image you expect or want to see? Do you perhaps wish to see a younger self, free of cares and wrinkles and puffy eyes? Do you gaze into the mirror carefully, looking over the individual details until the shaving, hair combing and makeup are complete? Would you honestly want to have a magical mirror that always told you the truth? Would you dare look into such a mirror?

Almost 500 years ago, Martin Luther held up the mirror of the Eternal to the pharisaic church practices of his time. Today, many churches remember this man who, without blinking an eye, gazed into God's mirror and changed the course of history. Martin Luther, born in 1483, studied law as a young man. He eventually became a priest and a monk. He was a brilliant teacher, but not very happy. He worried himself sick about how to secure his salvation. In this all-consuming concern, Luther merely reflected the Church of his day, a Church that was often guilty of praying the prayer of the Pharisee in the Temple. Preoccupied with preserving the institution, the Church forgot the simple truth of God's free grace, forgot the generous spirit of Jesus. Instead, it legislated heavy burdens of guilt on the people, burdens that could only be bought off with penance and even money. This greatly frustrated and angered Luther, and so he risked a trip to the mirror of the Eternal God: "Mirror, mirror, of the Most High, who is your grace for?" Searching the Scriptures, Martin Luther encountered the abundant compassion of God. Especially when studying Paul's letter to the Romans, Luther was struck by the free gift of God's grace, a free gift to tax collector and Pharisee alike. Is this the kind of truth we expect to find looking in the bathroom mirror on a Sunday morning, preparing to go to the "one true church"? Luther found it, because his spirit was too restless to leave well enough alone. And once he took hold of God's free gift of righteousness, he could not possibly remain silent about it. Luther spoke up. He took the official Church to task for its pharisaic practices, which encouraged the belief that one could buy one's way into heaven.

After a number of attempts to defend his position with the clerical and secular rulers of his day, Luther finally said: "Unless I can be instructed and convinced otherwise, with evidence from the Holy Scriptures – since I am captive to the Word of God – I cannot and will not recant, because it is neither safe nor wise to act against conscience." And then he added his famous words: "Here I stand. I can do no other. God help me! Amen." With these words Martin Luther was kicked out of the Church, and the Reformation as a

Protestant movement became a historical fact. The mirror of the Eternal God had become the weapon of choice claimed by friend and foe alike in the human quest to prove who's right.

Now, almost 500 years later, as a Christian family, we are in the process of healing our divisions – slowly. Carrying the burden of centuries of strife, we now realize on all sides that the mirror of the Eternal God indeed bestows grace and righteousness in abundance on all who come before that mirror in faith and humility. Now our church leaders are sitting down with courage before this Divine mirror in a spirit of repentance and reconciliation.

Whether it is the sin of division in our Christian tradition, or our own personal sin that we try so hard to hide from, gazing into the mirror of the Eternal requires courage, but most of all it requires the grace of repentance and humility. How willing are we to hear the truth? How willing are we to see God's truth? Our answer is directly proportional to our willingness to admit our own sinfulness. To gaze into the mirror of the Eternal is to look into God's eyes and to see reflected there the truth of who we really are. See that reflection and know it as the only truth that matters. Let us be willing to ask God's forgiveness and be prepared to let God change our image so that it conforms more closely to the image God intended.

We cannot do any of this ourselves. Tithing, like the Pharisee did (although it helps our faith community), or fasting twice a week, or any pious works we may practise cannot, by themselves, bring about conversion. All the talks between our various churches cannot in and of themselves restore our unity in Jesus Christ. Conversion begins deep inside ourselves, as God's love and mercy and grace transform our hearts. Gazing into the mirror of the Eternal, we see our sinfulness, and as we gaze upon our sinfulness, we see God and find our true selves.

This is the truth of repentance and humility. This is the blessing of repentance and humility: that we can stand before the mirror of the Eternal and know the Truth – the truth that sets us free. When we take hold of this Truth, which God's mirror reflects back to us, like the tax collector did, and like Martin Luther did, we will no longer need to stand apart like the Pharisee, afraid to be contaminated by the tax collector's sin. When we take hold of God's free gift of grace through faith, we can once again gather together as churches in common worship. Maybe it is this spirit of repentance and humility in you and me that allows us to share in praise and worship under one roof this morning. Letting God's mirror show us the truth, we know that we are all sinners. We no longer need to take comfort in presumptuous prayer. We will no longer set up barriers between "us" and "them." We will be able to stand among our neighbours, no longer despising them because they are tax collectors or "from that other church," because we now see ourselves in them. Like them, we too are totally dependent upon God's mercy and forgiveness and love. And like them, we are each thankful for God's mercy and forgiveness and love. This is the work of the Almighty: to exalt us in our humble and sinful reality, and to love us there without measure, so that we can turn around and love others without measure. Amen.

CHAPTER 15

The Fullness of Catholicity

Peter felt hurt because Jesus said to him a third time,
"Do you love me?"
And Peter said to him,
"Lord, you know everything;
you know that I love you."
And Jesus said to him,
"Feed my sheep."

(John 21:17)

Despite my best efforts to show good intentions and be sincere, and despite my best efforts to stay firmly connected to the Body of Christ, criticisms about my preaching seemed to come with the territory. At first I got upset when I heard them, which was always indirectly and after some time had passed. My preoccupation with what others thought siphoned energy away from my relationship with God and drained courage from my soul. Realizing that my focus was not in the right place, I went to see a priest for confession and absolution. I told him about fearing human opinion more than God's judgment. With love in his eyes he said: "Welcome to the experience of the clergy." I was not quite sure what he meant. He continued, explaining that all ministry is prey to the scorn of self-appointed critics in the Church. Priestly ministry, and preaching is a part of that, he said, evokes a strange mix of expectations in people. Parishioners all think they know what the priest is supposed to be about, and many expect him to be superhuman. When the priest falls short of these expectations, they are disappointed and sometimes angry. But he said I was not to be discouraged: we are in good company, the company of our Lord Jesus himself, who was grossly misunderstood, even by his own followers, to the point that it cost him his life. My penance was to pray with Jesus' experiences of betrayal, and to open myself up to intimate solidarity with his suffering.

This experience of confession guided and challenged me for a long time. The encounter provided an excellent tool for discerning the authenticity of my faith and my mission: to what degree was I able to graft my personal experience onto Jesus' own ministry, mission, suffering, dying and rising? If my experience could not be connected to the life of Jesus himself, then it was time to step back and seriously review what I was doing and why. Father Leonard's words from several years before echoed in my heart: we have to connect our life experience with the Paschal mystery. Our calling as Christ's disciples is most revealed not in the easy things, but in the ones that bring pain, exclusion and suffering. The challenge becomes to find redeeming qualities in the humiliation and criticism we endure in this life without letting that pain destroy us:

> The pain in my soul made itself known today in gentle, nudging ways, drawing my emotional attention to the quiet but steady stream of inner tears that runs ceaselessly and abundantly through the catacombs of my being. I do not always know when and how the tears make their presence felt, but today I tried to follow the inner course they travel. On the outside this inner attentiveness did not show much other than in a rather melancholy tone and mood this afternoon. This inner "being with" the tears in my soul constitutes my faithful response to God in this time of death and rebirth. Such faithfulness pushes me radically into the here and now – and that is enough, for God is my comfort and strength. (Journal entry)

Having lived for a long time out of one particular spiritual and religious mode made it difficult for me to break open and to accommodate new modes of being and doing. Leaving the old understandings behind was a death experience; often the new life was not even remotely visible yet. Moving into new ways of being Catholic was clouded by a deep sense of loss, the loss of old ways of being. Finally and surprisingly, I now connected personally with the experience of losing old ways that so many Catholics lamented after Vatican II. The mourning siphoned off my energy, even when tiny signs of new life became apparent. Yet the push outwards could not be stopped. I felt compelled to explore where few had gone before, driven by my lifelong desire to take "the road less travelled." Despite the initial criticisms and suspicion from a few, I indeed discovered companions on the journey. One of these was Pope John Paul II himself.

It is comfortable, predictable and secure to remain fully within one's own tradition. If we always look out onto the world through the same window, we always see the same scenery. More and more the pronouncements from Pope John Paul II himself showed a similar commitment towards claiming our common ground as churches and growing relationships of love with non-Catholics. Reading *Lumen gentium* and *Unitatis redintegratio* in the Vatican II documents, the 1993 *Directory for the Application of Principles and Norms on Ecumenism*, and the papal encyclicals *Tertio millenio adveniente* and *Ut unum sint,* I found strong affirmations for what was happening in my own faith experience and ministry:

> The ecumenical movement is a grace of God, given by the Father in answer to the prayer of Jesus and the supplication of the Church inspired by the Holy Spirit. While it is carried out within the general mission of the Church to unite humanity in Christ, its own specific field is the restoration of unity among Christians. Those who are baptized in the name of Christ are, by that very fact, called to commit themselves to the search for unity. Baptismal communion tends towards full ecclesial communion. To live our Baptism is to be caught up in Christ's mission of making all things one.[66]

Working towards Christian unity extended well beyond taking part in ecumenical activities. Mixed in with the sense of loss over old and comfortable "Catholic" ways of being was a significant overhaul of mind and heart. On a given Sunday at Mass I carried in my heart all those whom I had come to know in other churches, who gathered in their churches at that same time, many of them hearing the same Scriptures proclaimed. I included them at the time of intercessions; I prayed for us all, gave thanks for friendships and mutual trust being forged, and asked God's help in continuing to build bridges of love and understanding. Whenever the intercessions addressed prayers for church leaders, in my heart I included all Christian leaders. On Sundays when I preached in other churches, I took nothing for granted. Studying church history made me realize that the trust I enjoyed now was hard won. Every gesture of welcome was pure gift and healing balm from God.

The hardest feelings to deal with were the shame, guilt and hurt over carrying responsibility for the deep rifts in the Body of Christ. I brought these to the altar at the penitential rite at Mass, asking Jesus to carry this heavy load with us, all the while hanging my head in shame over the wounds. Jesus had enough wounds; why did we have to add so many to his already bruised and broken body? I cried in repentance, especially when non-Catholics found the courage to share their woundedness, which was often caused by insensitive treatments at the hands of Catholics. After I had preached in a Lutheran church, an older woman approached me with hands outstretched and tears in her eyes. Grabbing my hand, she shared how she grew up Catholic but was ruthlessly ostracized by her church once she married her Lutheran husband. Seeing and hearing a Catholic in a Lutheran pulpit that day, she felt God's healing fill her heart, and was moved to tears. She had prayed for this kind of dialogue and unity all her life. I have carried her, and countless others like her, in my heart ever since. We owe it to this woman, and to all those who have been hurt by our arrogance and divisions, to commit ourselves to healing. My own commitment to contribute my little bit to the bigger picture became ever stronger:

> Heeding Pope John Paul II's call for repentance, I find my heart filled with contrition and with prayers for forgiveness and mercy over the extent of our denominational strife over the centuries. The rupture in the Church, for which we all bear responsibility, is a slap in the face of Christ himself, who gave his life so that we may be one. How could we have turned things so backwards all this time? (Journal entry)

As I surrendered, in my own local surroundings, to God's call into ecumenical ministry, growing a heart and mind that could accommodate the whole Christian family, I observed with amazement equivalent movements occurring on a global scale. Besides the *Joint Lutheran/Catholic Declaration,* an ecumenical milestone, I watched with awe at the start of the Jubilee Year 2000 the opening of the Holy Door at Rome's Basilica of St.-Paul-Outside-the-Walls: Pope John Paul II accompanied by the Anglican Archbishop George Carey of Canterbury and the Orthodox Metropolitan Athanasios. Then, as if this was not enough, the formal papal apologies followed during Lent of that same Jubilee Year – the confession of sins on behalf of Catholics who contributed throughout history to the divisions among Christians, the rupture in the Body of Christ. I knew, from personal experience and conversion, that each of these steps came at great cost. It is never easy to give up old ways of knowing ourselves, others, God and the world. Pope John Paul II's actions were the fruit of a deep process of conversion that originated in his own heart; out of great humility and integrity, he then invited the entire Church to join him in the process of reconciliation and healing. It takes courage to do this, and deep faith.

> The [Second Vatican] Council calls for personal conversion as well as for communal conversion. The desire of every Christian community goes hand in hand with its fidelity to the Gospel. In the case of individuals who live their Christian vocation, the Council speaks of interior conversion, a renewal of the mind. Each one therefore ought to be more radically converted to the Gospel and, without ever losing sight of God's plan, change his or her way of looking at things. Thanks to ecumenism, our contemplation of "the mighty works of God" has been enriched by new horizons: the knowledge that the Spirit is at work in other Christian Communities, the discovery of examples of holiness, the experience of the immense riches present in the communion of saints, and contact with unexpected dimensions of Christian commitment. In a corresponding way, there is an increased sense of the need for repentance: an awareness of certain exclusions which seriously harm fraternal charity, of certain refusals to forgive, of a certain pride, of an unevangelical insistence on condemning the "other side," of a disdain born of an unhealthy presumption. Thus, the entire life

of Christians is marked by a concern for ecumenism; and they are called to let themselves be shaped, as it were, by that concern.[67]

There was no better source of inspiration and support than our own pope. Strengthened by his example, I continued to walk this ecumenical journey, praying to God to supply only the bread I needed for the day. In the process of change my heart, mind and soul expanded significantly. Without feeling threatened in my own foundations of faith, I made more and more room for others. This is what it means to grow a truly Catholic heart. Jesus called us to be fishers of people, together. We have spent far too much time ripping our fishing nets apart with our arguments, our arrogance and our ignorance. It is time to mend the nets, despite the criticism and misunderstanding from among our own. My yearning for unity and mending is grafted onto the great prayer of Jesus, that we may all be one. As long as I keep my eyes on him, our Lord and Guide, I trust the journey. The importance of contributing to the mending – however small that contribution might seem – in the company of our own church leaders does not escape me. I play a small part in a much bigger picture.

Sermon at the United Church, start of the Week of Prayer for Christian Unity

Isaiah 9:1-4, 1 Corinthians 1:10-18, Matthew 4:12-23

It is a great privilege for me to be here among you today, and to share with you on God's Holy Word. I don't know if my parents realize that this is the result of raising me to be a "good Catholic" – my ending up in the pulpit at the United church! It was hard enough for them to figure out what a good Catholic girl was doing at a Lutheran seminary. My parents may be even more puzzled if they realize that I end up not only in the United church pulpit, but also in the Lutheran one, in the Presbyterian one, and next week, in the Anglican pulpit. Is this the product of becoming a "good Catholic," or is this called "going fishing"? Some fellow parishioners of mine don't quite know what to make of this "strange" practice either: what is she doing, some of them wonder, preaching in those other churches? Is she searching for greener pastures, or is she trying to catch more people in *our* fishing nets?

These are not just my parents' puzzling thoughts. And these are not just my fellow parishioners' sincere concerns and questions. Such suspicious thoughts hide a deeper reality. Such critical questions reveal more than what's on the surface. Today, we start the Week of Prayer for Christian Unity. At the invitation of the Christian churches we examine who we are in Christ – together. Like Peter, Andrew, James and John we follow the One who has made us "fishers of people." How are our nets holding out? As Isaiah calls Jesus the light in the darkness, so have we committed ourselves to be the light of Christ in the world; are we "one light," receiving our energy from the same source, who is the Lord Jesus Christ, or has our Christian light exploded into a million factions like bright fireworks in a darkened sky, soon to lose their brilliance. Do we take Paul's admonitions to the Corinthians to heart, humbly realizing that we are all baptized into the one name of Jesus, or do we let our divisions rule our hearts, like the Corinthians did: I belong to Martin Luther, I belong to Bill Phipps, I belong to Pope John Paul II, I belong to John Wesley, I belong to the universe.

I received a letter this past week from a dear friend who belongs to one of the evangelical churches. She shared with me her joy in believing, her relationship with the Lord, and how her faith is deepening through and despite the struggles of life. My friend admits that she is not quite sure what ecumenical involvement is. But, she adds, that's okay, for she has "no need" for this. After all, she has found Christ in the caring church community around her. These are good things to share, and I rejoice with her. However, I could not help feeling a deep sadness as I read her words alongside today's Scripture lessons.

I am sharing my friend's words with you not so we can pick on the evangelicals. Nor am I here today to extol the virtues of my own tradition, in order to overshadow yours. We all have skeletons in the closet. My friend echoes the feelings of many Christians right across the board: we have "no need" for involvement with those in other churches. We can be quite comfortable where we are, even a little smug at times – who needs sister churches? Or perhaps we have become bitter over time: what's the use of even trying to attain unity among this bunch? One of my own brothers, raised as Catholic as I was, takes one cynical look at Christianity and says: "How do you justify your historical track record of exploitation and oppression of entire cultures, all done in the name of Jesus? How can you explain your in-house quarrelling, and even killing, in places like Northern Ireland, the former Yugoslavia, and now Russia? And you expect me to give my life for this and go fishing for people?" Then there are those who adopt a laissez-faire attitude to justify their exodus from organized religion: to each their own, it is just different, and that's all okay, let's all be happy.

Smoothing over real divisions in these ways makes for cheap and false unity. That is certainly not the kind that Paul supports. Neither of these positions strengthens anybody's fishing nets. Jesus' fishing nets are the promises of God. Today these nets are full of big holes, poked and ripped as they are by centuries of bickering over the very things that Jesus gave us precisely to unite us: his life, his body and his blood, his mission to carry the Good News of God's unending love to the ends of the earth.

It is a good thing that none of this evangelizing the world stuff depends on our human efforts alone. It is a good thing that, despite ourselves, God is in charge, and God is the ever faithful One. Despite ourselves, and despite our tattered fishing nets, Jesus still calls out to us: "Follow me, and I will make you fishers of people." It is not too late to be God's united light to the world. On the eve of the Third Millennium, we are still called to God through the person of Jesus the Christ. We have little choice – we need to stand together and learn to love one another as fellow human beings, as sisters and brothers in Christ. How can we proclaim a unifying Christ to a hurting world when our own house stands so divided, ready to collapse?

Slowly, oh so slowly, we are learning – we give thanks for God's patience and endurance in this matter. My years as a Roman Catholic student at a Lutheran seminary taught me a few things about how to stand together in our diversity. Strong in my Catholic faith, I was eager to explore the holy things of God. But, when it came to dialoguing with Christians from other traditions I was rather wet behind the ears. This changed rapidly as I sat in class not only with Lutherans and a handful of fellow Catholics, but also with Anglican, United Church, Pentecostal and Mennonite students. Together we cast our nets into the legacy of our Christian tradition. As we struggled with theological, historical, spiritual and ecclesial questions, some very interesting things were revealed to us all. One, we each brought to the discussion table the church stuff we grew up with: the beliefs that meant the most to us, and to which we clung most stubbornly, sometimes at the expense of another's position. Two, overemphasizing our own views in a patronizing way risked deforming the Gospel and undermining our sister or brother from another tradition. This lack of humility and this inability to listen with an open heart thus produced disrespect, judgment and disharmony. Three, the only way the Gospel remained intact is if we held all perspectives, with all their tensions and seeming contradictions, in full view. Four, it is only by humbly submitting ourselves to the scrutiny of the other that Jesus is revealed in our midst, calling us all to follow him and be fishers of people, each in the tradition we know best.

And so, even if my parents always considered me to be a "good Catholic," I am becoming a better Catholic by immersing myself in the ecumenical world. While some worry that I am searching for greener pastures, my world is becoming more "catholic" in the true sense of "universal," as I enter into relationships with members of sister churches. I am discovering a foundational unity in Christ, not a unity as in sameness, but one that enhances our unique gifts in such a way that we can shine together as a light in the world's darkness. I would not have discovered the breadth and depth of Christ's unity had I stayed comfortably within my own tradition.

You can see only so far if you always look out of the same window. The discovery of the richness of ecumenical life in Christ fills me with sadness for my evangelical friend, who feels so comfortably Christian within her own church family. It is at times like this, when you, as a United Church congregation, entrust to me, a Roman Catholic, the preaching ministry in your own sanctuary that I ache for my brother and all the cynics out there who have discarded the Christian baby with the tainted bathwater, and I want to say: see, we are trying to mend our tattered nets. My heart goes out to those who have found only cold darkness in our churches and have truly left for greener pastures, roaming the religious market with restless hearts.

Claiming our unity in Christ does not lead us to abandon our own tradition. Quite the opposite – claiming our baptismal unity in Christ calls for a deep embracing of all that is good and life-giving in our own tradition first. We cannot share with others what we do not first experience, claim, cherish and love.

We claim our particular tradition not as a weapon for hitting others, but as the gift we bring to the ecumenical table of the Lord. Secure in who we are in Christ through our belonging to one tradition, we will then, and only then, be free to find unity with our sisters and brothers everywhere. It is not easy, and it is not without pain – there is a lot of hurt to overcome, a lot of misunderstandings to clear up.

But, moving into the new millennium, we have little choice left but to mend our fishing nets and tie them together. Jesus himself will be our light, Jesus himself will be our glory, and in Jesus lies the hope for all the churches, and yes, for all of creation. Amen.

CHAPTER 16

Take and Eat

"This is my body that is for you.
Do this in remembrance of me."
In the same way he took the cup also,
after supper, saying,
"This cup is the new covenant in my blood.
Do this, as often as you drink,
in remembrance of me."
(1 Corinthians 11:24, 25)

In the years before my ecumenical ministry began, I took Mass for granted in a sense. Seeing the Eucharist as the sacrament of unity did not mean a lot to me. To be honest, I cared little about different church practices of Eucharist, Holy Communion or the Lord's Supper. I had no personal experience of "fenced" tables[68] (closed communion tables), and the pain that such prohibitions can create. Over the past ten years this changed considerably. Learning to live with eucharistic divisions has been a rocky road. Accepting that the Christian family does not share the eucharistic table became a hard and painful experience, for both personal and communal reasons. I confess I do not always understand or respect this situation. At times I jumped the fence and "danced on the wall," just like those who danced on the Berlin Wall in 1989 before this 30-year-old divide came tumbling down. Dancing on the wall offers an experience of what life could be like if the wall was not there. In other words, I have on occasion received Eucharist in another church – not frequently, yet without special permission. Whether these were promptings of the Spirit or merely desperate attempts to soothe the pain for myself remains a matter for discernment.

I know the theological and ecumenical arguments about sharing or not sharing Eucharist. Some appeal to different understandings of the Eucharist; others have to do with the theology and history of ordination and ministry. Whether shared Eucharist is the means to unity or the ultimate fruit of organic unity, my ecumenical formation and my resulting preaching ministry forced me to walk through this issue in a deeply personal way.

As a student I was a member of the seminary faith community. I knew the people well. We shared many things, including food, tears and laughter. I was there on my own account, immersing myself in the liturgical life of the student body. I received communion at the Lutheran table during those years, for in a sense I belonged at that table. The Lutheran communion table invited me to partake while my own church officially prevented me from accepting the Lutheran invitation. Yet, my conscience told me that I could not refuse to take and eat, to take and drink Christ's body and blood with my brothers and sisters. If I did, I betrayed the fellowship and love we shared as students, a love that made Christ's spirit evident among us. I partook in good faith, hoping and praying that my eucharistic participation would not attract public attention. Now going back for visits, the bond I once shared with fellow students is gone, since all have moved on. I no longer belong to that faith community, and I no longer "need" to receive communion at their table. I have moved into more formal ways of being present at the seminary (such as being the Catholic guest preacher), and I have developed a certain appreciation and understanding for observing the eucharistic boundaries that are presently in place.

When preaching in another church I participate in Mass that same weekend. I do this for two basic reasons. First, I truly cherish our Catholic eucharistic celebration. Over the years I attended services of Holy Communion and Holy Eucharist in Lutheran and Anglican churches. Good as these are, I invariably missed the Catholic Mass. I love the familiarity of ritual actions, and cherish the expression of meaning through song, gestures and prayers. I experience there a fullness of celebration that I have not found in another tradition. The Catholic Mass remains for me the fullest expression of Jesus' gift of self in the world.

Participating in Mass on those Sundays when I preached in another church kept me firmly connected to my own church. Preaching was a rather formal, public task, and I ended up representing my own tradition in the inviting church. Developing a sensitivity to public image and appropriate behaviour became important: ecumenical ministry was not about attending someone else's church service *instead* of my own. I used my Catholic identity deliberately in ecumenical circles. Compromising my Catholic practice could easily water down my ecumenical ministry. I could not represent that which I did not practise. I was not interested in jeopardizing my Catholic belonging or my public image. My denominational belonging played a key role in my Christian identity and my ecumenical involvements, much like a savoury spice that is added to the stew.

With a few exceptions, I did most of my preaching when the local pastor was away, and therefore in the absence of communion. Usually, a lay member of the congregation presided and I proclaimed the Gospel and preached the sermon. But one time things were different. I was invited to preach at the Anglican church as part of the Week of Prayer for Christian Unity. Not only was the regular parish priest there, but full Eucharist was being celebrated. Preparing in the sacristy, Ron, the Anglican priest, made it very clear that I was invited to the eucharistic table. I thought for a moment, and declined, asking if I could come up for a blessing instead. I did not decline because I had just received communion at an early Mass, which I had. I did not decline because I did not personally wish to receive communion in the Anglican Church. Rather, I was acutely aware of the public character of my presence. It felt important to abide by the regulations of my church, which prohibited me from receiving the Eucharist in another church. Deciding to respect these rules for Christian unity felt in keeping with my decision to attend Mass on the weekends I preached elsewhere. In my heart I lived a new reality of eucharistic communion. But in my head I knew that pushing or pretending unity would not contribute to the cause – it would simply betray an agenda of my own. Ecumenical ministry is deeply personal, but it is not private. This was God's church, and any steps towards Christian unity, including my preaching, were the work of the Holy Spirit. In the grand scheme of things, I was merely one servant among many.

Even though the decision to refrain from receiving communion at this Anglican Eucharist felt right, I was nevertheless apprehensive. I feared feeling a real sense of exclusion, and prepared to experience the pain of church divisions. Instead, God blessed me with quite another revelation:

> With trepidation I walked forward, into the sanctuary, and knelt at the communion rail with everyone else. I knew I would not receive, and Ron knew not to offer. Instead, I received God's blessing by the sign of the cross Ron traced on my forehead. To my surprise, I felt a powerful and paradoxical unity not only with all Christians but also with all church structures; this was where we were at humanly speaking. Instead of receiving Christ's body and blood in the bread and wine, I received a deep peace, which glowed through my whole being. Instead of feeling angry or upset that my tradition prevents me from full communion with the Anglicans, my mind's eye received clarity of thought, insight into the bigger ecumenical call, and an increased love for the Church. (Journal entry)

This was not the first time God had surprised me. Just when I thought I knew what the experience would be, God provided just the opposite, showing that every aspect of the ecumenical journey, including the times of tangible divisions, are nevertheless held by God's love in such gentle ways. I marvelled aloud to Ron later about the ecumenical opportunities for preaching that I enjoyed. His reply was matter-of-fact, yet most revealing: "It makes sense. You are the only one in this area who has our [theological, pastoral, liturgical] training and you are not responsible for a parish, so you are free to accept the invitations." These words revealed God's plan a bit more: a plan that could not unfold this way if I insisted on ordination to legitimate my call and if I felt obstructed by church regulations prohibiting women to be ordained. It was all so unusual, and so unprecedented, that it was hard not to employ existing interpretations. The opportunities for preaching came in most surprising ways. In order to let God use these opportunities, I needed to surrender completely any preconceived notion that I knew what this was all about. I continued to feel like Peter, with someone putting a belt around me, taking me where I did not expect to go (John 21:18).

Sermon at St. Paul's Anglican Church

Micah 6:1-8, 1 Corinthians 1:18-31, Matthew 5:1-12

I am greatly honoured by your invitation to break open God's holy Word in your midst. These invitations come to me from time to time. They arouse a certain amount of awe, surprise and fear; not the fear that paralyzes me, but rather a healthy fear of the Lord. I am not worthy of this task – never will be. I consider your call to preach a sacred trust, a trust that pushes you and me deeper into prayerful surrender to the One who has called us to be one people in Christ Jesus.

Sharing your Sunday worship is a powerful way to close off a very special week in our community. This little blip in the universe, seemingly unimportant has come alive a bit more with God's love.

A special week it was, this Week of Prayer for Christian Unity. I have been in more different churches that I normally am, and maybe some of you have too. We enjoyed fabulous lunches – we fed one another's bodies. We heard the Good News preached in every church, and we fed one another's soul. We shared laughter and made new friends with people we do not ordinarily meet. We shared our stories and learned to make room for one another. I think here in particular of Pastor Bill, who shared about the significant shifts taking place in his church, the Worldwide Church of God.

In the eyes of the world, our gatherings this week hold little meaning. They could be considered almost a waste of precious time. There were no VIPs present, except for our special guest, Janet Somerville, the General Secretary of the Canadian Council of Churches. She turned out to be a rather quiet, pleasant and humble woman, who came more to listen than to deliver a polished speech. There were no heavy financial deals to be negotiated, no big contracts to be signed. In the eyes of the world, this week's gatherings probably looked like utter foolishness, meant for people who have nothing else to do.

Paul's words to the Corinthians today could just as well have been written for us:

> Consider your own call, Christians of the Battlefords. Not many of you are wise by human standards, not many of you are powerful in the world's eyes. Not many of you are of noble birth. But God chose what is foolish in the world to shame the wise, chose what is weak in the world to shame the strong.

In the simplicity of our prayer and sharing times, in the nothingness of our gatherings, Jesus stood among us and said: "Blessed are you who seek healing and unity, for the kingdom of God shall be yours." For one week, we took down our church walls. For one week, we opened our hearts and risked entering one another's lives and, yes, risked entering one another's experience of God. For one week, we gathered in the name of the one Lord who gave his life so we might be one people united through one faith and one baptism. Experiencing such a week as the blessing of God's own reign, we cannot help but take off our shoes, for we stand on holy ground in one another's churches.

In Matthew's account of the Sermon on the Mount, Jesus is not just giving us his version of *Chicken Soup for the Soul*. When the Son of God declares blessed all those who have nothing, and who are nothing, we get a glimpse of the very nature of God, and of the place where all of humanity can find fullness of life.

St. Francis of Assisi found that place. After injury in battle had exploded all self-glorifying dreams, and a long illness had taken away the complacency of a rich man's life, it was especially the poor whom Francis started to see with new eyes. Before his conversion, Francis thought poverty to be the curse of the earth, a fearful mistake in creation. But as Francis embraced the richness of poverty, of nothingness, he tasted God's blessings in ways that had been inaccessible to him before. A shift of enormous proportions took place in Francis' experience and understanding of God. And he came to see that the curse of creation is not in poverty, but in wealth. The curse of creation is not in nothingness and littleness, but in power and possessions, in all those things that harden and poison the human heart. As a result, Francis deliberately embraced poverty as his vocation in life, and found in this radical move the blessings of God that set him free. "Blessed are the poor in spirit, for theirs is the kingdom of heaven." Places of poverty, places of meekness and mercy – that is where God prefers to hang out. Places of peacemaking and mourning are the places where God finds the most room to enter our lives and shower us with blessing, holy blessing. Even this week there were many places where ordinary, powerless women and men cried their eyes out for sheer pain and suffering: the thousands and thousands of people in Colombia, robbed of their homes because of the earthquake; the parents in the local hospital whose child was diagnosed with leukemia; the teenager in jail, who knew he had gotten himself into real trouble; the gas spill in Taylor, British Columbia, which saw a town being evacuated. Yes, while we gathered to pray in one another's churches, there were also lots of hot, salty tears of pain this week.

Jesus is not suggesting that poverty and suffering are justified. No, Jesus merely points out that it is in the times of poverty and suffering in our lives that our hearts are most open to receive God's loving mercy and grace. That is what being blessed is all about: opening ourselves wide and falling into God's loving arms with all the tears and pain that cut through our lives. "Blessed are they who mourn, for they will be comforted."

Living in this state of God's blessing causes a heart to grow in patience, compassion and mercy. Belonging to the community of Jesus this way makes those around us get caught up in God's glow by the love and service that radiates from us from the inside out. We don't always have to make radical choices like St. Francis did to live poor in spirit. Thousands of parents, ordinary people, patiently, and often at great expense, help their children through numerous days of skinned knees, birthday parties, rebellion and broken hearts. Men and women who continue cherishing and caring for their spouse who has Alzheimer's or terminal cancer display both poverty in spirit and God's abundant blessing. These are ordinary places of blessedness. But sometimes, living in Jesus' footsteps calls for extraordinary steps, just as St. Francis took.

Take Pierre Andrian, for example. Pierre is a bright young fellow from France who moved to Montreal only a few years ago. He was led to Canada because of his love for a woman, but that did not work out. Instead, Pierre ended up volunteering in one of Montreal's busiest soup kitchens, called Accueuil Bonneau – the one that burned down a year ago. Pierre got to know the guys who came in off the streets. He saw that they had nothing, absolutely nothing, to live for. He saw them spend their days drinking away government handouts. This is not the kind of poverty sanctioned by the Beatitudes of Jesus. An accomplished musician who studied at French conservatories, Pierre got a foolish dream – nothing of any value in the world's eyes. But remember: God chooses what is foolish in the world to shame the wise. God uses what is low and despised in the world to confound the rich and powerful. Pierre, our young Frenchman, invited the men off the street to form a choir. Only three men showed up for the first practice. Pierre persevered, showing the men respect and friendship, and eventually more came. Was this hard? Yes, especially for the men. Did they feel awkward? Yes, for the singing required them to be sober. Did they lose confidence? Yes, for they had so little to begin with. Now, 21 men between the ages of 19 and 65, formerly homeless and jobless, have rediscovered joy, belonging, dignity and respect, experiencing first-hand God's blessing of their poverty, which is much more than material poverty. Their first concert occurred some two years ago, to the noise of the trains in a Montreal subway station. That first concert raised $1300. Their songs speak of the harshness of life on the streets, about the lonely existence of the vagabond, and about the solidarity among those who share the streets. The men have exchanged their old rags for choir uniforms of clean white shirts and black pants.

Almost all the men agree that the choir has had a more therapeutic effect on them than years of counselling or staying in shelters could achieve. The choir has now made two CDs, has performed over 400 concerts, and was flown to Paris recently to encourage a similar initiative there. All this started with one man who had a foolish dream and pursued it. This dream demanded all the trust, courage and hope he could muster, demanded a true spirit of poverty and mercy. The men of Accueuil Bonneau have a new reason to live because someone looked beyond their tattered clothes and the smell of alcohol, and saw God's blessedness hidden in their scarred spirits. "Blessed are they who hunger and thirst for righteousness, for they will be satisfied."

Jesus calls us blessed in our purity of heart, in our moments of mourning and meekness, in our hunger and thirst for justice and peace. When we gather to express our yearning for Christian unity among the churches, Jesus is with us, calling us blessed. When we pray for patience and compassion in our weary hearts as we deal with challenges that often feel too heavy, Jesus is with us, calling us blessed. When we embrace voluntary poverty as a lifestyle for the sake of the Gospel, as St. Francis did, Jesus clothes us with God's holy blessing. When we look really hard to find the beauty of the human spirit in those who are rejected and forgotten, as Pierre Andrian did, Jesus declares our lives blessed.

And so it is that what is foolish and weak becomes God's own holy dwelling place. What are only little blips in the universe, like our community of the Battlefords, become radiant lights, shining with Jesus' mercy and love. It is the only hope the world has, even if in its foolishness it often turns away from that which it despises, and ignores that which holds so little significance. Maybe the upside-down view of God is right side up. "Blessed are the peacemakers, for they will be called children of God." Amen.

Without a deep faith in and appreciation of the centrality of Eucharist, I could not sustain the motivation to keep working towards Christian unity. Two experiences, both within the same week, revealed the necessity for this eucharistic orientation towards ecumenical ministry. First, I attended a unique interchurch Sunday worship service. Two faith communities, a Roman Catholic parish and a United Church congregation, celebrated their covenant agreement. The Catholic church was packed to the rafters with members from both faith communities. In order to host this unique celebration, the parish cancelled one of its three Sunday Masses. This decision, which was made by the parish priest, upset a few parishioners. But the parish priest was firm, citing Jesus' own words to illustrate that putting aside Eucharist in order to be reconciled to fellow Christians is as much God's work as is celebrating Mass: "So when you are offering your gift at the altar, if you remember that your brother or sister has something against you, leave your gift there before the altar and go; first be reconciled to your brother or sister, and then come and offer your gift" (Matthew 5:23). Refraining from Eucharist for the purpose of reconciliation reinforced the centrality of the Eucharist as strongly as celebrating Mass itself did. The message was clear. We are not taking our divisions lightly, and we are not rushing to the table before clearing the air. The Eucharist is too important to be treated in a trivial manner.

A few days after participating in this joyous celebration, I met with a dear Mennonite friend who worked as an assistant pastor. She was obviously preoccupied and was hesitant to tell me about it. She and the senior pastor had celebrated Holy Communion in their Mennonite congregation the Sunday before, something that Mennonites do only a couple of times a year. Their normal procedure consists of passing the bread and wine while everyone remains seated in the pews. But this time the congregation was invited to come forward to receive Communion, making for a very different experience. My friend was embarrassed to tell me that many criticized the change as "too Catholic" and "a stampede," and a few other not-so-nice terms. It was obvious this rather small change touched a nerve in the members of the congregation. My friend, who had come to deeply love the Eucharist and the Catholic celebration of it, felt hurt on my behalf and on behalf of all Catholics.

Both stories reveal the same truth: Eucharist is central to our faith in Jesus Christ our Lord. It is vital that we take personal and ecclesial responsibility to clear up the divisions that keep us apart at the table, a table prepared by the Lord himself in the offering of his body and blood. My experience tells me that it is in the process of forging relationships of love and fellowship, of entering into a covenant with one another, as individuals and as congregations, that our desire to share one table increases. I have experienced this process many times, most poignantly in personal friendships.

Bruce and I were fellow students at the Lutheran seminary. We shared often, and deeply, about our faith and about our traditions' understandings and practices. We attended the same classes, shared laughter, food, and heavy discussions, and socialized with each other's family. More than once we saw one another's tears, struggling as we each did to make sense of God's foolish act of calling us to ministry. We grew in our friendship, allowing the other to touch God in the core of our self-identity. Lutheran and Catholic, we experienced unity in our God-given diversity.

Several years after I graduated, I attended Bruce's installation as pastor in the first parish to which he was called. I was deeply moved throughout the worship service, a service that included the celebration of Eucharist with Bruce as presider. The experience of pain over the eucharistic division between our traditions burned a hole in my heart. I was torn to pieces: my church did not allow me to receive, yet not receiving Christ's body and blood from the hands of my dear friend, ordained and just installed, felt like betraying an entire relationship of trust and faith, a relationship that had been deeply affected by the presence of Jesus in our hearts. My church told me to regard Bruce's ordination as invalid and not in keeping with the apostolic succession; yet my heart knew Bruce to be ordained in the sight of God and with the blessing of his church authorities. The only church teaching offering me some comfort and reassurance in this particular situation was that the freedom of conscience is to be respected at all times: "Man has the right to act in conscience and in freedom so as personally to make moral decisions. 'He must not be forced to act contrary to his conscience. Nor must he be prevented from acting according to his conscience, especially in religious matters.'"[69]

Ultimately, it is not our place, as individuals or as a church, to judge the decisions of another, especially those decisions that emerge from a commitment to sincere, faith-filled and courageous soul-searching. Even then, sometimes it is hard to know what motivates us. How do we know whether a certain decision is the prompting of the Holy Spirit, a public statement of disagreement with the status quo, or simply a desperate attempt to soothe our own pain?

In a mist of tears I knelt at the communion rail and received Christ's body and blood from my friend, the new Lutheran pastor. Lord, O Lord, have mercy on us all.

PART V

Called to Preach

Women's Collective Pain

She visits me sometimes
no, rather she
butts in uninvited
bursts open
the door of my
soul
creating havoc
with her strident
penetrating look
spilling hot red
blood all over my
papers and books
my pots and pans
all over the
Bread and Wine…
burning fire in
her belly
in my belly
roaring and thundering
anger of the ages
tainting red all
that I touch…

Other times
her broken spirit
knocks shyly
on the window of
my existence
aching for a home
in the eyes of my
soul
once she locks me
into her gaze
centuries of pain
centuries of silence
throw her in
violent labour
lamenting, piercing
screams for mercy
awakening me
ruthlessly
crucifying
contractions, birthing
tears of many
of so many

CHAPTER 17

Blessed Pain

*As he came near and saw
the city, he wept over it, saying,
"If you, even you, had only
recognized on this day the things
that make for peace."*
(Luke 19:41-42)

For young children, pain, and dealing with pain, is very concrete. Countless times one of my children came into the house crying because he or she was hurt. A hug, a kiss, an acknowledgement of the hurt, and soon my son or daughter was off playing again. For a child with a terminal illness, pain is immediate and clear. Children live in the here and now, without much baggage from the past or much worry about the future. Somewhere in the course of living, however, we lose this capacity to be so fully present to today. For many adults pain, especially emotional pain, involves much more than what happens on any given day. Somewhere in the process of growing up things get very muddled.

It is difficult for outsiders to see how much pain we carry on the inside of our lives. It is even more difficult for us to deal with our own pain if we do not acknowledge its presence. For a time I honestly believed there was no pain in my life, as if God had forgotten to give me a cross to bear. I discovered the hard way that this was not the case.

Not long ago I had a sudden muscle spasm in my lower back. There was no need to guess whether I was hurting or not; everyone saw that I was unable to move and heard my moaning. I thanked God for a son who is over six feet tall and solidly built, so that I could put my arms around his neck and drag myself around without causing him discomfort. Friends helped me to the hospital, where a doctor prescribed muscle relaxants and sent me home. The kids ran errands, and others brought food. All the while I was visibly and audibly in pain, not knowing which way to sit, stand or lie down without hurting. For several days the busyness of life simply stopped dead out of sheer necessity, and everything I hoped to accomplish was put on hold. Those around me were helpful, understanding and patient. Without much questioning they moved into caring mode, and all I had to do was to receive graciously: something, I found out, that is infinitely harder for me than giving.

Unlike my muscle spasm, my inner pain was much more difficult to diagnose and to validate. Inner emotional and spiritual pain is highly subjective, especially pain supposedly caused by deeply loved and cherished religious institutions. Coming to terms with this type of pain continues to be rather complicated for me. The pain felt by legions of faith-filled women in the Catholic Church is distrusted at the best of times, and sometimes least validated by women like myself:

> I cannot get worked up about these women who complain that the Church has no room for them. I have always felt at home in the Church, and have found places in the Church to be of service. Not willing to take political and militant positions on issues like women's ordination, I avoid those who argue such cases. I question what motivates them. If God truly wishes for women to take on more leadership in the Church, I am sure he will find a way to make this known to the powers that be. Meanwhile, as a woman I serve gladly, recognizing that at least all the informal leadership in parishes belongs to women anyway. (Journal entry before seminary)

I took courses on counselling women, feminist therapy, women and Christianity, and women's spirituality. In spite of insights gained through these courses, I retained a critical stance towards things feminist. Some textbooks were filled with as many biases as the very patriarchal systems they took to task, only in reverse. I was annoyed that for the most part Christianity was portrayed in such courses as negative and oppressive to women. There was no room in feminist-oriented courses to legitimate my experience of liberation and emancipation through the Gospel of Jesus. I managed to keep a comfortable distance from the pain that so many women in the Church articulated, and I quietly doubted its validity. Like Thomas who doubted the risen Jesus, I could not believe unless I felt the pain in my own bones. Never again will I make such a statement in front of the risen Christ who appears with the wounds of the cross.

It was not the volume of feminist discourse at the seminary that created the pain. There was, in fact, very little of this. It was not because other women told me of their pain with church structures that I copied them. In fact, I quietly thanked God that I did not share their agony. Rather innocently and trustingly, and with deep love and desire, I opened myself wide to the learning and studying of the holy things of God and the Church: theology, liturgy, history, spirituality, sacraments, pastoral care. The learning helped me grow in my womanhood, and set ablaze a love and passion so great that the desire to serve in a leadership ministry grew and grew. In some ways I felt seduced, as if God had beckoned me under false pretense, for I soon joined the company of countless other women in history who experienced that same beckoning and could not respond fully within the existing church structures. I did not expect this to happen, nor was I aware that such a certain pool of collective pain existed. Pope John Paul II acknowledged the reality of collective pain incurred by sin in the course of history, as shown by his March 2000 prayers of forgiveness and reconciliation. I inadvertently tapped into the collective pain by growing deeper in the desire to respond to God's call to preach and by feeling the need to have this call affirmed, clothed and mandated by church authorities – a mandate that did not exist in my tradition without full ordination. The emerging pain had to do with the faith community dimension of ministry, and with the reality of the communion of saints, with whom, as our church teaches, we remain connected across time. For among those saints were the legions of nameless women who spent their entire lives in painful invisibility yet in deep faithfulness to what they came to know as true and good.

[Because of this invisibility] women were denied knowledge of their history, and thus each woman had to argue as though no woman before her had ever thought or written. Women had to use their energy to reinvent the wheel, over and over again, generation after generation. Men argued with the giants that preceded them; women argued against the oppressive weight of millennia of patriarchal thought, which denied them authority, even humanity, and when they had to argue they argued with the "great men" of the past, deprived of the empowerment, strength and knowledge women of the past could have offered them.[70]

I argued intensely with the pain. As Elizabeth Kübler-Ross describes in her writings, there are various stages that people go through in times of grief and loss. In my case, I tried to run, to ignore, to distrust, to avoid, to bargain, to fight, to rationalize, to judge what was solidly lodging itself in my very being. No matter what I tried, the pain remained, as if someone had left a wildcat on my doorstep, which jumped into my house and was bound to live there. Whether I liked it or not, the best thing to do was to enter into a relationship with the pain, accepting that it was there to stay:

I cannot stand the wildcat circling my legs any longer! She roams around my life, wreaking havoc with every sense of meaning and love on which I have built my primary relationships, my marriage and my church. She ambushes me at the most inopportune times, drawing the tears from the underground streams of my soul onto my face, soaking every move with my baptismal calling, and blinding every bit of vision and hope I try to hang onto. On my better days I like to think that we have tamed one another somewhat, or entertain the hope that maybe she has left me, or wonder if she got lost and cannot find me anymore – until I feel once again the pain of being nailed to the church door. I don't want the pain. Take the wildcat away. I don't have the strength, the courage or the energy to handle her any longer. I wish things were just the way they used to be. I should never have fed that wild desire to study the holy elements of my faith. (Journal entry)

While still studying, especially that last year, the pain over my call's ecclesial invisibility ambushed me at regular intervals, finding me in tears over "nothing at all." When the tears did not flow on my cheeks, they flooded the inner tributaries of my soul, making me fear that God's call to preach was about to drown and take its place with all the other unclaimed gifts of women. I did not know what to do except to surrender once again, and to connect the pain and the tears to Jesus himself. Staying close to Jesus, especially on days when I felt overwhelmed, gave me the rope I needed to hold onto to keep my head above the salty water. Even if I had trouble accepting and validating this painful turmoil, I knew that Jesus took note and held my soaked face and soul in his loving hands.

Again, my fundamental relational and extrovert orientation became my greatest obstacle. Even though I wanted so badly, I was completely at a loss for how to share with someone the depth of this journey to the cross of suffering. I kicked and screamed in solitude, for as with the preaching call itself, this experience of pain reinforced the notion that I was utterly alone, with only Jesus to turn to. In prayer and discernment, however, it became clear that absorbing this pain to its fullness was a necessary part of embracing my self-identity as a Christian woman in the Catholic Church. Embracing the pain as gift joined me to the communion of saints, especially women, in past, present and future. Ultimately the process of mingling my loving passion for church ministry with the passion of Christ on the cross would bear fruit in compassion and resurrection living. Did not Christ himself absorb all the pain and suffering of humanity as he hung on the cross? Why was I surprised to find myself on the road to Calvary?

> Jesus said to them: "Are you able to drink the cup that I drink, or be baptized with the baptism that I am baptized with?" They replied, "We are able." Then Jesus said to them: "The cup that I drink you will drink; and with the baptism with which I am baptized, you will be baptized." (Mark 10:38)

Every time our faith becomes incarnate in the fullest sense of that word, we who claim to be true believers are caught off guard. When our Christian involvement becomes too hot to handle, we tend, with Peter, to flee and deny rather than bear the tension and pain of the Lord's suffering and death within the events of our life. Later on I learned that one of the principles of humility as written by St. Benedict in the fifth century reads: endure the journey and do not grow weary. Well, I was on the journey, all right. There was no map. There was no blueprint. There was no instruction manual. Though many have gone before us, passing through the dark night of the soul, as St. John of the Cross called it, the journey feels new and threatening and all-consuming each time. I dragged my feet as much as Jeremiah did, as much as anyone does who resists giving up control. Slowly but surely, I learned that staying close to Jesus protected me from bitterness and anger, and from being destroyed by the pain altogether. In time, I learned to speak the pain in prayer, in my journal, to others, and even in my sermons and homiletic reflections. The collective pain of women throughout Christian history became my teacher and unchosen companion, guiding me into the mystery of Christ's suffering. The distinctive features of my personal pain were that a formal discernment process of the call I experienced was inaccessible to me, that the Church was indifferent to whether I had anything to offer (other than my volunteer labour in the parish), that the faith community continued to call me forth in spite of the lack of institutional mandate, and that I was limited in how I could respond to the community's call. In my attempts to meet others who had had similar experiences, I found some unexpected companions on this painful road, some of whom want nothing less than full ordination.

I spoke with several women religious who, because of a shortage of priests, "pastored" parishes in remote areas. Their stories echoed the same sort of deep pain I experienced. Under current regulations, for example, lay people in such positions are prohibited from offering the sacrament of anointing to dying parishioners. Finding a priest was often impossible; in any case, the sick person and his or her family regarded "Sister" as the pastor. Yet she could not formally fulfill the priestly sacramental function required for anointing. This dilemma caused immense pain, for the pastoral need was great. Another sister shared about similar pain when it came to sacramental confession. People in the community she served developed a pastoral relationship with her. At times when someone desired to return to God in sacramental confession, Sister, their "pastor," was forced to decline as she did not have a sacramental mandate. Refusing the sacramental function because one is prohibited by the church structures from exercising it is one thing. Being approached by the community for precisely this role caused excruciating pain. One sister wondered out loud if parish-based pastoral work was becoming too painful for her, because she could do nothing to still the sacramental hunger. Here in Western Canada, especially in rural areas, Catholics are receiving the sacraments less and less – in part because the rule over who can be ordained takes precedence over the baptismal right of Catholics: the right to the sacraments.

While solutions to this sacramental crisis are not clear, those of us who find ourselves in these dilemmas are called to great courage, wisdom and patience alongside those who give themselves to political lobbying, activism and public criticism. Consistent with my tendency to be involved with people rather than political issues as ends in themselves, I prefer to stay close to the work in the pastoral trenches, however frustrating and painful its institutional limitations can be. Activism divorced from spiritual grounding cannot bear good fruit, even in the Church. Carol Lee Flinders examines at length the reconciliation necessary, for example, between spirituality and feminism. In her book *At the Root of This Longing*, she writes:

> Feminism catches fire when it draws upon its inherent spirituality. When it does not, it is just one more form of politics, and politics has never fed our deepest hungers. What a Gandhi knew, a Mother Teresa, a Dorothy Day, is that when individuals are drawn to a selfless cause energy and creativity come into play that simply do not under any other circumstances.[71]

While working on the margins of new experiences in the Church I trod with courage and care. More than anything I needed to foster my spiritual connection with God. When the pain overwhelmed me, I resorted to prayer with all the energy I could find, pouring my tears into God's own heart. Even in times of great pain there remained the call to fullness of life. Strange as it may sound, there was a richness to living pain in its fullness as part of my calling. The tension thus created was never easy to live, but the call to live the tension was as real as the pain invading my peace of mind:

The intensity of the day is still with me. The rawness and the pain were not new, but their depth reminded me forcefully of their unrelenting presence. Today also served as a reminder of much integration yet to be done.... I am still so out of sorts, with tears flowing constantly on the inside, as if they will never stop. As well, tears flow quickly on the outside and I feel like moaning and groaning. I have little success in focusing, even at work. The pain of having to keep so private what is meant to be so public is unbearable. The pain of being forced to keep to myself that which is given precisely to be poured out in the community of faith is tearing me to shreds. Resolution and peace will only return once I drag myself into the intimate encounter with God. (Journal entry)

I learned how not to become a victim of pain or of my position in the Church. I learned to use pain to grow in solidarity with others who feel invisible, marginalized and silenced in the Church. I learned to ask God to transform pain, and to ask without reserve. The One who specializes in transforming pain, and even death itself, would hold my tears as well, if only I surrendered them radically. This surrender was extremely difficult when anger, bitterness, judgment and resentment risked poisoning my thinking and my feeling.

Homiletic Reflection on Ascension Sunday

Acts 1:1-11, Ephesians 1:17-23, Matthew 28:16-20

I remember the school trips I went on when my children were in elementary school. One of those trips took us to the International Children's Festival. My memory contains flashes of mobs and mobs of children, colourful artistic events, and lots of music and dance. Yes, there were lots of happy noises out there in the park along the river. But there is one memory that clashes with the others: as I was standing in line with some of the kids to get popcorn or drinks, I suddenly heard a shrieking sound. I turned around and saw a boy of maybe four or five pointing upwards, with big tears in his eyes. His yellow balloon was soaring up and up into the blue sky – getting smaller and smaller, until it disappeared from our sight. Before I turned my eyes away from the sky I heard the child's mother lecturing him: "I told you this would happen if you weren't careful!" I felt sorry for the little boy, who by now was crying even more. For us grown-ups it was just a balloon. For the little boy it was his prized possession of a happy day – and now it was gone. We adults forget, don't we? We forget what it was like to be a child. Losing his balloon was painful for that little boy, just as painful as some of the letting go we as adults face whenever we lose anything or anyone that is of great value to us.

Here in our local community in the Saskatchewan parklands we are about to lose something that has been precious to us for a very long time: the school board has decided to close our school at the end of this school year. Like the balloon was to the little boy, the school has been our prized possession here for many years. Maybe we realize its value even more now that it is about to close. We will mourn and maybe even be angry. But when the appointed time comes, a real letting go is needed, a letting go of what once was, so that we can make room for the new that is to come. We don't know at this time what that newness will look like, but we cannot cling forever to the past in ways that prevent the future from unfolding.

Jesus knows the blow we feel in losing something, whether it is our balloon, our school, or someone we love. Jesus knew that his disciples would need all the comfort and reassurance possible in order to believe that the death of their Lord was not the end. Just as we need reassurance that our community can survive a school closure, so Jesus spent enormous amounts of time and energy reassuring the disciples that they would not be abandoned. We have heard some of those words over the past few Sundays:

"I am the gate for the sheep."

"I came that you may have life, and have it abundantly."

"Do not let your hearts be troubled."

"I will go and prepare a place for you."

"I will not leave you orphaned."

"Wait for the promise of the Father, the Holy Spirit, the Advocate."

The disciples did not realize what these words really meant at first. When Philip, after all this time with Jesus, still asked to see the Father, he clearly had not gotten the message. When the disciples ask Jesus in today's reading of Acts whether he had come to restore the kingdom of Israel, they clearly did not get it. When the mother scolded the child for not being careful enough with the balloon, she clearly did not get it. The loss for the child was enormous. The loss of our school can feel enormous. When we think that the school closure means the end of our community, we are blinded by the pain of the loss and cannot see past this. The loss of their Lord would feel even more enormous to the disciples; Jesus tried hard to prepare them for this.

When loss and grief start upsetting our lives, we start to understand the need for Jesus' Ascension, and the meaning of his words of comfort. The blessing and authority given to the disciples in Matthew's Gospel, and given to us as Christians, can only take effect when we learn to truly let go of the things that hurt us and to let go of the things that are most dear to us. The authority to baptize, to teach and to heal happens when we let go of the things that hold back new life in us. Learning to live the Ascension in the very fabric of our lives requires the kind of letting go that hurts in our bones. In a lot of ways, that is what happened to Myra.

I met Myra in Fr. Ron Rolheiser's new book called *Seeking Spirituality*. This is what Rolheiser says about her:

> I met her in one of the theology classes I taught. She was a woman in her late forties who seemed to have enough reasons to be really happy. She was healthy, attractive, very bright, a published artist, married and the mother of two healthy teenagers. But despite all these outside appearances, Myra was far from happy. Inside her was a cancerous anger that consumed her life, threatening to choke off every opportunity for happiness and fulfillment which presented itself. Her presence in class was a continual disruption for us all

and every one had to tiptoe around her for fear of triggering her anger.

One day after class, she shared her story with me. It turned out to be a tragic one: Her father had been an alcoholic, and one night when she was nine years old, he had raped her. This was now forty years later and still she clung; she clung to the hurt of what she lost when she was nine years old.

"Something inside me died," Myra said. "The spirit left me at age nine, and I have had no real enthusiasm for life ever since. Oh, I managed to bury it at times, to leave it behind, to pretend, to act normal, like everyone else. I got good at going through the motions – even got married and had kids – and for awhile I even thought it was behind me. I remember coming home for my dad's funeral, and seeing him there in the coffin. He looked peaceful, more peaceful than I'd ever remembered him. I kissed him – I forced myself to make my peace. He was dead now, and I wanted to let him and it go. But neither the memory nor the hurt died, it didn't go away. The older I got the more I hurt. I ended up getting angrier and angrier. I began to fight everyone, including my family. Anger is threatening to ruin my marriage, to ruin my relationship to a church I love so dearly, to ruin every chance for happiness. But something ruined me long before all this."

Myra was clearly hurting, and she was at wit's end as to how to let go of that death of spirit which she had suffered forty years previously. Like Jesus, she too had been crucified, killed by the sin of humanity. And like Jesus, she was not dead. Even though the shadow of death loomed large, she was at the same time teeming with life, life which called for release – but she seemed unable to let go.

Myra needed Ascension in the best sense of that word. Fr. Rolheiser continues:

When I saw her again, a year or so later, she told me that Ascension is exactly what took place for her, shortly after she had shared in the class I taught. Encouraged by another woman who had been abused, Myra risked her life and gave herself over to a comprehensive healing journey: Grief therapy helped lessen the shock to her psyche, physical massage helped lessen the shock to her body, the place where memories of the violation were stored. And good spiritual guidance helped lessen the shock to her soul. She recalled in particular one session with a doctor, a psychologist, a nurse, and a priest, one of whom said to her: 'Jesus gave the disciples forty days to grieve and adjust. He has given you forty years! It is time to let go.' It was at that time that Myra grasped in body, mind and soul what Ascension was all about. Today she walks the earth upright, with a fuller and a blessed spirit – the spirit of someone who has tasted death in her bones and rose again into new life. Through the healing of her wounds, leaving scars, she now embraces the authority of one who is sent out, reaching out in particular to others who seek healing from abuse.[72]

Walking through the valley of our own death – in the losses, hurts and betrayals – is never easy. Coming out at the other end with a renewed spirit of life is even more difficult. But if, by the grace of God, we do make it through, the Spirit of truth will rest upon us, just as Jesus promised. The marks of the cross become sacred blessing, the blessing of the One who was crucified for us, the One who died for us and then rose again and is seated at the right hand of the Father. It is our suffering, grafted onto the suffering of Christ that becomes the ground for blessing and authority. Only when we surrender our pain can new life break through. Only pain that is lived fully and offered as holy sacrifice can carry the authority of Christ. Amen.

I found great consolation in Ron Rolheiser's words in the final chapter of *Seeking Spirituality,* where he speaks about the need to live tension for the sake of the Church, for the sake of God's reign. Rolheiser calls this the gift of life in the tension and the pain. In light of my unlikely calling to preach I found myself at the heart of my beloved church, slowly growing in compassion, love and for-giveness. None of this was automatic, and none of it became easier with time. Success on this kind of journey is not measured in politi-cal results or in earthly vindication, but rather by the degree of faith-fulness in that little part of the long journey entrusted to us, a jour-ney extending far beyond our lifetime. The journey itself connects us to the timeless Body of Christ, and leads into transformation towards perfection and consummation at the end of time.

The real value of carrying tension for the sake of love is that it is a gestation process. By pondering as Mary did as she stood helplessly beneath the cross and by sweating blood as Jesus did in the garden at Gethsemane, we have the oppor-tunity to turn hurt into forgiveness, anger into compassion, and hatred into love…. Accepting to carry tension for the sake of God, love, truth, and principle, is the mysticism that is most needed in our day. Almost everything in our culture invites us to avoid tension and to resolve it whenever possi-ble, even at the cost of some of our more noble instincts…. Jacques Maritain, the great Catholic philosopher, once stated that one of the great spiritual tragedies is that so many peo-ple of good will would become persons of noble soul if only they would not panic and resolve the painful tensions within their lives too prematurely, but rather stay with them long enough, as one does in the dark night of the soul, until those tensions are transformed and help give birth to what is most noble inside of us – compassion, forgiveness, and love.[73]

CHAPTER 18

Only a Woman

Just then his disciples came.
They were astonished that he was speaking
with a woman, but no one said,
"What do you want?"
or, "Why are you speaking with her?"
(John 4:27)

The most important yet the most difficult requirement of preaching was the letting go. I learned quickly that words spoken in public take on a life of their own. People listen to the preacher from the context of their own hurts and joys, their own ideologies and spirituality, their own biases and judgments. Comments afterwards showed how different people heard different things while being part of the same assembly. At first this was hard to accept. I wanted to ensure that the meaning I wanted my words and stories to have was honoured. But there was more going on than simply what words I spoke in public.

Sometimes comments, reaching me indirectly and weeks later, indicated that some were preoccupied more with who the preacher was than whether I had anything meaningful to say. A priest in a neighbouring parish told me one day about being approached by well-meaning parishioners, asking whether he knew that I write my own reflections, whether he was aware of their contents, and whether he approved of my preaching. On another occasion people spoke with suspicion to a pastoral assistant in another parish (who in turn told me) about my preaching in other churches. They quizzed her about whether I was indeed, as rumour had it, "leading worship" in other churches (which I was not), and whether the bishop knew about these unusual escapades (which he did). And what was I doing in a Protestant seminary, "turning away" from my church? Their tone of voice and choice of words suggested that they were trying hard to find fault with what I was doing.

I felt vulnerable occupying this unique position in ministry, both in and outside my own church; I was more than aware that there was no precedent for what I was doing, which left me open to criticism and misunderstanding. I took these types of comments personally. Every time I heard one, I wanted to run and hide in a hole, never to come out again. "I have become a laughingstock all day long; everyone mocks me," I prayed to God with Jeremiah (Jeremiah 20:7).

In some ways these reactions were not surprising. Even with the frequency of Sunday Celebrations of the Word increasing in rural parishes, very few people took on the daunting task of writing and delivering their own homiletic reflections. Because the Church had not undertaken to call forth the gifts of the laity in the area of preaching, many simply lacked confidence or remained unconvinced that preaching was a valid and valuable ministry for those with the proper skills, training and insights. The assembly's ecclesial and sacramental imagination was already severely tested by the absence of Sunday Mass. The increasing shortage of priests offered new challenges in this part of the Catholic world. For decades, if not centuries, we had no need to change our understanding of church, sacraments and our own baptismal calling as the people of God. Even my offer to help others to prepare homiletic reflections was taken up by only a few, the argument being that "Father" was better suited and a more legitimate instructor.

Being a non-ordained woman preaching my own reflections, and offering to instruct others in a ministry so strongly identified with ordained priesthood, made me prone to misinterpretation even while a begrudging respect formed. My presence as a preacher unconsciously challenged people's deep and unexamined assumptions both about ordained priesthood and about the role of the laity. As long as an adequate supply of priests is available, such assumptions remained invisible and unchallenged. The present scarcity of sacramental ministers in the modern Western world evokes a variety of reactions: some cling to the few priests we have and demand more of them, others shrug their shoulders and abdicate responsibility, still others tentatively open themselves to something new. It is important to pray for more vocations to the priesthood, and it is important to recommit ourselves to fostering a religious climate in which young people can hear and respond to God's call to ministry. But in addition, we need to expand our store of temporary solutions to the present scarcity of ordained priests.

As a woman preacher in the Catholic Church, I was viewed with suspicion, admiration, fear and great expectation, all at the same time. For some, my presence in the pulpit was refreshing, and fuelled a hope for a renewed and more inclusive model of church leadership in the future. For others, the only legitimate preacher was the priest because he was the only one inspired by God to exercise this ministry. Any other person in the pulpit was by definition inadequate, and should merely read a homiletic text prepared by the priest or taken from a book of homilies written by a priest. Having someone read the priest's homily was still the preference in many parishes, as if this gave the lay person legitimacy in the role of "preacher." Even though he was supportive, my own parish priest also felt uncomfortable with the new way of thinking that the phenomenon of lay preaching forced upon him. He tried to reassure those who approached him and questioned the legitimacy of my preaching ministry that I was trustworthy and that the bishop was well-informed of my activities.

The spiritual and emotional demands requiring me to show enormous integrity, unwavering faith and faithfulness, wrapped in deep love and respect, were acute. I carried within me the tension of the community forced into new things; of knowing myself called to preach, yet having no automatic and formal church mandate to do so other than my baptismal commitment; of experiencing the inspiration of the Holy Spirit in preparing to preach, yet not always having my words recognized by the community because of its preoccupation with the fact that I was the "wrong" vessel.

Once I was asked in a class – long before this preaching business ever started – what biblical image I identify with the most. Without much thinking I chose the one of a prophet (or maybe, the image chose me) and the Scripture passage I chose to illustrate my experience was the one where God calls Jeremiah. Little did I know… I sat on the riverbank behind the seminary this morning, watching the weir. I saw in the flow of water my journey with God of the past few years: for a long time the water calmly moves along, until it gets to the sharp drop-off where it thunders down. Now wild, swirling currents throw me around, and I am unsure of where the water is going and what it sounds like. With Jeremiah I find myself saying: "Ah God, do not call me, for I do not know how to speak – I am only a woman." Yet, with an insistence and authority similar to Jeremiah, God answers from the deep below the currents: "Do not say 'I am only a woman and I do not know how to speak'; for you shall go to all to whom I send you, and you shall speak whatever I command you. Do not be afraid, for I am with you to deliver you," says the Lord. Then the Lord put out his hand and touched my mouth… (from Jeremiah 1:7-9). And I kick and scream, for I still do not want this call. It is just too new and upsetting, both for me and for the faith community. (Journal entry)

My talks with Father Leonard were helpful, as was reading Fr. Kenan Osborne's book on the theology and history of lay ministry in the Roman Catholic Church. Both encouraged honesty and perseverance at this time of discernment and challenge. Both helped me ground the legitimacy of my call in baptism and confirmation. For, as Osborne points out, Christ himself issues the basic call to ministry, not the Church. The Church can only affirm and celebrate what has already taken place in the intimate relationship between Christ Jesus and the one called; this is the basis of Vatican II's sacramental theology as addressed in *Lumen Gentium*:

> Every Christian has both the right and obligation to fulfill these *tria munera* (threefold baptismal anointing with Christ into priest, prophet and king) primarily within the community called church and secondarily within the socio-political society in which he or she lives…. *Lumen Gentium* in article 33 speaks of the vocation of all Christians (in the threefold ministry and mission of Jesus) "given to all without exception; it is given with one's incorporation in the People of God, in the one body of Christ, under one Head, Christ."… It is, therefore, Christ in and through the sacra-

ments (of baptism and confirmation), not a pope, not a bishop, not a priest, who both calls and commissions a person, whether male or female, to such a Christian vocation.... The Christian's mission and ministry, a sharing in Jesus' own *tria munera*, arise from the sacramental initiation of baptism-confirmation-Eucharist. The sharing in these *tria munera* is present in virtue of the call and commissioning of the Lord himself, not by a clerical delegation or deputation.[74]

In a book preceding the one on lay ministry, Osborne comes to similar conclusions when reflecting on the ordained priesthood:

The following stress in the documents of Vatican II is consistently maintained. The call to ministry is ultimately not from a Church official but from the Lord himself. The officials must, of course, discern in faith whether the Lord is actually calling an individual or not, but the call and the commission is in the last analysis from the Lord. In today's world, it would seem, the Lord might indeed be calling a woman to priestly ordination. In other words, if the call is not directly from the bishop or some other Church official, but from the Lord himself, and even if the commissioning is from the Sacrament (of Holy Orders), not from delegation, and therefore, from the Lord himself, then great care must be exercised by all Church officials in their discernment of Christ's call and commissioning. This is not to downplay the role of the Church in the selection and ordination of ministers but it is rather a caution, based on the very theology of Vatican II, not to absolutize historical data.[75]

I gleaned some key insights from all my reading and studying. The most important one was that the theology to explain and validate what I experienced is and has always been "on the books" in Roman Catholic understanding, and was explicitly formulated in a new way at Vatican II. One of the greatest problems was, and continues to be, that very little of this theological and sacramental understanding trickled down to the common understanding and experience of the majority of ordinary Catholics. Couple this omission with most Catholics' predominantly ahistorical understanding of church (as if church has always been the way we have known it in our lifetime), and there was a lot of room for misunderstanding and rejection of that which may in reality be quite old – namely, being on fire with the Gospel and desiring to spread this around. My strong need to feel secure in my own church battled with this fire in my body to preach the Good News. In some ways I did not want to upset the comfortable faith of well-meaning and devout Catholics merely by who I had become and what I was doing in the liturgy. Yet, if no one was trying to give flesh and bones to what our church teaches about baptismal calling, then how are those in the pews ever going to learn? Spending time in prayer with Mary, the Mother of God, I grafted my response unto hers: "Here I am, the servant of the Lord. Do with me what you will." Like Mary, I learned to surrender. The lessons in humility were not easy, yet they were necessary. Nothing had ever seemed so hard, yet nothing had ever felt so pregnant with new life.

The challenge became how to foster the confidence among the laity that the gifts needed for the liturgical well-being of the faith community are present in the members of that community. God does provide, especially in our time of need. Could it be possible that God provided in ways other than through an ordained priest? Offering workshops and other types of training and modelling good lay-led liturgies, including good preaching, helped. At one of the workshops we had a Sunday Celebration of the Word in the presence of two ordained priests. Their presence felt like a blessing and a mandate, helping people to feel more comfortable with the necessity and the liturgical validity of such services. I was the preacher on this occasion.

I was nervous about preaching with ordained Catholic clergy present. Time and again while I prepared I called on God to help rein in the anxiety, for it risked becoming a serious distraction. The Gospel, which was the story of Jesus' encounter with the Samaritan woman at the well, posed additional "distractions," upping the ante for me. Ironically, my encounter with Jesus over my preaching was similar to the Samaritan woman's experience of encountering Jesus and entering this highly unlikely dialogue with him, a Jew and a man. Even though my experience of this spiritual encounter was valid, it alone could not dictate what I would say to the community. I had to take into account the reality of the gathered assembly, an assembly that found itself without Eucharist through no fault of its own.

As the words slowly formed in secret and in solitude, it was almost as if God handed me what the faith community needed to hear. And once again, Jeremiah walked beside me, this time as God's reluctant prophet plagued by doubt over his worthiness and his mission:

> I have the distinct sense that God put the words into my heart; not the many words I could have said about this, my favourite Gospel passage, but rather the words that those listening need to hear. The consequence of such a calling is, then, that I am required to yield constantly, letting go of my own agenda and my own preferences, insofar as they obstruct God's holy activity…. This is the lot of the prophet: the one with the clear, sharp vision of God (not his or hers), a vision consuming her whole being, the one called to hand over the vision to the people and hand over her whole being to God…. One who is fully in tune with both who God is and where the people are, while at the same time being plagued by fear and insecurity about both the message and mission as soon as the spotlight moves onto herself. Jeremiah is indeed a true model for me: no prophet was ever so sure of his words and so unsure of himself. (Journal entry)

I wondered if the doubt, the anxiety and the feelings of unworthiness would ever diminish. I felt fragile, unworthy, vulnerable, fearful. At the same time I knew enough about spiritual discernment to realize what the features of God's activity looked like. In other words, the very presence of such feelings authenticated God's own activity, making it clear that I did not operate out of my ego, or my own agenda, nor was I on some kind of power trip. As my own weaknesses tried to interfere with the preaching, St. Paul spoke to me as he did to the Corinthians: "But we have this treasure in clay jars, so that it may be made clear that this extraordinary power belongs to God and does not come from us" (2 Corinthians 4:7).

Homiletic Reflection on the Third Sunday in Lent

Exodus 17:3-7; Romans 5:1-2, 5-8; John 4:5-42

Here we are, doing Sunday liturgy without the usual leadership of our pastor. Many of us deplore the fact that we have to resort to a Sunday service without the celebration of the Eucharist. After all, we are a eucharistic people. Breaking bread and sharing wine is what we are about. God is revealed to us in the risen Christ, made present in the Eucharist. Some of us will go elsewhere to find a Mass, feeling forced to choose between celebrating Eucharist and celebrating with our local community. Some of us would like to believe that the shortage of ordained leaders in our church is only temporary. So we will just wait it out. We are in a time of transition that challenges us all to stretch and grow. And so now we learn about lay-led liturgy. Our bishop affirms the centrality of the Sunday gathering for us Christians, even in the absence of a priest. The Canadian bishops have expressed their affirmation by publishing the official liturgical book for conducting Sunday Celebrations of the Word and Hours. Given all this, what do the Scripture readings have to say to us today?

Water runs through the readings, especially the first one and the Gospel. Living water flows from a rock struck by Moses. Water from a most unlikely place. Jesus offers living water to a Samaritan woman. Water for a most unlikely person. Water is essential for living. We who live off the land know this. Crops that suffer drought look withered, stunted, dead. And poor crops affect many lives in a province like ours. The people of Israel grumbled in the wilderness, for they thirsted for water. We grumble in our wilderness, wondering: "What will happen to our Church with the dwindling number of priests?" The Samaritan woman bears the heat of the day as she makes her way to the well to draw water. Like that thirsty woman, we bear the heat of our daily trials and commitments as we come once again to the wellspring of our faith, the Sunday gathering. Even in our church community we easily get caught up in the busyness of parish life. We forget to stand still and drink deeply from the well of living water. Or we sit back passively, lacking living water, wondering and complaining:"Why don't we get much out of Mass anymore?""Why do 'they' keep changing things on us?"

Jesus *is* the Living Water. Jesus offers Living Water to the Samaritan woman. Jesus offers us Living Water in the sacrament of baptism. Baptism is God's Living Water. Baptism calls us all to share in the mission and ministries of the Church, ordained and non-ordained alike. Richard McBrien, one of today's leading theologians, has written about the close connection between baptism and ordination. McBrien points to times throughout the history of the Church when baptism enjoyed a much larger meaning than merely the erasing of original sin. Baptism was radical immersion in Christ's dying and rising to new life through conversion. This radical baptismal understanding lifted up the calling of the laity in the life of the Church. Baptismal calling to ministry and service was recognized and honoured, alongside the role of service and leadership of the ordained. Vatican II restored this prominence of the baptismal call to serve. We are called into a faith community that drinks deeply from the wellspring of God's Living Water, the Body of Christ crucified, died and risen. If all of us are alive to our baptism, from our midst some will answer the call to ordained ministry. Praying for priestly vocations is not enough. We ourselves are called to be living communities of faith, communities from which God can indeed call forth leaders. This living water, this deep meaning of water, is the first gift to us from today's readings.

A second striking element is that Jesus talks to a woman, and a foreign, unclean Samaritan at that. The story itself comments on this most controversial aspect. Both the woman and the disciples wonder aloud why Jesus bothers to talk to her at all. Women had no social status of their own. Samaritans were openly despised by the Jews. Jesus breaks all taboos and norms by addressing a Samaritan woman and engaging her in conversation. She is the most unlikely person he should be talking to. And yet, not only does Jesus engage her in serious dialogue, he offers her living water. Most shocking of all, Jesus reveals to this outsider his mission as the Messiah. This yields a jumble of jarring questions, even in Jesus' day: Does Jesus not belong to the Jews alone? Does God belong to the Jews or the Samaritans? What about the fact that a woman's word had no authority?

With fewer priests, who will lead us in worship? We, like the Samaritan woman, do not immediately see who waits for us. But look closely now. Jesus addresses each one of us, a most unlikely bunch of people indeed. Jesus is calling us, affirming what God promises at baptism. Jesus says: "Your lives are indeed caught up with me. I call you to witness and share Good News with one another. I call you to proclaim justice to a broken, hungry world." But we wonder, "How is it that the Lord should talk to us?" I lack worthiness. You lack self-confidence. She lacks courage. He lacks training. Here, our second reading offers a gift in our searching worries. In his letter to the Romans, Paul states that we are justified and deemed worthy by our faith in the One who died for us even though we are sinners. Paul reassures believers. God does not ask us to be superhuman before we can be called to ministry and service. God calls for faith, faith active in serving lives. God does not require human perfection, God calls for faithfulness. Equally, God does not respect our rules – cultural, social, religious – when it comes to calling people to proclaim Good News to the faith community. Jesus broke every rule by talking to the Samaritan woman. Jesus can still break rules today in order to pour out God's waters on a thirsty, parched creation. Listen to Christ's voice. Drink from the Living Water. Let us join the company of the Samaritan woman and be compelled to go and tell our people. The Samaritan woman's people recognized her words – not as hers, but as God's very own self-revelation. Let us embody our beliefs so people will ask Jesus: "Stay with us awhile…"

These are good gifts for our journey now, here in Saskatchewan, at this time of transition, growth and baptismal calling. Let us ponder them. Let us be encouraged and enlightened by them. God's faithfulness to us, to creation, endures. God is faithful and calls us to faithful hope. Beyond any lament, we rejoice that we are united and free to drink from the living water. In these living waters, in our redeemed community, God is truly doing a new thing in our time. God brings forth water from unlikely places: a rock in the desert, a conversation with an outsider by a well, an anxious church community. God offers living water to unlikely people: the grumbling Israelites, the Samaritan woman, the anxious Romans, yes, even us. Let us come together around Christ our rock and "boast in our hope of sharing the glory of God." Amen.

I shared the text of this reflection three times: at the workshop with the priests present, at the Sunday Liturgy without Eucharist, and in the local weekly Catholic newspaper. The text, the child of my soul, was literally gone, swept up by God's own Spirit to do God's work in the world. When that happened, the words almost ceased to be mine, for they took on the life of God. As the Incarnation shows us, God's Word takes on the qualities and features of our human condition: as we are deeply affected when God touches us, in turn God's Word is affected by the particularity of our humanity. In my experience of preaching, the Word of God chose to come to the faith community in and through the reality of who I was before God and in the world with all my gifts and shortcomings: a white European turned Canadian, a woman in mid-life, a Christian, a mother, wife and community member. That Word of God kindled a blazing fire of passion and compassion, of profound loneliness and communion, of painful insight and love. Like a mother who finds it hard to let go of her child, it hurt to part with the words of my soul, which were scattered into hearts and minds, and received in so many different ways. My only consolation was that my letting go increased God's own breath in and through the preached words: "For this reason my joy has been fulfilled. He must increase, but I must decrease" (John 3:29b-30).

CHAPTER 19

Already / Not Yet

*"The kingdom of heaven is like yeast
that a woman took and mixed in with
three measures of flour
until all of it was leavened."*
(Matthew 13:33)

Good preaching is more than an innate gift and far from simply magical. I learned tricks of the trade, one of which is paying attention to the use of words. In the first homiletics class, considerable time was devoted to raising our awareness about the importance of language. Words used well have a certain power. Words used well in preaching can have a transforming power, letting us in on the kingdom of God here, now and yet to come. As part of course requirements I read Annie Dillard's *Teaching a Stone to Talk* and Kathleen Norris' *Dakota*. Both authors are masterful wordsmiths. I observed carefully how they used words, and how the crafting of their sentences created impact. After enjoying my own initial emotional response to their stories, I employed the tools offered in class to dissect their skills and to study why authors like these succeed in speaking to the heart.

The main purpose of preaching is to facilitate in the hearer an immediate experience of the Word of God in a way that speaks anew in every time and place. One of the most basic ways that humans process information is through the imagination. In a sermon, we activate and guide the imagination by always using the present tense of verbs. When speaking about Jesus, using the present tense makes his message acutely active in the here and now, instead of removed from us by twenty centuries. Present tense engages and makes it harder to maintain distance. Even when the present tense feels artificial to me as the preacher, the words adjust to the hearer's ability and need. I saw this happen many times and I have come to call this God's activity in the Holy Spirit:

> Something happens between the preacher's lips and the congregation's ears that is beyond prediction or explanation. Sermons that make me weep leave my listeners baffled, and sermons that seem cold to me find warm responses. Later in the week, someone quotes part of my sermon back to me, something she has found extremely meaningful – only I never said it. There is more going on here than anyone can say. Preaching is finally more than art or science. It is alchemy, in which tin becomes gold and yard rocks become diamonds under the influence of the Holy Spirit. It is a process of transformation for both preacher and congregation alike, as the ordinary details of everyday lives are translated into the extraordinary elements of God's ongoing creation.[76]

Besides engaging listeners by using the present tense, I needed to acknowledge the local reality of the faith community. Using stereotypical, trite or generic examples in preaching sounded inauthentic and impersonal; it allowed hearers to keep their distance. Worse yet, if such examples prevail Sunday after Sunday, people may begin to suspect that the preacher had not wrestled with the texts or had even lifted an entire homily from a book or the Internet. Even when I borrowed from someone else's sermon, I needed to appropriate the words for myself as the preacher for a specific faith community. Offering another's words as my own inevitably felt, and sounded, phony. In each preaching act I needed to open myself to God's Word in the same way as the faith community was invited to do through the Word proclaimed and preached.

I remember one occasion when I was given a sermon to "preach." It had been distributed by the diocese and addressed the need to pray for vocations to the priesthood. It was a "suggested sermon" given to me with the best intentions, with the comment that I could "save myself the headache" of putting something together myself and that I could just "preach" this one. "How convenient," said my parish priest with a smile. This task and the way it was presented did not sit right with me at all. First, I did not consider putting together a homiletic reflection a "headache." In fact, I cherished every invitation to prepare and preach. Second, everything in me revolted against what I was asked to do, for several reasons. To be given this text by someone who preaches as part of his priestly calling, and who I thought knew the demands that good preaching made on the preacher, was confusing. This kind of text was not a homily, but more a "reading after the Gospel." Reading a canned sermon was not preaching according to my understanding. My formation objected, and my experience contradicted the comments made. I did not only object to the canned sermon, I also reacted strongly to the content. The words sounded like a guilt trip for not praying hard enough to God for vocations to the priesthood. The purpose seemed to spur us on not to ignore God's call in our sons, asking us to give our sons to the Church in the service of God. A glaring lack of respect towards the faith community was communicated in two ways: first, by the choice and tone of the words, and second, by the fact that this sermon did not touch on the Scriptures for that day, nor did it seem to reveal good news. The content, the choice of words, the style: all felt like a violation of my learning, my understanding and my experience of call and ministry.

> The power of words has a disconcerting effect on me. The words in this sermon on vocations make me tremble. So much of its content clashes with my experiences: my commitment as a Christian parent, my training in preaching, and my own questions around ministry and church leadership. I ask God to forgive me for backing out – I just cannot do it. Am I asked to bite my tongue and close my heart as I read this to the gathered assembly on Sunday? I pray, and search my conscience, pray and plead for wisdom. God, help me. (Journal entry)

I declined the task. Despite prayer and willingness to obey, I was not able to detach myself from the topic, the style and the words. I cannot speak words in a disembodied manner – the power of these words violated my being. In the end someone else in the parish read the sermon, someone who felt at peace with the assignment. That made neither the sermon nor my withdrawal from the task right, but I had no authority to do anything else. I opted to maintain my own sense of authenticity and integrity.

Words carry worlds of meaning. The way we use words, and the choice of our words, bring into being our lives and the world around us. Language calls us into life and relationship. Words give birth to human yearnings, pains and desires. Words can pierce the heart and damage the soul. It is no accident, therefore, that God chose to dwell among us as the Incarnate Word. In light of the power of words, the beginning of John's Gospel is no surprise: "In the beginning was the Word, and the Word was with God, and the Word was God" (John 1:1). Our Christian faith claims God as the Word-made-flesh, the embodied Word enfolding all our words, our worlds and our realities.

An inner appropriation accompanied my technical understanding of good preaching. The words I used in preaching insisted on being "incarnate," i.e., becoming fully a part of my very being. Like a goldsmith lovingly heating the precious metal and moulding it into something special, the preparation process for preaching heated up the words inside me, moulding them long enough to form me into something new. Once my soul opened to conversion and felt nourished by the words to be preached, the sermon was ready to be offered to the faith community. Using words well in preaching became an invitation to live fully in the here-and-now reality of God's reign while acknowledging the fullness of this reign awaiting us at the end of time. The invitation to "live in the kingdom" even while awaiting the fullness of the kingdom arose directly out of the call to preach, and had a profound effect on my way of being in the world and in the Church.

I have never understood preachers who claim to "stay out of" their sermons, preaching the word of God and the word of God alone. It is not possible, but there is no reason why it should be possible. By choosing Christ to flesh out the word, God made a lasting decision in favor of incarnation. Those of us who are his body in the world need not shy away from the fact that our own flesh and blood continue to be where the word of God is made known. We are living libraries of God's word. Our stories are God's stories. Sometimes they are comedies and sometimes they are tragedies; sometimes faith shines through them and other times they end in darkness, but every one of them bears witness to the truth of God's word. Preachers cannot "stay out of" their sermons any more than singers can stay out of their songs. Our words are embodied, which means we bring all that we are to their expression.[77]

We are indeed living libraries of God's Word, as reading the words of Jesus tells us. God made an irreversible decision to become flesh in stories about sowers and seed, about women and yeast: "The kingdom of heaven may be compared to someone who sowed good seed in the field" (Matthew 13:24). "The kingdom of heaven is like a mustard seed" (Matthew 13:31). "The kingdom of heaven is like yeast" (Matthew 13:33). Preaching is an all-encompassing endeavour that employs the elements of our lives – seed, yeast, oil, water, bread, wine – and uses them to reveal the Word-made-flesh, breaking both preacher and hearer open into the fullness of God. Sometimes I felt like the person in Matthew's Gospel who found a treasure in the field and went and sold all he had in order to buy the field. Throwing my own personal experiences into the divine mix, I placed all that I was and had to offer at the service of the preaching task. At other times I felt like the woman who mixed yeast into the measure of flour: the yeast dissolved yet it was responsible, even essential, for the rising of the dough.

Every era in the history of Christianity has to confront its own questions and challenges. Every era probably felt that its particular challenges were unique and unprecedented. This is both true and not true. We are new to the challenges, but the Church as a whole is not. That is why studying church history had such a liberating effect on me. Learning about the great debates, questions and disagreements in the course of history allowed me to see the Spirit of God at work in the Church over time. Taking the long view of history greatly helped me to understand the need for debate, tension and questions. The Spirit of God often uses our human struggles for truth to nudge us further on this journey towards the kingdom at the end of time. Understanding that God is at work in the midst of tension and times of transition was freeing and energizing for me.

One of the big questions in our particular time and place seems to be our understanding and experience of ministry and church leadership. Like others in the Church I do not always know where to turn. I feel caught between my desire to return to the "flesh pots of Egypt" (the way things used to be, just as the Hebrew people complained to Moses in the desert) and what feels like a disintegrating and unknown tomorrow. We have indeed centralized too much ministry in the clerical system while failing to foster adequate catechesis about the ministry and calling of all the baptized. The present tensions surrounding these questions may well be the Spirit's way to wake us all up from a comfortable and complacent Christianity. As someone for whom ordination is not open, and as someone whose passion for ministry spills over from my baptism, I feel caught in this tension. Mary Catherine Hilkert speaks of this tension that is evoked by the challenge of conversion:

> This process of conversion will call the community and its leaders to think differently – to imagine new models of preaching that draw on the experience of the assembly gathered to worship, new understandings of authority that are more consonant with the gospel, new images of human community and the larger beloved community of creation, new images of Christ, and even new images of God.[78]

It is precisely at disintegration points, when old models fall apart and cherished understandings crumble, that God has the best chance of fashioning something new. I clung to this notion in faith, even though I risked being judged and misunderstood, at times even by good Christian people. My greatest enemy was my own fear. At times the power I gave to negative vibes, even the slightest ones, was out of proportion to the faith to which God called me as the "something new" occurred in and through my preaching. I was as afraid as the disciples who gathered in the upper room even though they knew Jesus their Lord had risen from the dead. Yet despite their fear, the Spirit "breathed on them" and tongues of fire rested on each of them. In that stunning revelation, God was indeed doing a new thing. God is still doing a new thing. Casting aside fear and doubt, I open myself to God's Spirit and strive to be God's yeast in the dough.

Homiletic Reflection on Pentecost Sunday

Acts 2:1-11, John 20:19-23

Today, Pentecost Sunday, we end our celebration of the 50 days of Easter. Pentecost remembers the coming of the Holy Spirit and the mandate of the Church to be sent out. In a couple of weeks, our younger parishioners will celebrate the sacrament of confirmation. As a community we are invited today to reflect on our own confirmation, on the presence and action of the Holy Spirit in our lives and in our church. Who are we as God's Spirit-filled church? How does the Holy Spirit breathe on us here in rural Saskatchewan? How does the Spirit call forth the diversity of gifts needed in a church in transition, in a broken and famished world?

From that first Pentecost on, we have been Spirit-filled people of God. Sealed with the sacrament of Confirmation we have joined the disciples in the Spirit of Christ. With the disciples we are sent out to proclaim Good News, to forgive sins. Granted, we do not always live up to this radical calling. Many times we do not feel the Spirit, we do not act in the Spirit. We too, at times, fear "the authorities": maybe not the ones "out there," but surely the ones in ourselves. Some of us come to Mass out of duty and to assuage guilt. We can judge ourselves, and others, harshly when life treats us unfairly. We fail to forgive many times, especially in our families, in our communities. We refuse to participate in the liturgy because we do not consider ourselves worthy. We reduce our faith to a set of rules to follow. Or we are so busy living good and pious lives that we get tricked into trusting our own efforts to make it into heaven. Before we know it, oh so subtly, we betray Christ as much as the disciples did. Rather than choose a different band of supporters, though, Christ breathes his Spirit in us and pushes us out the door, sends us as the Father sent him.

Despite all our legalisms, we are still a Spirit-filled people. We do not always recognize the One who appears among us, the One whose Spirit fills our being. Only when he shows us his hands and his side do we see the Lord. By the scars of the crucifixion we truly know that it is the Lord among us. This scarred and holy presence stands among us in the most surprising places. As a faith community without Eucharist today, we feel incomplete, as if we are at a party without food and drink. Yet Christ stands among us. Our incompleteness becomes the wound that binds us to Jesus. The Lord is among us when we gather on the first day of the week. The Lord is among us when we open ourselves to the Living Word from Scripture. The Spirit of the Lord rests on us when we truly hear one another in love, each in our "own language." The Lord is present in us when we reach out to those in need. The Lord is among us when we show the fruits of his indwelling Spirit, right through the scars of death in our lives.

Even outside of our Sunday gathering, Christ comes and stands in our midst with scars and words of peace. Christ stood among the 120 women with whom I gathered a few weeks ago. They gathered to remember, share and celebrate stories of life as prairie women. They gathered to express a common prairie bond before God. The diversity was stunning: Christians of all traditions, non-Christian, Native, white and Métis, religious sisters and secular seekers, young and old, urban and rural. How would we ever hear one another, each in our own language? There was hesitation at first; divisions and distinctions were evident. Slowly, over the three days, wounds and scars were shared – the wounds in our hands, our hearts, our sides. The Spirit opened the ears and hearts of all to hear, to receive, and to celebrate our common bond before God. Hearts were changed and friendships were born. Jesus, holding in unity and love the mosaic of our differences, stood among those gathered, saying: "Peace be with you…." Gradually we do recognize the One among us.

Jesus, standing among us, speaks peace. Limited, flawed and poor at listening as we are, Jesus brings peace to us who are made whole and worthy through his death. This peace is a costly kind. It is costly because it comes with the scars of the cross. Jesus' peace comes with the full knowledge of our own sinfulness. Jesus speaks peace right into our fear of pain and death, right into our fear of doing the wrong thing, even in this Sunday liturgy. In the midst of our own betraying and betrayed lives, Jesus speaks peace. Not a peace meaning absence – absence of war, pain and strife. Rather, Jesus' peace carries a fullness – the fullness and faithfulness of God's presence among us. Jesus speaks, and is, our peace.

And so with the disciples, we rejoice and are sent forth. We are sent forth in the Spirit of the risen Christ, in the Spirit of forgiveness. As a community of faith reborn in the Spirit we are sent to be God's forgiveness and mercy in the world. We become God's absolution, scarred and broken, but forgiven, a forgiveness that knows no bounds. This forgiveness is so extensive that we are a new creation – every day. This forgiveness is so powerful that, should we retain sins, they would be retained. Just as the water of baptism recreates us in God, so the Spirit now pushes us out the door to extend that new life in Christ to the world. We rejoice, are sent forth and live the mercy of God, both within and outside the community of faith.

A forgiven and forgiving community lives in the joy of the resurrection. It embraces diversity rather than imposing uniformity. A community in God's mercy cherishes a variety of gifts while knowing itself to be one body. There are those who clean the church, those who plan and lead liturgy, those who provide lunches on Sundays and at funerals, those who prepare and lead music, those who visit the sick, and many more. We are that community. We are that Spirit-filled people. We call forth the gifts in each of us, without distinction. With our present shortage of ordained leaders, calling forth one another's gifts becomes acutely important. As Paul tells us, the store of our gifts is meant for the common good. Baptized in one Spirit, we are made whole and one in Christ Jesus.

Sealed with the Holy Spirit in confirmation, we are mandated to serve the community and to be pushed out the door into the world. Living in the radical light of this risen Lord will make heads turn at the sight of a forgiven and forgiving community.

As we leave here today, we take Christ's Spirit into our hearts in a new way. In the morning, when we splash water on our faces to wake ourselves up, we remember our baptism and our confirmation. See and feel Jesus' breath warming us from the inside out: Receive the Holy Spirit. Taste the forgiveness of a merciful God. Pray for the community of faith, that we may truly live as God's Spirit-filled people. Amen.

CHAPTER 20

Waiting for Light

When they entered the temple,
the chief priests and the elders of the people
came to him as he was teaching and said,
"By what authority are you doing these things,
and who gave you this authority?"
(Matthew 21:23)

Lay preachers, at least in a Catholic context, are caught between a rock and a hard place. In theory, the only possible answer to the question "By whose authority do you stand here and speak to us?" is this: the power of Jesus, my baptismal anointing into the mission of Christ, and the authority handed by the faith community itself. Yet most Catholics do not recognize this as a typical Catholic answer. While evangelical lay preachers in the nineteenth century claimed the authority to preach publicly, Catholics in the twenty-first century continue to distrust lay preaching. While Protestant traditions have emphasized preaching by downplaying its sacramental connection to Eucharist, Roman Catholic tradition downplayed preaching in order to overemphasize the sacrament of the Eucharist. It was only in the twentieth century that preaching was restored as a normative part of the Catholic liturgy; more specifically, since Vatican II there has been a greater recovery of the connection between the Word proclaimed and preached and the celebration of the Eucharist. The intimate connection that now exists between Word and sacrament may well add to the Catholic hesitation to trust lay preaching. Yet part of a prophetic vocation – of which lay preaching can well be one – is to announce "hard words." God's Spirit is the source of unity, peace and joy. But God's Spirit is also the "new thing," that which disturbs, troubles and upsets us in times of change. Growing an ability to let the Spirit move and disturb, while claiming that same Spirit's peace in times of turmoil, can sometimes lead to places beyond our wildest dreams.

A few years ago three urban Catholic parishes in my area decided to initiate a first-ever Advent ecumenical service. I was not part of the planning committee, but because of my connections with the Protestant clergy, I played an informal advisory role for the organizers who were new to ecumenical initiatives. I was pleased that more Catholics were taking an interest in ecumenism. As the planning progressed, several Protestant clergy joined the committee and were prepared to take an active role in the service. One evening, Dean, the committee's chair, phoned, inviting me to consider preaching at this ecumenical event. Catching my breath, I replied that, first, I was not on the committee and second, I felt that one of the Protestant clergy ought to be asked to preach. Dean then told me that it was the Protestant clergy who had highly recommended me for the job, since I preached in the pulpits of several of their churches. For them, this simple fact established my credibility, validity and trustworthiness.

I was taken aback by the request. My first thought was, "God, what are you doing?" I recognized again the surprising yet definite call from the faith community to break open the Word of God. Again, the authority was handed to me without my asking, expecting or looking for it. This kind of "ordaining" activity from the grassroots was an integral part of the ministry of church leadership, whether ordained or not. This invitation was unique for several reasons. For one thing, I was to preach in the presence of several ordained clergy, including Catholic priests, who were presiding together over this ecumenical service. In addition, many Catholics in the gathered assembly seldom heard lay preaching. Sunday Celebrations of the Word in the absence of a priest occurred less often in the city than in the rural parishes. Seeing a Catholic laywoman in the place where a priest usually stands would truly be a new experience for many. It was of utmost importance to model good lay preaching, to be authentic in my communication, and to include an appropriate sign from the ordained showing support and permission for me to occupy this role in the worship service. Once again I found myself in the company of nineteenth-century women who claimed a call to preach:

> [Claiming a divine call spurred] women to act as agents of change and to search for avenues to express that sense of vocation. A woman's call served a number of functions in her life and ministry; it was her impetus to begin preaching, her refuge and solace when her ministry was challenged or rejected, and one way to account for the fruits of her labor. The ongoing struggle to practice ministry in the face of opposition served to heighten her conviction that this was indeed God's will, whatever others might say. Her call was shared as testimony to edify and encourage others and often identified as a turning point in personal religious experience.[79]

I sifted and sorted through the delicate issues arising from the invitation, recommitting myself to walking with God in a spirit of humility and gratitude as so many women preachers had done before me, albeit in different churches. An unusual process of preparation settled in, presenting new challenges alongside the ever-demanding solitary prayer time:

> How can this be? I yield to your Spirit, O God, and doors open in most unexpected ways. I am stunned. I feel in my bones that you are dead serious, God, when you say, "Nothing is impossible, just let me show you." I cry, and tremble in fear. I cover my face and take off my shoes, for I stand on God's Holy Ground, asked to be the burning bush in a church aching to heal its own divisions and strife. Or am I making too much of this? Am I moving into self-centredness, with a twinge of self-pity? Lord God, take my tears as an offering of self. Calm the storm, Lord; smooth the waters. I offer all the turmoil and pain over not knowing, all the fear of making the wrong choices, all the temptations to make this my ego trip. (Journal entry)

It was not enough to accept the invitation to preach. It was not enough to have the bishop's blessing for my ecumenical involvements. I felt a deep need to seek the support and mandate from the local Catholic leadership. I took nothing for granted. Since this was a non-eucharistic liturgy, there was no canonical problem giving the preaching task to a layperson. However, I did not want to step on anyone's toes. I went to discuss the matter with a Catholic priest. He admitted this situation was unique and offered me his support and encouragement, adding that it does not seem easy for Catholic priests to gain the trust of the ecumenical community. He hoped that my lay involvement was forming a bridge between the churches.

Despite all the affirmations in the world, I remained uncomfortable with the position I occupied in the local Christian family. I felt like a pioneer all over again, like I did when I moved to this vast country from tiny, crowded Holland. There was, however, a big difference between the adventuresome spirit that characterized that move and my mid-life need for stability and predictability. As a young adult, I was making new choices and exploring new territory. Now in mid-life, I just wanted to slow down and simply continue on paths I had chosen earlier in my life. I was discovering that this was not possible. The road was to be created, not followed. One of the hardest parts was allowing God's Spirit to redefine where, and to whom, I belonged in relationship to God, others, myself, the Church. My formation in ministry and church leadership resulted in a changed relationship with both clergy and laity, making me belong to both groups and to neither at the same time. Moreover, I felt forced to shed the false security of thinking that the direction of my life even remotely "belonged" to me.

I appreciated anew Jesus' response when one enthusiastic follower said, "I will follow you wherever you go." And Jesus said to him, "Foxes have holes, and birds of the air have nests; but the Son of Man has nowhere to lay his head" (Luke 9:57-58). In some ways, I belonged everywhere and nowhere. I belonged in my Roman Catholic tradition, yet moved about freely in other sanctuaries. I belonged with the laity, yet in some ways I also belonged with the clergy, because of a formation that had profoundly changed my self-identity, a change that my tradition calls an "indelible mark on the soul." The experience of the Advent ecumenical service – an experience requiring a most delicate balancing act in humility and wisdom – highlighted all these aspects:

Something deep inside me pushes to claim my experience of call as more than what my church allows for women. Yet I feel equally strongly about respecting my church's present position on ordination and letting my experience shine as a witness of passionate lay ministry. I yield to both, and let change unfold in God's love and in God's time. The painful crucible, formed deep in my being, at times seriously jeopardizes my capacity to keep loving the Church and surrendering to God. (Journal entry)

As in the past, I felt compelled to seek God's forgiveness. The temptation to use events for my own benefit was simply too obvious to ignore – seeking the Church's sacrament of reconciliation helped my heart to surrender. The words of St. Paul to the Corinthians became my constant prayer: "My grace is sufficient for you, for power is made perfect in weakness" (2 Corinthians 12:9). In my feelings of fear and trembling, in my inadequacies and lack of trust, I called on God's power. In my own failing to live up to the words to be preached, I called on God to redeem, restore and transform my soul.

I learned about the difference between false and real humility, which is much like the difference between God's and Satan's angels of light. The twelve principles of humility that St. Benedict developed in the fifth century in his Rule for monastic life became clear, relevant and alive. I grew in my awareness of God at all times, in all places and in all things (1st principle). Preaching taught me to let go of the notion that I was in charge of the world (2nd principle), to submit to the authority of the community and of Scripture (3rd principle), to endure the journey and not grow weary (4th), to confide in one person, confessing my sinfulness and my intimate journey with God (5th), and to be content with nothing (6th). I was learning about the freedom that comes when I am willing to take a "one down" position regarding the other (7th principle), when I wait for endorsement of the community before making any move in ministry (8th), when I learn to withhold words that may hurt another (9th), and when the tendency to ridicule is reduced to zero (10th) while always ensuring that I speak gently (11th). According to Joan Chittister, "the twelfth degree of humility describes the human being with the humble heart.... we 'manifest humility in our bearing no less than in our hearts.'"[80] Real humility grown and tended to in these twelve ways fosters a calm dignity and integrity wrapped in courage. It gives one strength to follow through on the challenge ahead, without needing to show off or to cling to the outcome. Real humility gives equal weight to both gifts and faults. Paradoxically, false humility feeds pride and judgment of self and others, denies gifts and callings, as well as dismisses God's ability to use us as instruments of grace.

At one time I feared the passion that made its way from my inward being out through my mouth. Preaching made that passion flow through my veins, and I was embarrassed to show the gathered assembly. At one time I feared claiming the authority to preach. After all, I belong in the pew and I could get by trying very hard to make better pies for the church supper. Through time, experience and intentional prayer and reflection, however, I recognized that such feelings fostered false humility, which in turn discounted the power of God to use ordinary women and men to do extraordinary things. By the time the Advent ecumenical service came around, I lived in a truce of sorts between God's call and the nagging feelings of fear and embarrassment. I was prepared to roll with the experience and let God use the event, letting the chips fall where they would, abandoning myself in trust to God's own Holy Spirit.

> The dangerous memories of the words and deeds of Jesus are often the cause for profound transformation. The gospel of one who was himself despised and rejected takes on new meaning and power as women begin to reflect the prophetic message and liberating lifestyle of Jesus. In the midst of the painful and unjust social and ecclesial situations, many women continue to experience the power of resurrection. Some are discovering and creating new ways to announce the good news to those grieving and weeping. Still others speak with joy and conviction of their vocation to preach. Like Mary Magdalene, they have moved beyond grief, loss, and confusion to announce the truth of their experience of the crucified and risen one.[81]

Is this what the power of resurrection feels like to a woman pushed by God's Spirit to occupy a central place in announcing the

Good News of Jesus died and risen? Is this how Mary Magdalene felt when she ran to the disciples and announced: "I have seen the Lord" (John 20:18)? I sat in the sanctuary with 13 ordained clergy (some of whom were female), and was the only layperson involved in leading the service. After the proclamation of the Gospel, while over 300 people looked on, the three Catholic priests gathered around me, prayed a blessing and "sent" me to the pulpit. It was the strongest, most visible and public mandate I had ever experienced. Several people held back tears, somehow unable to articulate what moved them. My own husband commented that this was the most powerful preaching he had heard me do. Much later I wondered about the connection between mandate and quality of preaching: the stronger the formal recognition was, the greater was my courage to let God speak. Here was a prime example of something much bigger than it appeared at first glance. God acted, and God moved hearts, without much regard for propriety and human-made restrictions. All I could feel was wonder, bewilderment and gratitude. Did this really happen? It was the strongest expression of God's Spirit breaking through barriers, of churches and otherwise, that Christians in this city ever experienced. One single prayer kept welling up in my heart: "My soul magnifies the Lord, and my spirit rejoices in God my Saviour" (Luke 1:46-47).

Homily for Advent Ecumenical Service

Isaiah 9:1-6, John 1:1-5

Here we are, at the start of the church year, gathered together in one church, gathered together to wait – for that is what Advent is about: waiting. In our culture, waiting is not something we do well. With computers that work faster and faster, with telecommunications that put the world at our fingertips, waiting can be excruciating in our world. We hate to wait for anything. That becomes even more evident when Christmas decorations show up in our stores in November, even before Remembrance Day. Not only do we not wait well, our society is no longer Christian – that's strike two against us sitting in church tonight. Everything around us forms this conspiracy: skip Advent, go straight to the reason for the season and buy your little hearts out. There are, after all, only so many shopping days left, all these cards to write, gifts to buy, wrap and mail, to say nothing of the cleaning, the decorating and the partying – all for the big day of Christmas. Who wants to wait and watch? We have better things to do.

Yet the liturgical calendar insists on Advent. Like the nine months of waiting before the birth of a child, God insists on Advent, and our souls need Advent. Like a whisper sent into the commercial chaos and into our non-stop lifestyles, Advent invites us to be really foolish: come on, pause in the midst of the busy-ness, listen between the lines of the songs and the ads blaring in the malls and on the radio, and hear the invitation. The awesome gift of God's presence comes wrapped in hectic days of preparation. For despite all the secular co-opting of the Christmas season, the heart of Christmas remains the heart of God.

And despite all the "things" we can buy for one another, the true longings of our heart find ultimate fulfillment in God's promise of salvation. God insists on Advent, and our souls need the waiting more than we let on. Beneath the tinsel and gift buying we have an aching need to remember the stories that witness to God's coming. Like the chosen people of Israel, we too need to hear those stories: the ones that move us from darkness into light. It is this remembering and this telling that help us believe anew in the power of faith and faithfulness, in unity and friendship and fidelity, in compassion and courage and discipleship.

"The people that walked in darkness have seen a great light; on those who live in a land of deep shadow a light has shone." These words remind me of a woman I met recently. Yvonne Johnson grew up knowing full well the realities of darkness: from early childhood on she knew abuse of all kinds, neglect, poverty and violence. She was the child of a Native woman and a Norwegian father. She suffered personal and cultural discrimination, and has the scars on her flesh, bones and soul to prove it. Love? What is that? She had never experienced it. Because she had never been loved, Yvonne was terrified: would she be capable of loving her own children? Yet, to her great surprise, her children became the light in the darkness of her violent and painful life.

Despite all the odds, Yvonne felt within her a swelling of something beautiful that came from somewhere, from Someone. She tried desperately to hang onto and nurture within her this capacity to love. But her violent and abusive environment kept grabbing from her every attempt at trying to love and to discover some sense of inner and outer peace. In 1992, Yvonne was charged in Alberta with first-degree murder.

She was sentenced to life in a federal penitentiary. Robbed of her children – the one hope for the light of love – and now, locked up, behind bars, Yvonne at first turned suicidal and sank into utter depression. Yet, strangely enough, her incarceration became an unexpected light in the darkness. Not in a big, flashy way, as in one moment pinpointing when salvation occurred. No, the light came blurred and slowly, much like the dawning of a new day that is still shrouded in thick mist. Behind locked doors and barbed wire, the cycle of abuse, addiction and neglect stopped. For the first time in her life, Yvonne had time and space to think, to pray and to remember. She discovered that her spirit – that core of her being, her soul, which is part of God – was not completely crushed. Just like the people of long ago heard Isaiah's promise, Yvonne was stunned to discover that she was not alone, that God, the great Manitou, had not abandoned her. Somehow God heard her cry of desperation and would come to set her free. Prison became God's sanctuary where faint hope was rekindled, confidence was cautiously restored and Yvonne was able to take hold of her life. Yvonne started to write down her memories, however ugly and painful that process was. The writing became God's vehicle of liberation. She desired deeply to know that her personal pain, and the cultural pain of her Native brothers and sisters, was not in vain, and so she suffered the pain of remembering. In the writing God turned her scars and oozing wounds into redemptive suffering. With the help, encouragement and mentoring of Rudy Wiebe, a well-known Canadian writer, Yvonne gave birth to her dream: together they wrote and published Yvonne's life story. Their book, called *Stolen Life,* was released earlier this year.

I met Yvonne through reading her book. The reading was not easy: its content is harsh and graphic. But its witness to the power of God's light breaking through utter darkness is equally compelling and overwhelming. Yvonne is still serving time, now at the Native healing lodge in Maple Creek. But her spirit is set free, and her dignity as a child of God has been restored. Like Jesus, whose arms on the cross stretched out to embrace the entire universe in his death, Yvonne's story of pain and suffering stretches out over Canada, and now belongs to God and to us all.

John's Gospel says this: "The light shines in the darkness, and the darkness did not overcome it" (John 1:5). In the dark of winter, in the dark of the pain in our lives, we are irresistibly drawn into the very heart of God, which overflows with infinite love for each of us, for God desires nothing more than to set us free. Sooner or later, amidst the pain and the tears, sometimes in the most unexpected places, like behind the bars of a federal penitentiary, God's light breaks through the darkness, and the darkness does not overcome it.

Our life may not look as bleak as Yvonne's, but our hearts can hurt just as much and our eyes can shed just as many tears. Ever felt the agony of raising teenagers in our promiscuous society? Ever been told that someone you love has only a little time to live, because cancer is eating away at their body? Ever felt the shock of learning that a teenage friend was raped and got pregnant? Ever felt the humiliation of being stuck in a job, with no prospects for another career? Ever felt the pain of church divisions right in your own backyard, in your own heart? Sometimes the darkness settles in so thickly around us, we have trouble expecting any ray of light – ever. The people of Israel wandered in the desert for several generations before they experienced the light of reaching the Promised Land. It took Yvonne 40 years of living in hell before the morning dawned on her soul. It took Lutherans and Roman Catholics almost 500 years to reach consensus on some basic tenets of the faith, and to embrace one another as sisters and brothers in Christ – something we did officially only a month ago. Some of us here tonight are still waiting for the light, with doubt nibbling at our hope – maybe the light will never come, we think. Yet, Isaiah, Yvonne and John tell us tonight, "Hang on, sit tight, stand firm in your pain. No darkness is too dark for the Word of Life. In Christ, the Word made flesh, the light shines in the darkness, and the darkness did not over-come it."

It is this dimension of Christmas that is missed so easily amidst the sentimental tunes playing in the shopping malls. Advent waiting is not make-believe. It's not about hoping for that one perfect gift. Christmas faith is not a trip down memory lane to that time long ago when angels sang and shepherds watched their sheep. Telling the Advent stories of light piercing the darkness is about the ancient and ever-new fulfillment of God responding to the cry of those who long for freedom. God *does* bring light in the darkest of times. God *does* feed hope when all is hopeless. Celebrating the birth of this one child affirms that in this child, the Christ, salvation still becomes flesh and dwells among us. All who claim Jesus as Lord embrace anew God's own Spirit of adoption. As the ones called to bring Christ to the world, we share in his ongoing ministry of love, of service, of saving grace. Our shared faith in Christ Jesus is the bond that unites us across church boundaries. We are all taking risks by being here tonight – the risk that we may recognize the Christ child in one another, and be filled with love and mercy for those in all the Christian churches. The risk we take by gathering here tonight is outweighed by the blinding light that our common witness in Jesus can be in our dark and hurting world. Our shared faith and the love of God sustain us and make us shine, offering the hope that with him and in him we can make our world a better place.

This is why year after year, century after century, we pause in the midst of winter darkness to celebrate the triumph of light and life and hope. We look back to ancient times in order to see more clearly the events in our life here and now. We listen to the words and wisdom of the prophets. And tonight we are listening and pray-ing and singing with those whom we might be meeting for the first time, yet whom Jesus knows as our sisters and brothers. We tell and retell the stories about the struggles and hopes of others, and we hope that our lives too may be blessed by the same wonder-filled news that now, in our own day, place and time, a saviour is given to us – a saviour who empowers us to live more fully, to forgive more deeply, to love more fiercely.

This saviour, Jesus Christ, is the reason that we reach beyond the boundaries of our churches, beyond the boundaries of our lives, and learn to embrace one another as sister, as brother. The saving grace of this holy season is that, in Jesus, we are all brought close to God and to one another. Yes, Advent does come at the worst possible time. And Advent does risk getting lost in the bustle of commercialism. But we cannot afford to lose out on the waiting, to skip the times of prayer and remembering. Our spirit drinks deeply from God's promise. Advent does come when we need it the most. Amen.

Blessing

And there is One
who wrestles with me in the dark of night
until daybreak and,
seeing that I cannot be mastered, says:
Let me go, for day is breaking.
But I answer: I will not let you go
unless you tell me your name and
bless me.
And the Stranger holds me
in tight grip and suspense
as tears of blessing
soak my heart, mind and soul.
Tell me your name, I insist
while fighting to get loose.
Nothing but the mantle of
integrity and faithfulness
to cover me, warm me, dress me
for I wrestle and am strong with God.
No name, only Blessing
and then, left alone
as day breaks...
(adapted from Genesis 32:26–30)

Epilogue

The journey continues, and who knows where it leads? I have tried to capture it in the chapters of this book, and invariably I could have said or explained things differently. In sharing my experience of call and of preaching, I have tried to stay away from limited interpretations as to what this is all about in the hope that I can talk about these things without pushing a political agenda of sorts, feminist or otherwise. No doubt opinions will vary as to whether I succeeded in this.

When publishing a book, words and ideas are "out there" to survive on their own and to speak to whoever reads them. In that sense, completing the book finishes my part of the task. The rest lies with God's Holy Spirit, which is alive and well in this time of transition in the life of the Church. I have learned that things are simply not always what we think they are or should be. I have found that, too often, our personal insecurities, hurts, agendas, egos and power trips do not allow the Spirit the radical freedom of movement necessary when a new thing is happening. This is not meant as an apology. It is simply a realization that writing is an act of faith, hope and love: I write about my experience of faith, in the hope that it may have meaning for others, and that my story, even if challenging to some, will be received in love. Reading the story makes you a part of it now, with your own questions and musings in your heart, questions about where we are going as a church, and how we can be fruitful and faithful to the call of Jesus Christ to preach the Gospel to all nations and at all times.

I have always struggled with the effects of dualistic thinking: yes/no, right/wrong, good/bad. More often than not we live in an ambiguous mix of "both/and." This struggle to integrate and balance is played out in my experience of the call to preach, to lead the faith community, and to celebrate the sacraments. I cannot separate these things. But trying to hold both these aspects as part of one call creates profound challenges. As a Roman Catholic, I cannot believe that a separation of one call into three distinct ministries is possible.

Yet, more and more, we see this separation as increasing numbers of men and women find themselves meeting the pastoral needs of the faith community and preaching to their own congregations without the Church's sanction of the sacrament of Holy Orders. My Catholic understanding of one call prevents me from promoting lay preaching as an end in itself, i.e., as divorced from ordination. If I pursue that line of reasoning, I risk contradicting present Catholic teaching on the ordination of women, since this would mean that I claim a call to ordained ministry. I have in this book only pursued the preaching aspect of the call. However, if I maintain the emphasis on a call to preach as separate from a call to lead the faith community and to celebrate the sacraments, I reflect more of a post-Reformation or even an Evangelical position rather than the contemporary Catholic Church's or Vatican II's renewed understanding of priestly ministry. Either way, the story remains incomplete and open to misinterpretations and criticism.

All I can hope for is that in the reading a bond has formed between writer and reader, a bond that can best be described as an intimate partnership of words and ideas read in a spirit of openness and compassion. We all need courage, patience and humility to let the Spirit do the rest.

Each time we negotiate a new chapter in our spiritual and psychological maturing, we bring to bear all our past experiences in a comprehensive process of reinterpretation in order to make sense out of what presents itself here and now. When I look back to discover the time when and where this call to preach was first planted in my soul, a particular time and place emerges in my memory. I am 17 years old, living in my Dutch hometown of Rijen, and I am happily involved with the parish youth group. With this group of young committed Christians, I am engaged in intense soul-searching for the purpose of writing "sermons" and of preaching the Good News in all the wild ways we employed back then. The fire of the call was kindled in those years, even if the name of the call eluded me at the time. In my attempts to keep responding to that fire in my soul, I spent time in France, at Taizé and in Jean Vanier's L'Arche communities. Eventually I found my way to Canada, into a countercultural, back-to-the-land lifestyle for the sake of the Gospel, and in various ministries in the Church. Next, God's fire led me to the seminary, where I, like Jacob, wrestled with the Lord at night and was given a new name. How I continue to interpret this new name, and to live with its intense demands and creative flames, is related in this book.

I never did get my degree in pastoral counselling. God did not intend that direction for me, despite my arguments to the contrary. Instead, I worked for nearly four years as the editor of *Our Family* magazine, a national Catholic publication owned and supported by the Missionary Oblates of Mary Immaculate, St. Mary's Province. After 53 years, this magazine ceased publication in February 2002. I am immensely grateful for the experience the editor's job gave me. Without it, I would likely not have developed the confidence and skills required to write this book. In hindsight, the hand of God is visible in what initially looked to me as unlikely work in the Church. Following my editorship, I worked as Pastoral Associate in a large parish. Preaching was not part of my ministry there, but journeying with adults in their relationship to God in both individual and communal ways in turn formed and informed my understanding of the preaching ministry. I now work half-time for the Diocese of Saskatoon in Ministry Development and Parish Renewal. As this book reaches the store shelves, I am embarking on a new phase in this journey with preaching. Under the auspices of the Minnesota-based organization *Partners in Preaching*, which exists to support and train Catholic lay people called to the preaching ministry, I am preparing to teach preaching to lay people. (For more information, contact www.partnersinpreaching.org.) I am further involved in retreat work, spiritual direction, Christian healing touch, pastoral counselling, public speaking and hospital chaplaincy.

Back on the farm, we continue to draw water, chop wood and grow food. A second home in the city accommodates life with our three growing and thriving young adults. Our sons, ages 21 and 19, have jobs and run their own lives. Our daughter has only a couple of years left in high school. They are turning out to be very fine young people who are dreaming of an ambitious future in which they, too, hope to make a difference in the world. Jim and I remain active in our Catholic parish, and in the wider church. Jim keeps busy on the farm, growing plants and collecting and selling organic garden seeds (www.prseeds.ca). I keep busy with words through writing, editing and preaching. God is good, and I am growing in my ability to "come home" to God within my soul as much as is possible in this life.

I invite you to visit my personal website: www.malotg.com

Selected Bibliography

Archdiocese of Chicago. *The Liturgy Documents: A Parish Resource.* Chicago: Liturgy Training Publications, 1991.

Bausch, William. *Storytelling the Word: Homilies and How to Write Them.* Mystic, CT: Twenty-Third Publications, 1998.

Belenky, Mary Field, Blythe McVicker Clinchy, Nancy Rule Goldberger, Jill Mattuck Tarule. *Women's Ways of Knowing: The Development of Self, Voice and Mind.* New York: Basic Books, 1986.

Bepko, Claudia, and Krestan, Jo-Ann. *Singing at the Top of Our Lungs: Women, Love and Creativity.* New York: Harper Collins, 1993.

Brown Taylor, Barbara. *The Preaching Life.* Boston: Cowley Publications, 1993.

———. *Bread of Angels.* Boston: Cowley Publications, 1997.

Buttrick, David. *Homiletic Moves and Structures.* Philadelphia: Fortress Press, 1987.

Chittister, Joan. *Womanstrength: Modern Church, Modern Women.* Kansas City: Sheed & Ward, 1990.

———. *Heart of Flesh: A Feminist Spirituality for Women and Men.* Ottawa: Novalis, 1997.

———. *In Search of Belief.* Liguori, MO: Liguori Publications, 1999.

Conroy, Maureen. *Looking into the Well: Supervision of Spiritual Direction.* Chicago: Loyola Press, 1995.

Coombs, Marie Theresa, and Nemeck, Francis Kelly. *Discerning Vocations to Marriage, Celibacy, and Singlehood.* Collegeville, MN: Liturgical Press, 1994.

De Mello, Anthony. *Taking Flight: A Book of Story Meditations.* New York: Bantam Doubleday, 1988.

De Sola Chervin, Ronda. *Prayers of the Women Mystics.* Ann Arbor, MI: Servant Publications, 1992.

Eddy, Corbin. *Who Knows the Colour of God? Homilies and Reflections for Year C*. Ottawa: Novalis, 2000.

English, John J., SJ. *Spiritual Freedom: From an Experience of the Ignatian Exercises to the Art of Spiritual Guidance*. Second Edition. Chicago: Loyola University Press, 1995.

Flannery, Austin, OP. *Vatican Council II: The Conciliar and Post-Conciliar Documents*. Collegeville, MN: Liturgical Press, 1975.

Flinders, Carol Lee. *At the Root of This Longing*. San Francisco: HarperCollins, 1998.

Hilkert, Mary Catherine. *Naming Grace: Preaching and the Sacramental Imagination*. New York: Continuum, 2000.

Johnson, Elizabeth A. *Friends of God and Prophets: A Feminist Theological Reading of the Communion of Saints*. Ottawa: Novalis, 1998.

Lathrop, Gordon W. *Holy Things: A Liturgical Theology*. Minneapolis: Augsburg Fortress Press, 1993.

Lerner, Gerda. *The Creation of Feminist Consciousness: From the Middle Ages to Eighteen-Seventy*. New York: Oxford University Press, 1993.

Libreria Editrice Vaticana. *Catechism of the Catholic Church*. Collegeville, MN: Liturgical Press, 1994.

Lisieux, Thérèse of. *The Story of a Soul: Autobiography of St. Thérèse of Lisieux*, translated by John Beevers. New York: Doubleday, 1957.

Malone, Mary. *Women Christian: New Vision*. Dubuque, IO: Brown Co., 1972.

McBrien, Richard. *Catholicism: New Edition*. San Francisco: HarperSanFrancisco, 1994.

McNamara, William, OCD. *Mystical Passion*. Rockport, MA: Element Books Ltd., 1991.

Meehan, Bridget Mary. *Praying with Passionate Women: Mystics, Martyrs and Mentors*. New York: Crossroad, 1995.

Merton, Thomas. *The Seven Storey Mountain*. New York: Harcourt Brace, 1970.

Milton, Ralph. *Sermon Seasonings: Collected Stories to Spice up Your Sermons*. Winfield, BC: Wood Lake Books, 1997.

Minus, Paul M. Jr. *The Catholic Rediscovery of Protestantism: A History of Roman Catholic Ecumenical Pioneering.* New York: Paulist Press, 1976.

Noffke, Suzanne, OP. *The Prayers of Catherine of Siena.* New York: Paulist Press, 1983.

Noren, Carol M. *The Woman in the Pulpit.* Nashville: Abingdon Press, 1992.

Norris, Kathleen. *Amazing Grace: A Vocabulary of Faith.* New York: Riverhead Books, 1998.

———. *Dakota: A Spiritual Geography.* New York: Houghton Mifflin, 1993.

Osborne, Kenan B., OFM. *Ministry: Lay Ministry in the Roman Catholic Church, Its History and Theology.* New York: Paulist Press, 1993.

———. *Priesthood: A History of the Ordained Ministry in the Roman Catholic Church.* New York: Paulist Press, 1989.

Parachini, Patricia A. *Guide for Lay Preachers.* Chicago: Liturgy Training Publications, 2000.

Pearson Mitchell, Ella, ed. *Those Preaching Women.* Valley Forge, PA: Judson Press, 1996.

Perri, Willliam P. *A Radical Challenge to Priesthood Today.* Mystic, CT: Twenty-Third Publications, 1996.

Prokes, M. Timothy, SSND. *Women's Challenge: Ministry in the Flesh.* Denville, NJ: Dimension Books, 1977.

Puhl, Louis J., SJ. *The Spiritual Exercises of St. Ignatius, Based on Studies in the Language of the Autograph.* Chicago: Loyola University Press, 1951.

Rolheiser, Ronald, OMI. *Seeking Spirituality: A Spirituality for the Twenty-First Century.* London: Hodder & Stoughton, 1998. (Also published under the title *The Holy Longing.* Toronto: Doubleday, 1999.)

Schneiders, Sandra M. *Beyond Patching: Faith and Feminism (Anthony Jordan Lectures).* New York: Paulist Press, 1991.

Siena, Catherine of. *Set Aside Every Fear: Love and Trust in the Spirituality of Catherine of Siena.* Notre Dame, IN: Ave Maria Press, 1997.

Smith, Christine. *Weaving the Sermon: Preaching in a Feminist Perspective*. Louisville, KY: Westminster/John Knox Press, 1989.

Thielicke, Helmut. *A Little Exercise for Young Theologians*. Grand Rapids, MI: Eerdmans, 1962.

Trible, Phyllis. *God and the Rhetoric of Sexuality*. Philadelphia: Fortress Press, 1978.

Troeger, Thomas H. *The Parable of Ten Preachers*. Nashville: Abingdon Press, 1992.

Uhlein, Gabriele. *Meditations with Hildegard of Bingen*. Santa Fe, NM: Bear & Co., 1983.

United States Catholic Conference. *Fulfilled in Your Hearing: The Homily in the Sunday Assembly*. Washington, D.C.: Author, 1982.

Vandezande, Gerald. *Justice, Not Just Us: Faith Perspectives and National Priorities*. Toronto: Public Justice Resource Center, 1999.

Vanier, Jean. *Becoming Human: Massey Lecture Series*. Toronto: Anansi Press, 1998.

Whitehead, James, and Whitehead, Evelyn. *A Sense of Sexuality*. New York: Doubleday, 1989.

———. *The Promise of Partnership: A Model for Collaborative Ministry*. San Francisco: Harper Collins, 1991.

Notes

Introduction

1   *America*, Vol. 184, No. 7, March 5, 2001.

2   The seminary I attended is part of the ELCIC, the Evangelical Lutheran Church in Canada. This is not to be confused with the Evangelical Lutheran Church – Missouri Synod.

3   Kenan B. Osborne, OFM (New York: Paulist Press, 1993), 601-602.

4   Thérèse of Lisieux, *The Story of a Soul: Autobiography of St. Thérèse of Lisieux* (New York: Doubleday, 1957), 155.

Chapter 1

5   Helmut Thielicke, *A Little Exercise for Young Theologians* (Grand Rapids, MI: Eerdmans, 1962), 24.

6   Joan Chittister, *Heart of Flesh: A Feminist Spirituality for Women and Men* (Ottawa: Novalis, 1997), 42.

7   *Heart of Flesh*, 11.

Chapter 2

8   Barbara Brown Taylor, *The Preaching Life* (Boston: Cowley Publications, 1993), 76.

9   David Buttrick, *Homiletic Moves and Structures* (Philadelphia: Fortress Press, 1987), 64.

10   Gordon W. Lathrop, *Holy Things: A Liturgical Theology* (Minneapolis: Augsburg Fortress Press, 1993), 194.

11   Vatican Council II, *Constitution on the Sacred Liturgy,* #52.

12   Vatican Council II, *Third Instruction on the Correct Implementation of the Constitution on the Sacred Liturgy,* #13.

Chapter 3

13   Joan Chittister, *In Search of Belief* (Liguori, MO: Liguori Publications, 1999), 161.

14   Adela Torchia, "U.S. Bishops Looked at Lay Ministry," *Western Catholic Reporter,* Nov. 20, 2000, 16.

[15] National Conference of Catholic Bishops, *Lay Ecclesial Ministry: State of the Questions* (Washington, D.C.: Author, 1999).

[16] Marie Theresa Coomb and Francis Kelly Nemeck, *Discerning Vocations to Marriage, Celibacy and Singlehood* (Collegeville, MN: Liturgical Press, 1994), 22–23.

[17] *Heart of Flesh*, 27.

Chapter 4

[18] This is the official liturgical name in the Roman Catholic Church for Sunday worship in the absence of a priest which includes a distribution of communion consecrated at an earlier Mass. The name for the service is taken from the ritual book published by the Canadian Conference of Catholic Bishops in 1995, *Sunday Celebrations of the Word and Hours.*

[19] Mary Catherine Hilkert, *Naming Grace: Preaching and the Sacramental Imagination* (New York: Continuum, 2000), 146.

[20] Carol M. Noren, *The Woman in the Pulpit* (Nashville: Abingdon Press, 1992), 9.

[21] *The Preaching Life*, 77–78.

[22] *The Woman in the Pulpit*, 23.

[23] *Homiletic Moves and Structures*, 142.

[24] This is a slight paraphrasing/summary of a longer paragraph from Dietrich Bonhoeffer, *The Cost of Discipleship* (New York: MacMillan, 1963), 289.

Chapter 5

[25] *Lumen gentium*, #50.

[26] Elizabeth A. Johnson, *Friends of God and Prophets: A Feminist Theological Reading of the Communion of Saints* (Ottawa: Novalis, 1999), 91–92.

[27] Quoted in *Friends of God and Prophets*, 28–29.

[28] Mary Malone, *Women Christian: New Vision* (Dubuque, IO: Brown Co., 1972), 56–57.

[29] Catherine of Siena, *Set Aside Every Fear: Love and Trust in the Spirituality of Catherine of Siena* (Notre Dame, IN: Ave Maria Press, 1997), 125–127.

[30] Carlo Carretto, *I, Francis* (Maryknoll, NY: Orbis, 1983), 22–23.

Chapter 6

[31] William McNamara, *Mystical Passion* (New York: Crossroad, 1983), 56.

[32] James Whitehead & Evelyn Whitehead, *A Sense of Sexuality* (New York: Doubleday, 1989), 66.

[33] *Homiletic Moves and Structures,* 64.

Chapter 7

[34] Ronald Rolheiser, *Seeking Spirituality: A Spirituality for the Twenty-First Century* (London: Hodder & Stoughton, 1998), 85.

Chapter 8

[35] Sr. M. Timothy Prokes, SSND, *Women's Challenge: Ministry in the Flesh* (Denville: Dimension Books, 1977), 47.

[36] "Combined fertility," an expression adopted in Natural Family Planning, refers to the male and female physiological processes rendering women and men fertile, thus making conception possible.

[37] *Women's Challenge,* 31.

[38] *Women's Challenge,* 47.

[39] *Women's Challenge,* 43.

[40] James Nelson, *The Intimate Connection* (Philadelphia: Westminster Press, 1988), 126.

Chapter 9

[41] *Ministry,* 604.

Chapter 10

[42] Anthony de Mello, *Taking Flight: A Book of Story Meditations* (New York: Bantam Doubleday, 1988), 63.

[43] Gerald Vandezande, *Justice, Not Just Us* (Toronto: Public Justice Resource Centre, 1999), 76.

[44] *Justice, Not Just Us,* 76.

[45] Thomas Merton, *The Seven Storey Mountain* (New York: Harcourt Brace, 1970), 387.

[46] *Seeking Spirituality,* 170.

[47] *Seeking Spirituality,* 171.

Chapter 11

[48] *The Story of a Soul,* 109.

[49] *Discerning Vocations,* 212-214.

[50] *The Woman in the Pulpit,* 20.

[51] *Ministry*, 600.

Chapter 12

[52] *In Search of Belief*, 161.

[53] *In Search of Belief*, 161.

[54] William Perri, *A Radical Challenge to Priesthood Today* (Mystic, CT: Twenty-Third Publications, 1996), 2-3.

[55] *Universal Prayer, Confessions of Sins*, Rome, March 12, 2000.

Chapter 13

[56] *Catholicism*, 787.

[57] The paper I wrote for that final exam was later worked into an article on the *Joint Declaration* that was published three times: in two different Catholic publications and in the *Canada Lutheran* to mark the official signing of the *Joint Declaration*.

[58] Joint Declaration paragraphs 14 and 15, p. 39, *Justification by faith through grace: Study resource for congregations and parishes,* CCCB and ELCIC, 1999.

[59] Carlo Carretto, as quoted in Rolheiser, *Seeking Spirituality*, 122.

Chapter 14

[60] *Directory on Ecumenism,* #107.

[61] *Ut unum sint*, #2.

[62] Vatican II Documents, *Decree on Ecumenism*, #4.

[63] The Worldwide Church of God, founded by H.W. Armstrong, published *The Plain Truth*. The doctrinal upheaval occurred after Armstrong's death.

[64] Congregation for the Doctrine of the Faith, *Dominus Iesus* (1999).

[65] *Decree on Ecumenism,* #4.

Chapter 15

[66] *Directory for the Application of Principles and Norms on Ecumenism*, #22.

[67] *Ut unum sint*, #15.

Chapter 16

[68] "Fenced" table is an expression from the early church, meaning that the communion table is open only for those who are baptized.

[69] *Catechism of the Catholic Church*, #1782.

Chapter 17

[70] Gerda Lerner, *The Creation of Feminist Consciousness: From the Middle Ages to Eighteen-Seventy* (New York: Oxford University Press, 1993), 166.

[71] Carol Lee Flinders, *At the Root of This Longing* (San Francisco: HarperCollins, 1998) 325.

[72] *Seeking Spirituality,* 141–143. Reprinted with permission.

[73] *Seeking Spirituality,* 212–213.

Chapter 18

[74] *Ministry,* 540, 546.

[75] Kenan Osborne, OFM, *Priesthood: A History of the Ordained Ministry in the Roman Catholic Church* (New York: Paulist Press, 1989), 354.

Chapter 19

[76] *The Preaching Life,* 85.

[77] *The Preaching Life,* 79.

[78] *Naming Grace,* 173.

Chapter 20

[79] *The Woman in the Pulpit,* 27.

[80] *Heart of Flesh,* 105.

[81] *Naming Grace,* 145–146.

Marie-Louise Ternier-Gommers